What Readers Are Saying About Web Development Recipes

Solid practices you can take into your everyday web development process. Web designers and developers with a hunger for picking up a collection of quick and expertly described techniques in areas like UI, testing, CSS, and jQuery will love this book. No words are wasted on trivial details; this is a book for proactive web developers who want to pick up some new ideas fast.

➤ **Peter Cooper**
   Editor, Ruby Inside, HTML5 Weekly, and JavaScript Weekly

I know of no other resource that even comes close to exploring so many interesting techniques for modern web development. These are real-world pragmatic recipes that you will actually use in your projects.

➤ **Matt Margolis**
   Manager, application development, Getty Images

Web Development Recipes is one of those rare books that is not only extremely practical but also incredibly useful for a wide range of readers. Everyone in all aspects of web design and development will find numerous tips and tricks that will be immediately useful in their day-to-day work.

➤ **Ray Camden**
   Developer evangelist, Adobe

This is probably the best general web development resource that I've read to date. Anyone new to the game can work through this book and gain a level of experience that normally takes years of freelancing. Even seasoned experts could learn some new tricks or explore areas of web development they haven't touched yet.

➤ **Steve Heffernan**
Creator, VideoJS

This is a design patterns book for modern web development, offering problem statements and solutions that can be applied to nearly any web development platform. It's a must-have for web developers who need to update their skills with the latest and greatest tools and techniques, and it's a library of solutions for those who are already up to speed. The authors have done an excellent job of condensing a tremendous amount of information into easy-to-understand, real-world solutions.

➤ **Derick Bailey**
Independent software developer, Muted Solutions, LLC

Web Development Recipes

Brian P. Hogan
Chris Warren
Mike Weber
Chris Johnson
Aaron Godin

The Pragmatic Bookshelf

Dallas, Texas • Raleigh, North Carolina

Many of the designations used by manufacturers and sellers to distinguish their products are claimed as trademarks. Where those designations appear in this book, and The Pragmatic Programmers, LLC was aware of a trademark claim, the designations have been printed in initial capital letters or in all capitals. The Pragmatic Starter Kit, The Pragmatic Programmer, Pragmatic Programming, Pragmatic Bookshelf, PragProg and the linking *g* device are trademarks of The Pragmatic Programmers, LLC.

Every precaution was taken in the preparation of this book. However, the publisher assumes no responsibility for errors or omissions, or for damages that may result from the use of information (including program listings) contained herein.

Our Pragmatic courses, workshops, and other products can help you and your team create better software and have more fun. For more information, as well as the latest Pragmatic titles, please visit us at *http://pragprog.com*.

The team that produced this book includes:

Susannah Pfalzer (editor)
Potomac Indexing, LLC (indexer)
Kim Wimpsett (copyeditor)
David J Kelly (typesetter)
Janet Furlow (producer)
Juliet Benda (rights)
Ellie Callahan (support)

Printed in the United States of America.
ISBN-13: 978-1-93435-683-8
Printed on acid-free paper.
Book version: P1.0—January 2012

Contents

Acknowledgments

They say nobody writes a book alone. The truth is that even when you have five authors, you still end up bringing many other people with you for the ride. Without the support of these people, we wouldn't have this book or the experience we gained from writing it.

Susannah Pfalzer, our wonderful development editor, did an amazing job wrangling five authors and making sure we didn't skimp on the little things, like complete sentences, introductions, useful transitions, and coherent thoughts. We set out to write a book that would expose the modern web developer to a wide and eclectic collection of tools, but Susannah was always there to make sure we delivered the "why" as well as the "how" and the book is much better for it.

With the five of us scurrying to get things out the door quickly, mistakes and inconsistencies crept in, but thanks to our technical reviewers Charley Stran, Jessica Janiuk, Kevin Gisi, Matt Margolis, Eric Sorenson, Scott Andreas, Joel Andritsch, Lyle Johnson, Kim Shrier, Steve Heffernan, Noel Rappin, Sam Elliott, Derick Bailey, and Kaitlin Johnson, we are proud to have a book that's so much better than it was when we started.

Special thanks to Dave Gamache for his advice on Skeleton, to Trevor Burnham for his feedback on CoffeeScript, to Steve Sanderson for setting us on the right path with Knockout.JS, and to Benoit Chesneau for quickly fixing some issues with the Couchapp installer.

David Kelly made our book cover, and while some of us would have loved to have the version of the cover with bacon on it, we're all very happy with the design you see instead.

We're all extremely grateful to Dave Thomas and Andy Hunt for giving us the opportunity to write for the Pragmatic Bookshelf. Their feedback helped immensely with a few of our more troubling recipes, but more importantly, they have created an atmosphere that puts the authors first. When you have that kind of support, everything else is so much easier.

Additionally, we want to thank our other business associates including Erich Tesky, Austen Ott, Emma Smith, Jeff Holland, and Nick LaMuro for their support and feedback throughout the process.

Brian Hogan

This is my third book for the Pragmatic Bookshelf, and while I only wrote a fifth of it, it was still the most challenging. My coauthors each stepped up in their own way at just the right time to make it happen, and I'm proud to share this book with them. Chris, CJ, Mike, and Aaron each brought amazing ideas and examples into this book, and I'm proud of what we have. Thanks, guys!

But even with the extra help this time, I still couldn't have done this without my wonderful wife, Carissa. Thank you for making sure I had the time to get this done. Thank you for taking care of the little things (and sometimes the big things that I'd forget).

Chris Warren

I can't thank my awesome wife, Kaitlin, enough for her support and understanding during many late nights and early mornings of writing and editing. You made some rough days infinitely more bearable.

Thanks to my coauthors for sharing in this experience. I've known these guys for a long time, and it was great to tackle writing a book for the first time with friends. Thanks especially to Brian, who has played a huge role in my professional development over the years, for getting me involved in this undertaking.

Finally, thanks to my parents for their encouragement and support when I was growing up, in both writing and programming. I haven't told you I've written this, and I'm excited to place a copy in your hands and show you what I've done.

Mike Weber

I'd like to thank Brian Hogan for being my mentor over the years and for getting me started as a web developer and now published author. Without him, I wouldn't be doing any of this.

I'd also like the thank my other coauthors Chris, CJ, and Aaron for going through this journey with me and helping me along the way.

I also want to thank my family for keeping me on task by constantly asking "How's the book coming along?"

And finally I'd like to thank my wife, Kaley, for putting up with my late nights away from her so we could finish the book.

Chris Johnson

To my wife, Laura, thank you for supporting me every step of this journey. You gave up spending time with me so I could work on writing, drove on trips so I could work, and gave up many summer activities so I could write.

To my parents, thank you for teaching me to work for things I want and to never give up. Dad, thanks for waiting on your startup so I could finish the book.

Thanks to Brian, Chris, Mike, and Aaron for collaborating on this; you have made me a better writer with your constant feedback and support. You guys kept me going when sections got tough, and I really appreciated that.

To the guys at work, thanks for being a sounding board and tech reviewing the book.

Aaron Godin

Brian, Chris, Mike, and CJ have each been an inspiration to me as well as individuals to look up to. Thanks for pushing me along, even when I was out of touch with it. To Brian especially, thank you for being the best mentor and friend I could hope for.

Thanks to Brian Long for always listening and taking interest. Thank you to Taylor for your caring attitude and motivation; you always were my foundation when things became difficult.

Finally, thank you to my parents, Bill and Cynthia, for your unconditional support, love, and understanding. You both have taught me to keep at the things I enjoy in life. Thank you for preparing me to take on the world and for being the wisdom I need in the most critical of times.

Preface

It's no longer enough to know how to wrangle HTML, CSS, and a bit of Java-Script. Today's web developer needs to know how to write testable code, build interactive interfaces, integrate with other services, and sometimes even do some server configuration, or at least a little bit of backend work. This book is a collection of more than forty practical recipes that range from clever CSS tricks that will make your clients happy to server-side configurations that will make life easier for you and your users. You'll find a mix of tried-and-true techniques and cutting-edge solutions, all aimed at helping you truly discover the best tools for the job.

Who's This Book For?

If you make things on the Web, this book is for you. If you're a web designer or frontend developer who's looking to expand into other areas of web development, you'll get a chance to play with some new libraries and workflows that will help you be more productive, and you'll get exposed to a little bit of that server-side stuff along the way.

If you've been spending a lot of time on the backend and you need to get up to speed on some frontend techniques, you'll find some good recipes here as well, especially the sections on workflow and testing.

One last thing—a lot of these recipes assume you've had a little experience writing client-side code with JavaScript and jQuery. If you don't think you have that experience, read through the recipes anyway and pick apart the provided source code. Consider the more advanced recipes as a challenge.

What's in This Book?

We've included a bunch of great topics to get you started on the path to more advanced web development. Each recipe poses a general problem and then lays out a specific solution to a scenario you're likely to encounter, whether it's how to test your site across multiple web browsers, how to quickly build and automatically deploy a simple static site, how to create a simple contact form that emails results, or how to configure Apache to redirect URLs and serve pages securely. We'll take you through both the how and the why so you can feel comfortable using these solutions in your projects. Since this is a book of recipes, we can't go into a lot of detail about more complex system architecture, but you'll find some suggestions on where to go next in each recipe's "Further Exploration" section.

We've organized the recipes into chapters by topic, but you should feel free to jump around to the topics that interest you. Each chapter contains a mix of beginner and intermediate recipes, with the more complex recipes at the end of each chapter.

In Chapter 1, *Eye-Candy Recipes*, on page 1, we cover some ways you can use CSS and other techniques to spice up the appearance of your pages.

In Chapter 2, *User Interface Recipes*, on page 33, you'll use a variety of techniques to craft better user interfaces, including JavaScript frameworks like Knockout and Backbone, and you'll look at how to make better templates for sending HTML emails.

In Chapter 3, *Data Recipes*, on page 111, you'll look at ways you can work with user data. You'll construct a simple contact form, and you'll take a peek at how to build a database-driven application using CouchDB's CouchApps.

In Chapter 4, *Mobile Recipes*, on page 153, you'll take user interfaces a step further and look at ways you can work with the various mobile computing platforms. You'll spend some time with jQuery Mobile, look at how to handle multitouch events, and dig a little deeper into how to determine how and when to serve a mobile version of a page to your visitors.

In Chapter 5, *Workflow Recipes*, on page 183, we'll show you ways you can improve your processes. We'll investigate how SASS can make your life easier when managing large style sheets, and we'll introduce you to CoffeeScript, a new dialect for writing JavaScript that produces clean, compliant results.

In Chapter 6, *Testing Recipes*, on page 227, you'll create more bullet-proof sites by using automated tests, and we'll show you how to start testing the JavaScript code you write.

Finally, we'll turn our attention to moving into production in Chapter 7, *Hosting and Deployment Recipes*, on page 267. We'll walk you through building a virtual machine so you have a testing environment to try things before you set up your real production environment, and we'll cover how to set up secure sites, do redirects properly, and protect your content. We'll also show you how to automate the deployment of websites so you won't accidentally forget to upload a file.

What You Need

We'll be introducing you to many new technologies in this book. Some of these are fairly new and somewhat subject to change, but we think they're compelling and stable enough to talk about at an introductory level. That said, web development moves quickly. We've taken steps to ensure you can still follow along, by providing copies of the libraries we use in these recipes with the book's source code.

We've tried to keep the prerequisites to a minimum, but there are a few things you'll want to get set up before you dig in.

HTML5 and jQuery

We'll use HTML5-style markup in our examples. For example, you won't find any self-closing tags in our markup, and you'll see some new tags like <header> and <section> in some of the examples. If you're not familiar with HTML5, you may want to read *HTML5 and CSS3: Develop with Tomorrow's Standards Today* [Hog10].

We'll also use jQuery, because many of the libraries we introduce in these recipes rely on it. In most cases, our code examples will fetch jQuery 1.7 from Google's content delivery network. There are a couple of cases where libraries will require specific versions of jQuery, and we'll be sure to point those out.

The Shell

You'll work with various command-line programs in these recipes whenever possible. Working on the command line is often a huge productivity boost, because a single command can replace multiple mouse clicks, and you can write your own scripts to automate these command-line tools. The *shell* is the program that interprets these commands. If you're on a Windows machine, you'll use the command prompt. If you're on OS X or Linux, that's the Terminal.

Shell commands will look something like this:

```
$ mkdir javascripts
```

The $ represents the prompt in the shell, so you're not meant to type it in. The commands and processes you'll use are platform-independent, so whether you're on Windows, OS X, or Linux, you'll have no trouble following along.

Ruby

Several recipes in this book require that you have the Ruby programming language installed. We'll be using some tools that require Ruby to run, such as Rake and Sass. We've included a short appendix that walks you through installing Ruby, which you can find in Appendix 1, *Installing Ruby*, on page 305.

QEDServer

Several of the recipes in this book make use of an existing product management web application. You can work with this application by installing QEDServer,[1] a stand-alone web application and database that requires very little setup. QEDServer works on Windows, OS X, and Linux. All you need is a Java Runtime Environment. Whenever you see us refer to our "development server," we're talking about this. It gives us a stable web application backend for our demonstrations, and it gives you a hassle-free way to work with Ajax requests on your local machine.

The examples of this book will run against the version of QEDServer that we've bundled with the book's code examples, which you should download from the book's website.

To use QEDServer, you start the server with server.bat on Windows or ./server.sh on OS X and Linux. This creates a public folder that you can use for your workspace. If you create a file called index.html in that public folder, you can view it in your web browser by visiting http://localhost:8080/index.html.

A Virtual Machine

Several chapters in this book use a Linux-based web server with Apache and PHP. You'll learn how to set up your own copy of this server in Recipe 37, *Setting Up a Virtual Machine*, on page 272, but we've provided a virtual machine that's already configured, which you can get from http://www.webdevelopmentrecipes.com/. You'll need the free VirtualBox[2] application to run the virtual machine.

Online Resources

The book's website[3] has links to an interactive discussion forum as well as a place to submit errata for the book. You'll also find the source code for all the

---

1. A version for this book is available at http://webdevelopmentrecipes.com/.
2. http://www.virtualbox.org/
3. http://pragprog.com/titles/wbdev/

projects we build. Readers of the ebook can click the box above the code excerpts to download that snippet directly.

We hope you enjoy this book and that it gives you some ideas for your next web project!

Brian, Chris, CJ, Mike, and Aaron

## CHAPTER 1

Eye-Candy Recipes

A solid application is great, but a couple of extra touches on the user interface can make a huge difference. If they're easy to implement, that's even better.

In this section, we'll use CSS to style some buttons and text, and we'll do some animations using CSS and JavaScript.

Recipe 1

Styling Buttons and Links

Problem

Buttons are an important element in our interaction with websites, and styling them so they match the look of our site can make a big difference in the overall design. Sometimes we want to use links and input buttons within the same context, such as a button to submit and a link to cancel a form, but we want those elements to match up visually. Additionally, it'd be great if we could have some stylistic control over our form buttons without having to create a graphic each time we needed one.

Ingredients

- A CSS3-compliant web browser, such as Firefox 4, Safari 5, Google Chrome 5, Opera 10, or Internet Explorer 9

Solution

Using CSS to style form elements or links is common enough, but by using a class and a few CSS rules, we create a style sheet that will make links and buttons match, giving us a consistent style across our elements without having to resort to using buttons for links or links to submit forms.

Since we want to achieve a common button appearance, we'll start by creating a simple HTML page with a link and a button on it.

cssbuttons/index.html

```
<p>
  <input type="button" value="A Button!" class="button" />
  <a href="http://pragprog.com" class="button">A Link!</a>
</p>
```

Note that each has a class of button assigned to it. We're going to use this class to style both the link and the input elements so that you can't tell one from the other on the page.

As we set up our button class, many of the attributes that are set apply to both the link and input elements, while a few will serve to bring consistency between the two.

First we'll apply the basic CSS attributes for both.

cssbuttons/css-buttons.css

```
font-weight: bold;
background-color: #A69520;
text-transform: uppercase;
font-family: verdana;
border: 1px solid #282727;
```

The result looks like this:

A BUTTON!   A LINK!

With just these basic attributes, we already have some consistency between the objects, as the following buttons show, but we're far from done. The font sizes don't match up, and padding is different. It's easy to tell that these are not the same type of element.

```
font-size: 1.2em;
line-height: 1.25em;
padding: 6px 20px;
```

A BUTTON!   A LINK!

By setting the font-size, line-height, and padding on the class, we override anything already set on the link and input elements. There are a still a few inconsistencies to address that give away that these two elements are not in fact the same.

```
cursor: pointer;
color: #000;
text-decoration: none;
cursor: pointer;
color: #000;
text-decoration: none;
```

By default buttons do not cause the cursor to change from an arrow to a pointer, while links do. So, we have to choose one or the other and apply it to both. Additionally, links pick up the default link color on the page, and linked text is underlined.

Zooming in on our buttons in the browser reveals that, while they're extremely close to the same height, the link is slightly smaller. This discrepancy will be clearer to users zooming in on mobile devices, so we want to make sure it's addressed.

```
input.button {
  line-height:1.22em;
}
```

We give a slightly larger line-height to input elements with a class of button. This tweaks the height slightly, bringing it in line with our link. There's no magic to finding out the necessary height to set here; just zoom in on the elements in your browser and play with the line-height until the buttons match up.

This removes the last discrepancies from our buttons, allowing us to focus on their overall look, which we could improve by rounding the corners and adding a bit of a drop shadow, like this:

```
border-radius: 12px;
-webkit-border-radius: 12px;
-moz-border-radius: 12px;

box-shadow: 1px 3px 5px #555;
-moz-box-shadow: 1px 3px 5px #555;
-webkit-box-shadow: 1px 3px 5px #555;
border-radius: 12px;
-webkit-border-radius: 12px;
-moz-border-radius: 12px;

box-shadow: 1px 3px 5px #555;
-moz-box-shadow: 1px 3px 5px #555;
-webkit-box-shadow: 1px 3px 5px #555;
```

We're adding three lines each for the radius and shadow attributes to ensure that the effect is seen in as many browsers as possible. Just the first line of each grouping (border-radius and box-shadow) is enough for modern browsers with CSS3 support, but -webkit-* and -moz-* increase compatibility with some older versions of Safari and Firefox, respectively.

For a final touch on the overall look of our buttons, let's add a subtle gradient for texture. We'll use this to our advantage shortly when we set the look of the buttons when they're pressed.

```
background: -webkit-gradient(linear, 0 0, 0 100%, from(#FFF089), to(#A69520));
background: -moz-linear-gradient(#FFF089, #A69520);
background: -o-linear-gradient(#FFF089, #A69520);
background: linear-gradient(top center, #FFF089, #A69520);
background: -webkit-gradient(linear, 0 0, 0 100%, from(#FFF089), to(#A69520));
background: -moz-linear-gradient(#FFF089, #A69520);
background: -o-linear-gradient(#FFF089, #A69520);
background: linear-gradient(top center, #FFF089, #A69520);
```

Once again, we have several lines that achieve the same effect across multiple browsers. In this case, we're creating a gradient for the background of our buttons. Note the -o-* prefix for Opera support, which isn't needed in the last set of CSS attributes.[1]

Finally, we want to add style to handle click events so that there is a visual indicator that the button has been pressed. Users expect that indication, and it can be disconcerting if it's not there. Although there are numerous ways to convey that the button has been pressed, the simplest is to reverse the gradient.

```
.button:active, .button:focus {
  color: #000;
  background: -webkit-gradient(linear, 0 0, 100% 0,
    from(#A69520), to(#FFF089));
  background: -moz-linear-gradient(#A69520, #FFF089);
  background: -o-linear-gradient(#A69520, #FFF089);
  background: linear-gradient(left center, #A69520, #FFF089);
}
```

There are several ways that we could reverse the gradient, but the easiest way to do it consistently across the different browsers is to swap the colors in each. By setting this background on .button:active and .button:focus, we ensure that, whether the link or the input button is clicked, the change happens.

CSS-styled links and input buttons allow us to style otherwise disparate elements and use them in the proper manner—links for navigating between pages and input buttons for submitting data—while presenting a consistent interface and not relying on JavaScript to make a link submit a form or a button outside of a form redirect to a page. This avoids breaking functionality in older browsers and lowering the overhead in understanding how a page is working.

Further Exploration

If a button is not available to the user, you could remove it from the interface, or you could add a disabled class to it. What would that class look like? Once you have a disabled button style that you like, what else would you need to do to truly disable it? Form inputs have a disabled attribute, but for links you're going to need to use JavaScript.

Also See

- Recipe 2, *Styling Quotes with CSS*, on page 6
- Recipe 28, *Building Modular Style Sheets with Sass*, on page 201

---

1. For help getting your gradient just right, check out http://www.westciv.com/tools/gradients/.

Styling Quotes with CSS

Problem

Quotations from experts and praise from customers carry a lot of weight, so we often draw attention to these quotations visually. Sometimes we'll offset the margins a bit, increase the font size, or use large curly quotes to really make the quotation stand out. On a website, we want to do that in a simple and repeatable fashion, while keeping the presentation of the quotation separate from the code.

Ingredients

- A web browser that supports HTML5 and CSS3

Solution

We typically use CSS to separate our presentation from content, and styling quotations shouldn't be any different. Modern browsers support some more advanced properties we can use to make our quotations stand out, without adding much additional markup to the page.

While we'll focus on styling quotations in this recipe, the techniques discussed can be applied in many other situations as well. For example, by combining the CSS we'll write with the code in Recipe 7, *Swapping Between Content with Tabbed Interfaces*, on page 45, we can further customize the style of our different examples, tweaking colors to help distinguish between different sets of data. We can also apply the ideas in Recipe 25, *Using Sprites with CSS*, on page 178 to add background images to our quotes or examples.

We've been asked to add some short customer reviews for the product pages of our store. They'll be only a couple of sentences long, but each product page will have several quotes, and we'll want them to stand out from the product description. First, let's look at the HTML and CSS techniques we'll pull together to make this happen.

We want to have a solid foundation to build our CSS upon, so we'll start by setting up our HTML structure. Using the <blockquote> and <cite> tags makes sense for wrapping the quote and the source, respectively.

```
cssquotes/quote.html
<html>
  <head>
    <link rel="stylesheet" href="basic.css">
  </head>
  <body>
    <blockquote>
      <p>
        Determine that the thing can and shall be done,
        and then we shall find the way.
      </p>
    </blockquote>
    <cite>Abraham Lincoln</cite>
  </body>
</html>
```

Now that we have good semantic markup for our quotes, we'll start styling them. First we'll do a simple approach; we'll put a border around the quote and increase the size of the text while putting a bit less emphasis on the author's name and sliding it to the right, like in Figure 1, *A basic quote style*, on page 8.

```
cssquotes/basic.css
blockquote {
  width: 225px;
  padding: 5px;
  border: 1px solid black;
}

blockquote p {
  font-size: 2.4em;
  margin: 5px;
}

blockquote + cite {
  font-size: 1.2em;
  color: #AAA;
  text-align: right;
  display: block;
  width: 225px;
  padding: 0 50px;
}
```

In this basic style, we set matching widths on our primary elements, the <blockquote> and the <cite>. We use an adjacent sibling selector on the <cite> tag to make sure we are styling it only if it comes immediately after a block-quote; otherwise, we'll leave other <cite> tags alone. Beyond that, we change the color of the author's name, adjust the padding to line everything up as we'd like, and end up with a simple but good-looking quote.

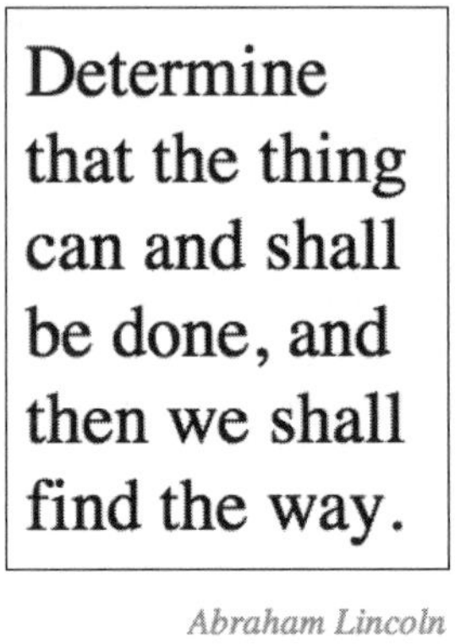

Determine
that the thing
can and shall
be done, and
then we shall
find the way.

Abraham Lincoln

Figure 1—A basic quote style

Now that we have our basic quote style established, we can start to get fancier. Rather than using a border, let's add a large " to the front of the quote to draw the eye and make it obvious what we're displaying, like Figure 2, *With quotes added by CSS*, on page 9.

cssquotes/quotation-marks.css
```css
blockquote {
  width: 225px;
  padding: 5px;
}

blockquote p {
  font-size: 2.4em;
  margin: 5px;
  z-index: 10;
  position: relative;
}

blockquote + cite {
  font-size: 1.2em;
  color: #AAA;
  text-align: right;
  display: block;
  width: 225px;
  padding: 0 50px;
}

blockquote:before {
  content: open-quote;
  position: absolute;
  z-index: 1;
  top: -30px;
```

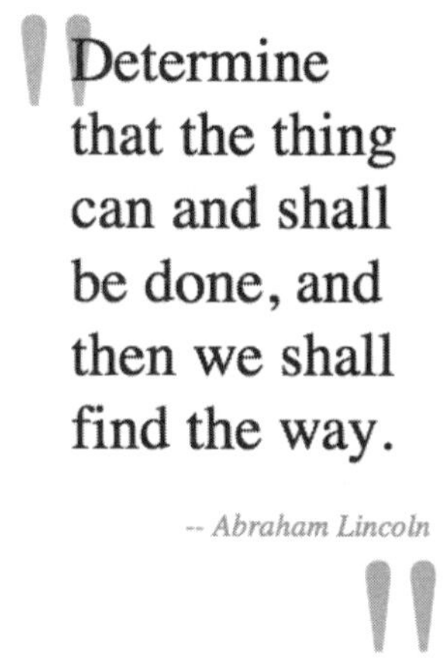

> Determine
> that the thing
> can and shall
> be done, and
> then we shall
> find the way.
>
> *-- Abraham Lincoln*

Figure 2—With quotes added by CSS

```css
  left: 10px;
  font-size: 12em;
  color: #FAA;
  font-family: serif;
}

blockquote:after {
  content: close-quote;
  position: absolute;
  z-index: 1;
  bottom: 80px;
  left: 225px;
  font-size: 12em;
  color: #FAA;
  font-family: serif;
}
blockquote + cite:before {
  content: "-- ";
}
```

This style inserts quotation marks behind our text, adds a – before the author's name, and removes the black border. To achieve this effect, we're using the :before and :after selectors, which allow us to insert content when specified tags are encountered on the page. Using the content attribute, we can specify what that content should be, whether it's open-quote and close-quote codes or a string.

With the quotes in place, we added a few more attributes, most of which are self-explanatory, such as color, font family, and font size. Be sure to pay attention to the z-index attributes that were added, as well as the position:relative;

attribute on blockquote p. Using the position attributes plus z-index lets us place the quotation marks behind the quote, so we don't need any extra space for the marks; plus, it looks cool to have the text overlaying them. We also position our blockquote:after along the bottom so that no matter how long the quote gets, the quotation mark stays at the end.

For our last style, we'll go all out and style the quotes to look like speech bubbles, taking advantage of some of cool CSS3 attributes to round the corners of the box and add a gradient to the background color, making our quote look like Figure 3, *In a CSS3-styled speech bubble*, on page 11.

```
cssquotes/speech-bubble.css
blockquote {
  width: 225px;
  padding: 15px 30px;
  margin: 0;
  position: relative;
  background: #faa;
  background: -webkit-gradient(linear, 0 0, 20% 100%,
    from(#C40606), to(#faa));
  background: -moz-linear-gradient(#C40606, #faa);
  background: -o-linear-gradient(#C40606, #faa);
  background: linear-gradient(#C40606, #faa);
  -webkit-border-radius: 20px;
  -moz-border-radius: 20px;
  border-radius: 20px;
}

blockquote p {
  font-size: 1.8em;
  margin: 5px;
  z-index: 10;
  position: relative;
}

blockquote + cite {
  font-size: 1.1em;
  display: block;
  margin: 1em 0 0 4em;
}

blockquote:after {
  content: "";
  position: absolute;
  z-index: 1;
  bottom: -50px;
  left: 40px;
  border-width: 0 15px 50px 0px;
  border-style: solid;
```

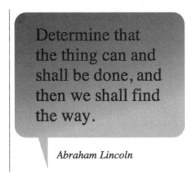

Figure 3—In a CSS3-styled speech bubble

```
  border-color: transparent #faa;
  display: block;
  width: 0;
}
```

Thanks to CSS3, we don't need images to put our quote inside a speech bubble. We start by setting a background color on the blockquote. This will be displayed in all browsers, even ones that don't support the CSS3 effects we're applying. Next we apply a background that has a gradient using the linear-gradient attribute and then we round the corners of the element by using the border-radius attribute.

Because different browsers use different syntax for linear-gradient and border-radius, we have to use multiple lines to get the same (or similar) effects across browsers. -moz and -webkit prefixes indicate code specifically for Firefox and WebKit-based browsers (e.g., Safari and Chrome), respectively. Finally, we add the CSS3 standard attribute, which covers all of our bases.

Very few changes take place in the blockquote p and blockquote + cite styles; we adjust sizes on a few attributes, but overall things stay the same. Font colors and sizes, as well as padding, can easily be adjusted here to better fit the style of the site.

Our final style element is the blockquote:after, which creates the bottom triangle of our speech bubble. We set the content to an empty string because there's no need for actual content here; we just want it for its borders. By setting the border widths to different thicknesses between the top and bottom, and left and right, we create a triangle. Multiple values can be set on any CSS attribute that can specify values for each side, in the clockwise order from top, right, bottom, left. We use this to set the sizes of the borders as well as the border-colors, with transparent borders on the top and bottom and color on the right and left.

Further Exploration

What other styles can you come up with for quotes? In our final example, we created a speech bubble. Swapping a border from right to left on the block-quote:after flips it on the vertical axis, but what would we have to do to move the author's name and the triangle to the top of the bubble?

Internet Explorer's gradient filter can create the same effects we used in our final quote style, but the process is a bit different. Gradients are applied directly to the object, rather than on the background-image as with the other browser. Using the documentation on this[2] from Microsoft, can you add support for older versions of IE?

Also See

- Recipe 1, *Styling Buttons and Links*, on page 2
- Recipe 25, *Using Sprites with CSS*, on page 178
- Recipe 7, *Swapping Between Content with Tabbed Interfaces*, on page 45
- Recipe 28, *Building Modular Style Sheets with Sass*, on page 201

---

2. http://msdn.microsoft.com/en-us/library/ms532997.aspx

Recipe 3

Creating Animations with CSS3 Transformations

Problem

For many web developers, Flash has been the go-to tool for developing sites with animations, but these animations aren't visible from the iPad, iPhone, and other devices that don't support Flash. In cases where the animation is really important to our customers, we'll need a non-Flash workaround.

Ingredients

- CSS3
- jQuery

Solution

With the advent of CSS3 transitions and transformations, we now have the option to define animations natively, without having to use plug-ins like Flash. These animations will work only with newer mobile browsers and the latest versions of Firefox, Chrome, Safari, and Opera, but the logo itself will be visible for all users, even if they don't see the animations. To make the animation work in other browsers, we would continue to rely on the Flash version.

Our current client's website originally had its logo done in Flash so that a "sheen" could be seen crossing the logo when the user loaded the page. He just got a new iPad, and he's frustrated that his animation doesn't display but even more worried that his logo doesn't show up. While the missing effect wouldn't break the entire site, the missing logo does remove some of the site's branding. We're going to make the logo visible in all browsers and add back the animation for browsers that support CSS3 transformations.

Let's start with the markup for the header that contains our logo. We'll add a class to the <img> tag so we can access it from the style sheet later.

csssheen/index.html

```
<header>
  <div class="sheen"></div>
  <img src="logo.png" class="logo">
</header>
```

To get this effect, we're going to create a semitransparent, angled, and blurred HTML block that moves across the screen once the Document Object Model (DOM) is loaded. So, let's start by defining our header's basic style. We want a blue banner that crosses the top of our content. To do this, we give our header the desired width and position the logo in the upper-left corner of our header.

csssheen/style.css

```css
body {
  background: #CCC;
  margin: 0;
}
header {
  background: #436999;
  margin: 0 auto;
  width: 800px;
  height: 150px;
  display: block;
  position: relative;
}
header img.logo {
  float: left;
  padding: 10px;
  height: 130px;
}
```

With our basic layout in place, we can add the decorative elements for the animation. Let's first create the blurred HTML element, but since this is an extra effect and has absolutely nothing to do with the content of our site, we want to do it with as little extra HTML markup as possible. We'll make use of the <div> with the "sheen" class that we defined in our markup to make this work.

csssheen/style.css

```css
header .sheen {
  height: 200px;
  width: 15px;
  background: rgba(255, 255, 255, 0.5);
  float: left;
  -moz-transform:       rotate(20deg);
  -webkit-transform:    rotate(20deg);
  -o-transform:         rotate(20deg);
  position: absolute;
  left: -100px;
  top: -25px;
  -moz-box-shadow:      0 0 20px #FFF;
  -webkit-box-shadow:   0 0 20px #FFF;
  box-shadow:           0 0 20px #FFF;
}
```

Figure 4—The "sheen" is visible and unstyled.

If we look at our page now (Figure 4, *The "sheen" is visible and unstyled*, on page 15), we see that we've added a thin, white, transparent line that's taller than our header. We're off to a great start. Now we want to reposition the sheen element so that it's blurred, starts left of the header, and is slightly angled.

This is where things get a little tricky. Because the various browsers are still deciding how to support transformations and transitions, we have to add the specific browser prefixes to ensure that each browser picks up on the style change. So even though, for what we're doing at least, each style declaration has exactly the same arguments, we need to add the various prefixes to ensure that each browser applies the style. We also want to add a nonprefixed style definition so our style will work when the CSS3 spec is agreed upon. For example, you'll see that we don't declare an -o-box-shadow style because newer versions of Opera don't even recognize that style anymore, and Firefox 4+ no longer uses the -moz-box-shadow style but still recognizes it and converts it to just box-shadow. However, we still keep the -moz-box-shadow style in place to support Firefox 3. In the code, on page 14, we had to sacrifice clean code for functionality.

With our styles in place, we're almost ready to animate our sheen element. Next we'll add the transition declarations, which we'll use for controlling the animation. For now, we'll have to rely on browser-specific prefixes.

```
csssheen/style.css
header .sheen {
  -moz-transition:     all 2s ease-in-out;
  -webkit-transition:  all 2s ease-in-out;
  -o-transition:       all 2s ease-in-out;
  transition:          all 2s ease-in-out;
}
```

The transition definition takes three arguments; the first tells the browser which CSS attributes should be tracked. For our example, we only want to track the left attribute since we're animating the sheen as it travels across the header. This can also be set to all to control the transition of any attribute changes. The second parameter defines how long the animation takes, in seconds. This value can be a decimal, like 0.5s, up to multiple seconds for a longer transition when slower changes are desired. The final argument is the name of the timing function to use. We just use one of the default functions, but you can define your own as well. Ceaser[3] is a tool that we could potentially use to define our own function.

Next, we need to add a style declaration that defines where we want the sheen to end up. In this case, it should end on the right side of the header. We *could* attach this to the hover event:

```
header:hover .sheen {
  left: 900px;
}
```

But if we did, then the sheen is going to go back to its starting spot when the user hovers away from the header. We want to make this a one-time deal, so we're going to have to use a little bit of JavaScript to change the state of the page. We'll add a special class to our style sheet called loaded, which positions the sheen all the way at the end of the logo, like this:

```
cssheen/style.css
header.loaded .sheen {
  left: 900px;
}
```

Then we'll use jQuery to add that class to the header, which will trigger the transition.

```
$(function() { $('header').addClass('loaded') })
```

When looking at Figure 5, *The "sheen" is styled but still visible outside of the header*, on page 17, you may be thinking that all you're doing is moving a blurry bar across the screen. But now that we're done styling the sheen, we can clean up the overall look by adding a single style tweak. We'll add a style of overflow: hidden;, which will hide the part of the sheen that hangs over the header.

```
cssheen/style.css
header {
  overflow: hidden;
}
```

---

3.   http://matthewlein.com/ceaser/

Figure 5—The "sheen" is styled but still visible outside of the header.

With all of our styles in place, we can trigger the entire animation just by changing a CSS class on an element. We no longer have to rely on a JavaScript animation suite or Flash for adding smooth animations to our websites.

This approach has the added advantage of saving our users' bandwidth. Although this doesn't affect most users, we don't always know when a user might visit our site from an iPad or another mobile device using cellular coverage. This approach means less files to download and therefore faster load times for our visitors. We should always keep site optimization in mind when developing websites.

In browsers that don't support these new style rules, our site will simply display the logo image. By separating style from content, we get the benefit of backward compatibility and better accessibility for users with screen readers, because the <img> tag contains the alternative text.

To make the animation work on all browsers, we could simply use this solution as a fallback to the original Flash solution, placing our <img> within the <object> tag that embeds the Flash movie.

Further Exploration

We covered only a few of the transformations and transitions that are available to us. There are other transformation options available like scaling and skewing. We can also get more fine-grained control over how long each transformation takes, or even which transformations we actually want to transition. Some browsers also give you the ability to define your *own* transitions. The built-in control that we're finally getting over animations is very exciting and well overdue.

Also See

- Recipe 1, *Styling Buttons and Links*, on page 2
- Recipe 2, *Styling Quotes with CSS*, on page 6
- Recipe 28, *Building Modular Style Sheets with Sass*, on page 201

Recipe 4

Creating Interactive Slideshows with jQuery

Problem

Just a few years ago, you'd probably create a Flash movie if you wanted to have an animated slideshow on your website. Simple tools would make this an easy process, but maintaining the photographs in the slideshow often means rebuilding the Flash movie. Additionally, many mobile devices don't support Flash Player, which means they can't see the slideshows at all. We need an alternative solution that works on multiple platforms and is easy to maintain.

Ingredients

- jQuery
- The jQuery Cycle plug-in[4]

Solution

We can build a simple and elegant image slideshow using jQuery and the jQuery Cycle plug-in. This open source tool will give our users a nice slideshow and only requires a browser with JavaScript support.

There are many JavaScript-based image cycling plug-ins, but what sets jQuery Cycle apart from the rest is its ease of use. It has many built-in transition effects and provides controls for the user to navigate through images. It's well-maintained and has a very active developer community. It's the perfect choice for our slideshow.

Our current home page is somewhat static and boring, so our boss wants us to build a slideshow showcasing the best of our company's photographs. We'll take some sample photographs and build a simple prototype to learn how the jQuery Cycle plug-in works.

We'll start by creating a simple home page template that will hold our image slideshow named index.html, containing the usual boilerplate code:

---

4.   https://github.com/malsup/cycle

```
image_cycling/index.html
<!DOCTYPE html>
<html lang="en">
  <head>
    <title>AwesomeCo</title>
      </head>
      <body>
        <h1>AwesomeCo</h1>
      </body>
    </html>
```

Next, we'll create an images folder and place a few sample images our boss gave us to use for the slideshow, which you can find in the book's source code folder under the image_cycling folder.

Next, we add jQuery and the jQuery Cycle plug-in to our <head> section right below the <title> element. We also need to add a link to a file called rotate.js, which will contain all of the JavaScript we'll need to configure our image rotator.

```
image_cycling/index.html
<script type="text/javascript"
  src="http://ajax.googleapis.com/ajax/libs/jquery/1.7/jquery.min.js">
</script>
<script type="text/javascript"
src="http://cloud.github.com/downloads/malsup/cycle/jquery.cycle.all.2.74.js">
</script>
<script type="text/javascript" src="rotate.js"></script>
```

Then, we add a <div> with an ID of slideshow and add the images inside, like this:

```
image_cycling/index.html
<div id="slideshow">
  <img src="images/house-light-slide.jpg" />
  <img src="images/lake-bench-slide.jpg" />
  <img src="images/old-building-slide.jpg" />
  <img src="images/oldbarn-slide.jpg" />
  <img src="images/streetsign-with-highlights-slide.jpg" />
  <img src="images/water-stairs-slide.jpg" />
</div>
```

When we look at our page in the browser, we will see something like Figure 6, *These images aren't cycling yet*, on page 20. This also shows us what our page will look like if the user does not have JavaScript. We see that all of the content is available to the user so they don't miss out on anything.

We haven't added the functionality to trigger the jQuery Cycle plug-in, so we just see the images listed in order. Let's add the JavaScript to initialize the

Figure 6—These images aren't cycling yet.

plug-in and start the slideshow. Let's create the file rotate.js and add this code, which configures the jQuery Cycle plug-in:

image_cycling/rotate.js
```
$(function() {
  $('#slideshow').cycle({fx: 'fade'});
});
```

The jQuery Cycle plug-in has many different options. We can make the images fade, fade with zooming, wipe, or even toss as they transition. You can find the full list of options on jQuery Cycle's website.[5] Let's stick with the fade function because it is simple and elegant. We defined it with the snippet inside of the cycle() call.

```
fx: 'fade'
```

Now that we have all the pieces in place, let's look at our page again. This time we see only one image, and after a few seconds, we begin to see the images rotate.

---

5. http://jquery.malsup.com/cycle/options.html

Adding Play and Pause Buttons

We now have a working slideshow. We show our boss the final product, and she says "That's great, but I would really like to have a Pause button to let customers pause the slideshow on an image they like." Lucky for us, the jQuery Cycle plug-in has this ability built right in.

We'll add these buttons to the page with JavaScript, since they're needed only when the slideshow is active. This way, we don't present useless controls to users who don't have JavaScript support. To do this, we'll create two functions: setupButtons() and toggleControls(). The first function will add our buttons to the page and attach click() events to each. The click events will tell the slideshow to either pause or resume. We'll also want the click() events to call toggleControls(), which will toggle the buttons so only the relevant one is shown.

```
image_cycling/rotate.js
var setupButtons = function(){
  var slideShow = $('#slideshow');

  var pause = $('<span id="pause">Pause</span>');
  pause.click(function() {
   slideShow.cycle('pause');
    toggleControls();
  }).insertAfter(slideShow);

  var resume = $('<span id="resume">Resume</span>');
  resume.click(function() {
    slideShow.cycle('resume');
    toggleControls();
  }).insertAfter(slideShow);

  resume.toggle();
};

var toggleControls = function(){
        $('#pause').toggle();
        $('#resume').toggle();
};
```

Notice that we are setting variables to our jQuery selectors. This allows us to manipulate the DOM in a much more succinct manner. We are also taking advantage of the way jQuery returns a jQuery object for almost all methods performed on a jQuery object, so we can chain our insertAfter() function onto our click() binding.

To trigger the setupButtons() function, we'll need to add a call to it below our cycle() call in the jQuery ready function.

```
image_cycling/rotate.js
$(function() {
  $('#slideshow').cycle({fx: 'fade'});
  setupButtons();
});
```

Let's check out the page in the browser again. We can see the Pause button show up on the page like in Figure 7, *Our rotating images with controls*, on page 23. Once our slideshow starts, we can click the Pause button, and we'll see the Resume button replace the Pause button as the transitions stop. When we click the Resume button, the images will begin to change again.

Further Exploration

This slideshow was easy to implement, and with all of the options that are provided at the plug-in's website,[6] we can extend the slideshow to include even more functionality.

To enhance the visual experience, the cycle plug-in has many transition settings, such as a shuffle, a toss, or an uncover transition. We can change our slideshow to use any of these by changing the value of the fx: option in our cycle() call. We can also cycle other elements besides images, including more complex HTML regions. These are just some of the possibilities baked into the Cycle plug-in, so go explore and try them.

Also See

- Recipe 3, *Creating Animations with CSS3 Transformations*, on page 13
- Recipe 35, *Testing JavaScript with Jasmine*, on page 255

---

6. http://jquery.malsup.com/cycle/options.html

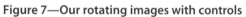

Figure 7—Our rotating images with controls

Recipe 5

Creating and Styling Inline Help Dialogs

Problem

We have a page with a lot of links to short, supplemental content elsewhere on our site. Just linking to these pages works, but it breaks the flow of reading to open the new browser while we're in the middle of a paragraph, so it would be great to display the content inline in a stylish way and leave the page only if absolutely necessary.

Ingredients

- jQuery
- jQuery UI[7]
- jQuery Theme [8]

Solution

Since we want our information to be part of the flow of the page while still working in older browsers, we'll use JavaScript to replace HTML links to our supplemental content and display that content inline on our page. Doing this will allow the content to remain accessible to browsers without JavaScript, while giving a more styled and smooth flowing experience to users with modern browsers and JavaScript enabled. And when we load this content, we will make it look good by displaying it with any of the jQuery animations, plus the regular and modal dialogs, such as Figure 8, *Modal dialog overlaying content*, on page 25.

Before we get to the JavaScript, let's create a basic page that will load jQuery, jQuery UI, and a jQuery theme plus give us our first link for our inline content.

inlinehelp/index.html
```
<html>
  <head>
    <link rel="stylesheet" href="jquery_theme.css"
    type="text/css" media="all" />
```

---

7.   http://jqueryui.com
8.   http://jqueryui.com/themeroller/

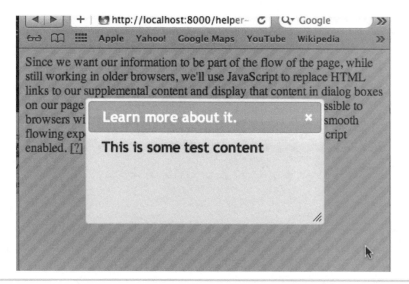

Figure 8—Modal dialog overlaying content

```
<script type="text/javascript"
  src='http://ajax.googleapis.com/ajax/libs/jquery/1.7/jquery.min.js'>
</script>
<script type="text/javascript"
  src='http://ajax.googleapis.com/ajax/libs/jqueryui/1.8.14/jquery-ui.min.js'>
</script>
<script type="text/javascript" src='inlinehelp.js'></script>
</head>
<body>
  <p>
    This is some text.
    <a href="test-content.html"
      id="help_link_1"
      class="help_link"
      data-style="dialog"
      data-modal='true'>
    Learn more about it.
    </a>
  </p>
</body>
</html>
```

We expect to add this functionality quite frequently throughout our site, so implementing it should be as easy as possible. Once everything is done, our helper links will look like this:

```
<a href="a.html" id="help_a" class="help_link" data-style="dialog">
  More on A
</a>
<a href="b.html" id="help_b" class="help_link" data-style="dialog"
  data-modal="true">
  More on B
</a>
<a href="c.html" id="help_c" class="help_link" data-style="clip">
  More on C
</a>
<a href="d.html" class="help_link" data-style="fold">
  More on D
</a>
```

Note that we are using data- attributes to declare the style and modal settings. This is part of the HTML5 specification, which allows custom data attributes on HTML elements. This lets us set information on our elements while maintaining valid markup.

The following code is an example of a simple setup for the script we're going to write, setting just a few options and then calling our displayHelpers() function. Once it's all set up, all we'll need to do to make a link display its contents inline will be to set a class on it, along with optionally setting an animation style and specifying if dialog boxes should be modal.

```
inlinehelp/inlinehelp.js
$(function() {
  var options = {
    helperClass:"help_dialog"
  }

  displayHelpers(options);
});
```

Using jQuery's ready() function, we make sure that the page has completely loaded before we start to manipulate the DOM. This ensures that everything is present on the page and we don't miss anything when our code starts to run. We set a couple of options here, which aren't required but help make our new links and dialog boxes look good. We then pass them in to the display-Helpers() and start to update the page there.

```
inlinehelp/inlinehelp.js
function displayHelpers(options) {
  if (options != null) {
    setIconTo(options['icon']);
    setHelperClassTo(options['helper_class']);
  }
```

```
  else {
    setIconTo();
    setHelperClassTo();
  }

  $("a.help_link").each(function(index,element) {
    if ($(element).attr("id") == "") { $(element).attr("id", randomString()); }
    appendHelpTo(element);
  });
  $("a.help_link").click(function() { displayHelpFor(this); return false; });
}
```

We start off by setting the icon or text that will be used to indicate there's something for the user to check out. We're going to expect these links to be relevant to the content around them, so it's OK to remove the actual text. We'll also set a class for our dialog boxes so that we can style them.

inlinehelp/inlinehelp.js
```
function setIconTo(helpIcon) {
  isImage = /jpg|jpeg|png|gif$/
  if (helpIcon == undefined)
    { icon = "[?]"; }
  else if (isImage.test(helpIcon))
    { icon = "<img src='"+helpIcon+"'>"; }
  else
    { icon = helpIcon; }
}
```

The setIconTo() function starts off by seeing whether there was a help_icon option passed at all. If there wasn't, we'll use the default option of [?]. If something was passed, we check whether it's a path to an image by seeing whether the string ends with any common image extensions. If it does, we want to insert that in to an <img> element. Otherwise, we can display the text as it was passed. If it turns out that we were passed a full <img> element anyway, it's no problem; it'll still be displayed.

Next we want to set the class for the dialog boxes so that they'll be styled when they're displayed, either by our own CSS or by using a jQuery UI theme.

inlinehelp/inlinehelp.js
```
function setHelperClassTo(className) {
  if (className == undefined)
    { helperClass = "help_dialog"; }
  else
    { helperClass = className; }
}
```

The setHelperClassTo() function checks to see whether a class was set in the options to use for the dialog boxes. If it was, we use it, but if not, we use our default of help_dialog.

We also want to make sure each link has an ID, because we will use this to associate the link with its respective dialog <div>. If a link doesn't have an ID, we should add one.

```
inlinehelp/inlinehelp.js
$("a.help_link").each(function(index,element) {
  if ($(element).attr("id") == "") { $(element).attr("id", randomString()); }
  appendHelpTo(element);
});
```

To ensure that IDs are present, we load any links on the page with the class help_link and inspect them to make sure they have an ID attribute set. If there isn't one, we generate a random string and use it as the ID.

```
inlinehelp/inlinehelp.js
function randomString() {
  var chars = "0123456789ABCDEFGHIJKLMNOPQRSTUVWXTZabcdefghiklmnopqrstuvwxyz";
  var stringLength = 8;
  var randomstring = '';
  for (var i=0; i<stringLength; i++) {
    var rnum = Math.floor(Math.random() * chars.length);
    randomstring += chars.substring(rnum,rnum+1);
  }
  return randomstring;
}
```

The randomString() function is a simple function that generates a random eight-character string containing letters and numbers. This should provide enough IDs to cover any links on the pages that don't have IDs on them already.

After ensuring that an ID is present, we call the appendHelpTo() function, which inserts our icon into the link and prepares the dialog elements that will hold the contents of the linked pages.

```
inlinehelp/inlinehelp.js
Line 1  function appendHelpTo(element) {
   -      if ($(element).attr("title") != undefined) {
   -        title = $(element).attr("title");
   -      } else {
   5        title = $(element).html();
   -      }
   -      var helperDiv = document.createElement('div');
   -      helperDiv.setAttribute("id",
   -        $(element).attr("id") + "_" + $(element).attr("data-style"));
  10      helperDiv.setAttribute("class",
   -        $(element).attr("data-style") +" "+ helperClass);
```

```
      helperDiv.setAttribute("style", "display:none;");
      helperDiv.setAttribute("title", title);

15    $(element).after(helperDiv);
      $(element).html(icon);
   }
```

When appendHelpTo() is called, it starts by inserting a <div> that will contain the contents of our linked page when the link is clicked. We give it an ID that is a combination of the link's ID plus the class that was set in the options at the beginning. We also set a few classes: the class as we specified in the options plus a class that will indicate the animation style to use. The final thing to do is to set the style of the <div> to display:none; because we don't want it to show up on the page until the link is clicked.

Line 3 of appendHelpTo() replaces the HTML of the original link with our icon, turning all of the links into inline [?]s or whatever was set in the options.

inlinehelp/inlinehelp.js
```
$("a.help_link").click(function() { displayHelpFor(this); return false; });
```

And now we call the final line of displayHelpers(), which gathers all elements with a class of help_link and overrides the normal response when one is clicked, instead calling the displayHelpFor() function and then returning false so that the normal click event does not fire.

inlinehelp/inlinehelp.js
```
function displayHelpFor(element) {
  url = $(element).attr("href");
  helpTextElement = "#"+$(element).attr("id") + "_" +
    $(element).attr("data-style");
  if ($(helpTextElement).html() == "") {
    $.get(url, { },
      function(data){
        $(helpTextElement).html(data);
        if ($(element).attr("data-style") == "dialog") {
          activateDialogFor(element, $(element).attr("data-modal"));
        }
        toggleDisplayOf(helpTextElement);
    });
  }
  else { toggleDisplayOf(helpTextElement); }
}
```

displayHelpFor() starts by getting the URL from the recently clicked link so we know what page we want to display. Next we build up the ID of the <div> that we inserted into the page earlier. This is where we will place the content from the URL of our link. But before we go to the trouble of loading that content, we should make sure we haven't already loaded it. If the <div> is empty, then we haven't loaded any content into it yet. If we have, there's no need to load it a second time, so we call the toggleDisplayOf() function. By not loading the content multiple times, we save the user from having to wait for the page to load again, and we reduce our own bandwidth costs.

However, if the content has not yet been loaded, we use jQuery's get() function to load the URL via Ajax and insert its content in to the <div>. Having done that, we check to see the requested style of inline text. If we are using the dialog style, we call the activateDialogFor() function, which prepares the dialog window in the DOM and sets any modal options as well.

```
inlinehelp/inlinehelp.js
function activateDialogFor(element,modal) {
  var dialogOptions = { autoOpen: false };
  if (modal == "true") {
    dialogOptions = {
      modal: true,
      draggable: false,
      autoOpen: false
    };
  }
  $("#"+$(element).attr("id")+"_dialog").dialog(dialogOptions);
}
```

This registers the dialog element with the page so that we are able to access it. After activation, we ensure that the dialog is closed by setting the autOpen: false option. We do this because we want to open it using the toggleDisplayOf() function so that we are being consistent with our other dialogs.

```
inlinehelp/inlinehelp.js
function toggleDisplayOf(element) {
  switch(displayMethodOf(element)) {
    case "dialog":
      if ($(element).dialog('isOpen')) {
        $(element).dialog('close');
      }
      else {
        $(element).dialog('open');
      }
      break;
    case "undefined":
      $(element).toggle("slide");
      break;
    default:
      $(element).toggle(displayMethod);
  }
}
```

`inlinehelp/inlinehelp.js`

```
function displayMethodOf(element) {
  helperClassRegex = new RegExp(" "+helperClass);
  if ($(element).hasClass("dialog"))
    { displayMethod = "dialog"; }
  else
    { displayMethod = $(element).attr("class").replace(helperClassRegex,""); }
  return displayMethod;
}
```

In toggleDisplayOf(), we finally display our new content. First we use the displayMethodOf() function to figure out how to display the content. We can use any animation method from the jQuery UI Effects library or the Dialog library, so first we check to see whether our link has a style of dialog. If it does, we return that; otherwise, we get the class of the link and remove our named class, which should leave us with just the animation style to use when displaying the content.

Back in toggleDisplayOf(), we use the display method to determine how to display or hide the content. If it's a dialog, we check to see whether it is already open using one of jQuery's helpers, isOpen, and open or close the dialog as is appropriate. If we were unable to determine the animation style, we default to slide and toggle the display of the element. Finally, if we do have a display_method, we toggle the visibility of our content using that method.

Once this code is in place, we can easily add new inline elements to our pages while giving us a great way to maintain compatibility with all browsers. Plus, our code is implemented loosely enough to handle any new animations that come along without having to make any changes beyond handling compatibility with new versions of jQuery.

Further Exploration

There are a few things that would be very nice to declare as options when we first initialize our code, specifically, the class for our helper links and the default animation. Right now both of those attributes are hard-coded, so we'll need to make sure there's still a default value if nothing is set, similar to how we set the class for our content <div>s or the icon text/image.

Right now we toss out the text of the original link and replace it with our icon. What could we do with it instead of discarding it completely? Setting it as a title would give our users some indication of what the page is about when they hover over the link and keep our page more in line with its original setup.

Also See

- Recipe 29, *Cleaner JavaScript with CoffeeScript*, on page 209
- Recipe 35, *Testing JavaScript with Jasmine*, on page 255

## CHAPTER 2

User Interface Recipes

Whether you're delivering static content or presenting an interactive application, you have to create a usable interface. This collection of recipes explores the presentation of information as well as some new ways to build more maintainable and responsive client-side interfaces.

Recipe 6

Creating an HTML Email Template

Problem

Building HTML emails is a bit like traveling back in time—a time before CSS, when everyone used tables for layout and <font> tags reigned supreme. A lot of the best practices we've come to know and love just aren't usable in HTML emails simply because the email readers don't handle them. Testing a web page on multiple browsers is easy compared to the amount of testing we have to do when we create an email that will be read in Outlook, Hotmail, Gmail, or Thunderbird, not to mention the various mail applications on mobile devices.

But our job isn't to complain about how difficult things are going to be; our job is to deliver results. And we have a lot of work to do. Not only do we need to produce readable HTML emails, we need to ensure we don't get flagged as spam.

Ingredients

• A free trial account on Litmus.com for testing emails

Solution

Designing HTML emails means discarding many current web development techniques because of the constraints of email clients. While staying aware of these limitations, we also need to avoid techniques that might get us marked as junk messages, and we need to easily test our email on multiple devices. We need to build something that is usable, readable, and effective on multiple platforms, and the best approach is going to be using good old trusty HTML with table-based layouts.

HTML Email Basics

Conceptually, HTML emails aren't that difficult. After all, creating a simple HTML page is something we can do without much effort. But just like web pages, we can't guarantee that the user will see the same thing we created. Each email client does something a little different when presenting email messages to its users.

For starters, many web-based clients, like Gmail, Hotmail, and Yahoo often strip out or ignore style sheet definitions from the markup. Google Mail actually removes styles declared in the <style> tag, in an attempt to prevent styles in emails from colliding with the styles it uses to display its interface. We also can't rely on an external style sheet, because many email clients won't automatically fetch remote files without first prompting the user. So, we can't really use CSS for layout in an HTML email.

Google Mail and Yahoo either remove or rename the <body> tag in the email, so it's best to wrap the email in another tag that can stand in for the <body>.

Some clients choke on CSS shorthand declarations, and so any definitions we do use need to be spelled out. This example:

```
#header{padding: 20px;}
```

might be ignored by older clients, so instead, we need to expand it:

```
#header{
  padding-top: 20px;
  padding-right: 20px;
  padding-bottom: 20px;
  padding-left: 20px;
}
```

Desktop clients such as Outlook 2007 and Lotus Notes can't handle background images, and Lotus Notes can't display PNG images. That might not seem like a big deal at first, but there are millions of enterprise users who use that as their primary client.

These aren't the only issues we'll run into, but they are the most prevalent. The Email Standards Project[1] has comprehensive lists of issues for the various email clients.

Partying Like It's 1999

When it comes down to it, the most effective HTML emails are designed using the most basic HTML features:

- They're built with simple HTML markup with minimal CSS styling.
- They're laid out with HTML tables instead of more modern techniques.
- They don't use intricate typography.
- The CSS styles are extremely simplistic.

In short, we'll need to develop emails as if the last ten years of web development didn't happen. With that in mind, let's code up a very simple email

---

1.   http://www.email-standards.org/

template using tables for layout. The application developers will take this template and handle all of the real content, but we'll need to figure out how to code up the template so that it's readable in all of the popular email clients.

Our invoice will have the typical items that we typically find on an invoice. We'll have a header and footer, as well as sections for our address and the customer's billing address. We'll have a list of the items the customer purchased, and each line will have the price, quantity, and subtotal. We'll need to provide the grand total for the invoice as well, and we'll have an area to display some notes to the customer.

Since some web-based email clients strip out or rename the <body> element, we'll need to use our own top-level element to act as the container for our email. To keep it as bullet-proof as possible, we'll create an outer table for the container and place additional tables inside of that container for the header, footer, and the content. Figure 9, *Our invoice mock-up*, on page 37 gives a rough example of how we'll mark this up.

Let's start by writing the wrapper for the email template, using an HTML 4.0 doctype:

htmlemail/template.html
```
<!DOCTYPE html PUBLIC "-//W3C//DTD HTML 4.01//EN"
         "http://www.w3.org/TR/html4/strict.dtd">
<html>
<head>
  <meta content="text/html; charset=ISO-8859-1" http-equiv="content-type">
  <title>Invoice</title>
</head>
<body>
  <center>
    <table id="inv_container"
      width="95%" border="0" cellpadding="0" cellspacing="0">
      <tr>
        <td align="center" valign="top">
        </td>
      </tr>
    </table>
  </center>
</body>
</html>
```

To ensure that our invoice shows up centered in the email client, we have to resort to using the very old and very deprecated <center> tag, since it's the only approach that comes close to working across all of the various clients. Don't worry, though; we won't be using <blink>.

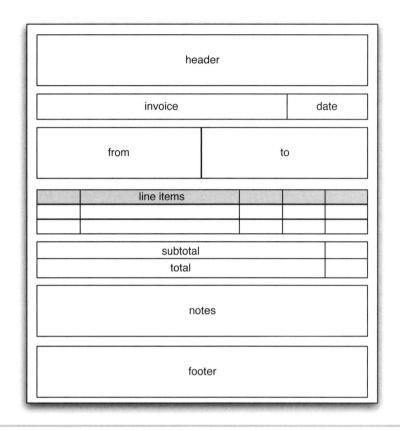

Figure 9—Our invoice mock-up

Next, we need to create the header. We'll use one table for our company name and a second table with two columns for the invoice number and the date.

htmlemail/template.html
```html
<table border="0" cellpadding="0" cellspacing="0" width="100%">
  <tr>
    <td align="center" bgcolor="#5d8eb6" valign="top">
    <h1><font color="white">AwesomeCo</font></h1>
    </td>
  </tr>
</table>

<table border="0" cellpadding="0" cellspacing="0" width="98%">
  <tr>
    <td align="left"  width="70%"><h2>Invoice for Order #533102 </h2></td>
    <td align="right" width="30%"><h3>December 30th, 2011</h3></td>
  </tr>
</table>
```

Since some of the web-based clients strip out CSS, we'll have to use HTML attributes to specify the background and text color. The first table has a width of 100 percent, but the second table has a width of 98 percent. Since our tables are centered on the page, this gives us space on the left and right edges so that the text isn't touching the edge of the outer table.

Next, let's add another table that contains the "From" and "To" addresses.

htmlemail/template.html

```html
<table id="inv_addresses" border="0"
       cellpadding="2" cellspacing="0" width="98%">
  <tr>
    <td align="left" valign="top" width="50%">
      <h3>From</h3>
      AwesomeCo Inc. <br>
      123 Fake Street <br>
      Chicago, IL 55555
    </td>
    <td align="left" valign="top" width="50%">
      <h3>To</h3>
      GNB <br>
      456 Industry Way <br>
      New York, NY 55555
    </td>
  </tr>
</table>
```

Next, we'll add a table for the invoice itself.

htmlemail/template.html

```html
<table border="0" cellpadding="2" cellspacing="0" width="98%">
  <caption>Order Summary</caption>
  <tr>
    <th bgcolor="#cccccc" align="left" valign="top">SKU</th>
    <th bgcolor="#cccccc" align="left" valign="top">Item</th>
    <th bgcolor="#cccccc" valign="top">Price</th>
    <th bgcolor="#cccccc" valign="top" width="10%">QTY</th>
    <th bgcolor="#cccccc" valign="top" width="10%">Total</th>
  </tr>
  <tr>
    <td valign="top">10042</td>
    <td valign="top">15-inch MacBook Pro</td>
    <td align="right" valign="top">$1799.00</td>
    <td align="center" valign="top">1</td>
    <td align="right" valign="top">$1799.00</td>
  </tr>
  <tr>
    <td valign="top">20005</td>
    <td valign="top">Mini-Display Port to VGA Adapter</td>
    <td align="right" valign="top">$19.99</td>
```

```
  <td align="center" valign="top">1</td>
  <td align="right" valign="top">$19.99</td>
  </tr>
</table>
```

This is an actual data table, so we'll make sure it has all of the right attributes, such as column headers and a caption.

Then we'll add one for the total. We need to use a separate table for this because, believe it or not, some email clients still have trouble displaying tables with rows that span multiple columns.

htmlemail/template.html
```
<hr>
<table border="0" cellpadding="2" cellspacing="0" width="98%">
  <tr>
    <td align="right" valign="top">Subtotal: </td>
    <td align="right" valign="top" width="10%">$1818.99</td>
  </tr>

  <tr>
    <td align="right" valign="top">Total Due: </td>
    <td align="right" valign="top"><b>$1818.99</b> </td>
  </tr>
</table>
```

We'll place another simple table to display the invoice notes next.

htmlemail/template.html
```
<table border="0" cellpadding="0" cellspacing="0" width="98%">
  <tr><td align="left">
    <h2>Notes</h2>
    <p>Thank you for your business!</p>
  </td></tr>
</table>
```

And finally, we'll add the footer, which we define as a single celled table with full width, just like the header.

htmlemail/template.html
```
<table id="inv_footer" border="0"
       cellpadding="0" cellspacing="0" width="100%">
  <tr>
    <td align="center" valign="top">
    <h4>Copyright &copy; 2012 AwesomeCo</h4>
    <h4>
       You are receiving this email because you purchased
       products from us.
    </h4>
    </td>
  </tr>
</table>
```

The footer is a good place to explain to the user why they got the email in the first place. For an invoice it's pretty obvious, but for a newsletter, we'd use this area to give readers some links to manage their subscription or opt out of future mailings.

With that, we've created a simple but readable HTML invoice. But what about those clients that can't handle HTML emails?

Supporting the Unsupportable

Not every HTML email client supports HTML email, and as we've learned, even those that do are inconsistent. We should provide a way for people to read the content on those devices, and the most common solution is to provide a link at the top of the message that links to a copy of the email that we host on our servers. When users click the link, they'll be able to read the message in their web browser of choice.

In our case, we can simply place a link to a copy of the invoice within the user's account. We'll want to place a link like that right at the top of the email, above the content table, so it's easily visible. As a bonus, some mail programs provide a preview, and this will let them jump right into the invoice without opening the email.

`htmlemail/template.html`

```
<p>
  Unable to view this invoice?
  <a href="#">View it in your browser instead</a>.
</p>
```

Third-party systems like MailChimp and Campaign Monitor provide this functionality by hosting the HTML email on their servers as static pages.

We could also construct a multipart email, sending both a plain-text version of the invoice as well as the HTML version. When we do this, we're actually inserting two bodies into the email and using a special set of headers in the email that tell the email client that the email contains both text and HTML versions. To do that effectively, we'd need to develop and maintain a text version of the invoice in addition to our HTML version. Alternatively, we could just place a link to the web page version of the invoice that we're hosting.

Sending multipart emails is beyond the scope of this recipe, but most web-based frameworks and email clients have options for sending out multipart messages. Wikipedia's entry on MIME[2] has a good overview on how multipart messages work.

---

2.   http://en.wikipedia.org/wiki/MIME

Joe asks:
Couldn't We Just Use Semantic Markup Instead of Tables?

Many standards-focused developers choose to avoid using tables in favor of semantic markup that relies on CSS to manage the layout. They're not concerned with the mail clients stripping out the CSS because the email will still be readable and accessible.

Unfortunately, if your stakeholders insist that the design of the email must be consistent across clients, standards-based web development techniques won't cut it. That's why we used a table-based approach in this recipe.

Styling with CSS

We used tables for layout because we can't rely on floating or absolute positioning with CSS, since many web-based email clients strip out CSS styles. To be honest, those web-based clients aren't stripping things out because their developers are mean-spirited standards-haters. They're doing it because if they allowed CSS, there's potential for the email's contents to conflict with styles in the web-based application.

However, there are two reasons we may still want to try to use CSS to make things look nicer. First, we want things to look nicer for people who actually have email clients that support CSS. But second, we can reuse this invoice template for the static page we talked about in *Supporting the Unsupportable*, on page 40.

Since many email clients strip off the <head> section of our document, we'll just place our style information in a <style> tag right above our container table.

Let's remove the margins around our heading tags so we can remove some of the wasted space. Let's also apply a background color and a border to our table and add some space between each of the inner tables, except for the footer, so things aren't so crowded.

htmlemail/template.html

```
<style>
  table#inv_addresses h3,
  table#inv_footer h4{
    margin: 0;
  }

  table{
    margin-bottom: 20px;
  }
```

```
table#inv_footer{
  margin-bottom: 0;
}
body{
  background-color: #eeeeee;
}
table#inv_container{
  background-color: #ffffff;
  border: 1px solid #000000;
}
</style>
```

With the styles in place, we have an invoice that looks like the one in Figure 10, *Our completed invoice*, on page 43. We're not done, though; we need to test things.

Testing Our Emails

Before we can show this off to the client, we need to see how this email works in some email readers. We can send it around a bit to our colleagues, or we could create accounts at Gmail, Yahoo Mail, Hotmail, and others to see how things look, but manual testing is time-consuming.

Litmus[3] provides a suite of tools that help people test web pages and emails. They support a wide range of email clients and browsers, including mobile devices. While the service is not free, it does provide a trial account we can use to ensure that our invoices work as expected.

Within a Litmus account, we can create a test that lets us choose the target clients. We can then email our invoice to some addresses Litmus provides, or we can just upload our HTML file through the web interface. Using the HTML upload doesn't provide a text fallback, so some of the test results will show only the HTML source, not a text fallback, but for our test, it's good enough.

Litmus takes our email, renders it on the target email clients, and provides us with a detailed report that looks like Figure 11, *The results of our test*, on page 44.

With the code we've written, it looks like we have an email invoice that looks fairly consistent across the major platforms and looks readable on most of the others.

---

3.   http://litmus.com/

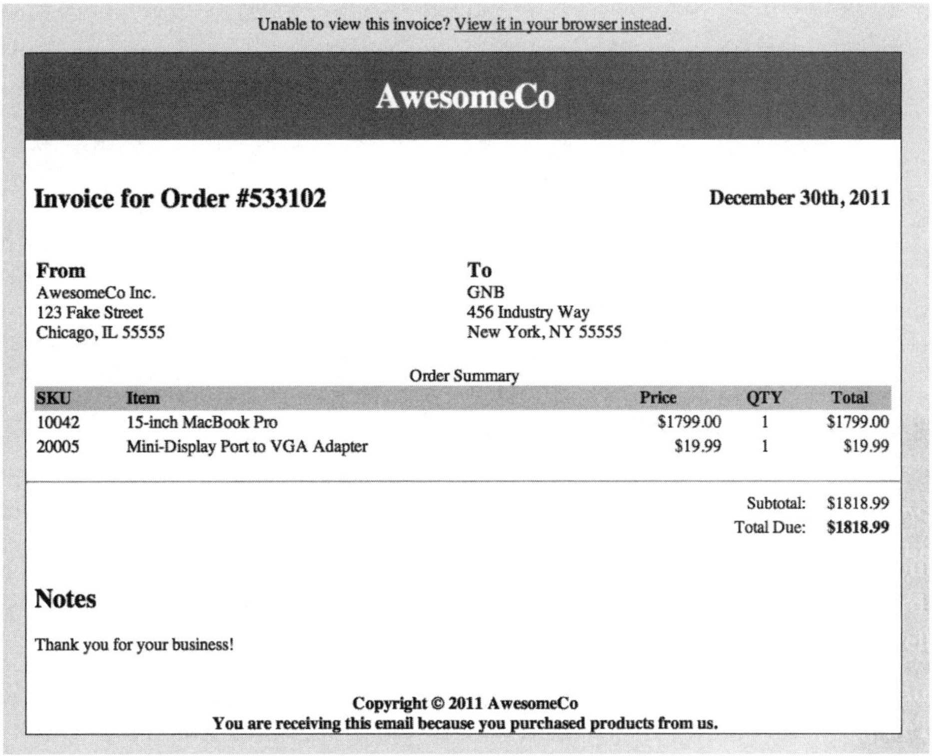

Unable to view this invoice? View it in your browser instead.

AwesomeCo

Invoice for Order #533102   December 30th, 2011

From   **To**
AwesomeCo Inc.   GNB
123 Fake Street   456 Industry Way
Chicago, IL 55555   New York, NY 55555

Order Summary

SKU	Item	Price	QTY	Total
10042	15-inch MacBook Pro	$1799.00	1	$1799.00
20005	Mini-Display Port to VGA Adapter	$19.99	1	$19.99
			Subtotal:	$1818.99
			Total Due:	**$1818.99**

Notes

Thank you for your business!

Copyright © 2011 AwesomeCo
You are receiving this email because you purchased products from us.

Figure 10—Our completed invoice

Images and Emails

We didn't talk about images in this recipe for two reasons. First, we'd need to host our images on a server and include absolute links into the email. The second reason is that most email clients turn images off, since many companies use images to track whether the email was opened.

If you do decide to use images in your emails, you'll want to ensure that you follow a few simple rules:

* Be sure to host the images on a server that will be available, and don't change the URLs to the images. You never know when someone will open the email you sent.

* Since images are often disabled by default, make sure you specify useful and descriptive alt attributes on your images.

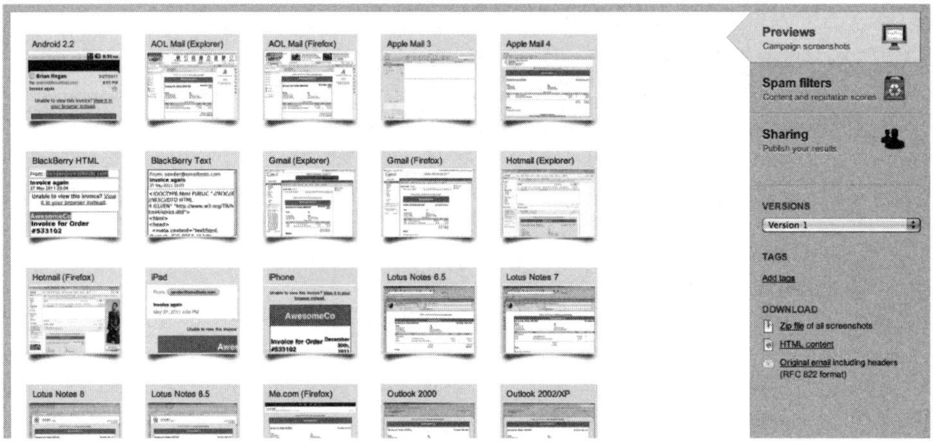

Figure 11—The results of our test

- Place the images into your email with regular <img> tags. Many email clients don't support images as table-cell backgrounds, and even fewer support images as CSS backgrounds.

- Because images are often blocked by default, it's a really bad idea to use images as the entire content of your email. It may look nice, but it causes accessibility problems.

Images in emails can be very effective when used properly. Don't be afraid to use them; just be mindful of the issues you will encounter.

Further Exploration

Our simple email template presents a readable invoice to our recipients, but it doesn't have to be as engaging as a marketing announcement or a newsletter might need to be. For that, we'd need to do more styling, more images, and more "exception handling" for various email clients.

MailChimp[4] knows a thing or two about sending emails. After all, that's its business. If you're looking to learn more about email templates, you can dig in to the Email templates MailChimp has open sourced.[5] They're tested on all of the major clients, too, and have some well-commented source code that gives more insight into some of the hacks we have to employ to make things work well across all of the major email clients.

---

4. http://www.mailchimp.com
5. https://github.com/mailchimp/Email-Blueprints

Recipe 7

Swapping Between Content with Tabbed Interfaces

Problem

We sometimes have multiple, similar pieces of information that we want to display together, such as a phrase in multiple languages or code examples in several programming languages. We could display them one after another, but that can take up a lot of space, especially with longer content. There has to be an easier way to let our users easily switch and compare without taking up an unnecessary amount of screen space.

Ingredients

- jQuery

Solution

We can use CSS and JavaScript to take the content on our page and turn it in to a slick tabbed interface. Each section of content will have a tab generated for it based on its class, and only one will be displayed at a time. We'll also make sure that we can have any number of tabs that we want so our design is very flexible. In the end, we'll have something that looks like Figure 12, *Our tabbed interface*, on page 46.

We've been asked to display product descriptions in multiple languages in an attempt to reach a wider audience. We'll build a simple proof-of-concept page so we can determine the best approach going forward.

Building the HTML

Let's start by building out the HTML for the elements we want to show our users. As a proof of concept, let's use two pieces of text, one in English and its Latin translation.

swapping/index.html
```
<!DOCTYPE html>
<html>

  <head>
    <title>Swapping Examples</title>
```

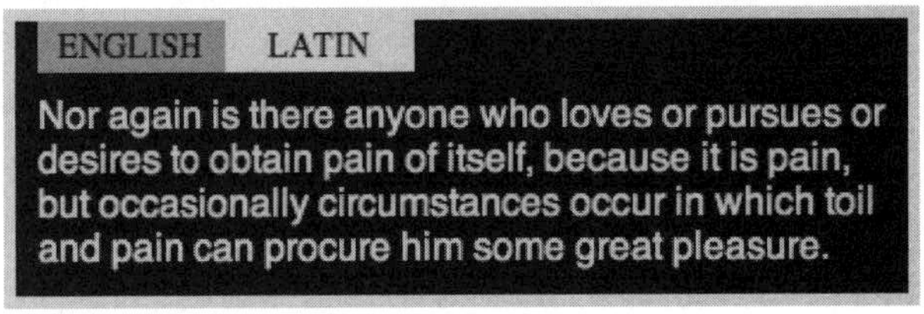

Figure 12—Our tabbed interface

```
<script type="text/javascript"
  src="http://ajax.googleapis.com/ajax/libs/jquery/1.7/jquery.min.js">
</script>
<link rel="stylesheet" href="swapping.css" type="text/css" media="all" />
<script type="text/javascript" src="swapping.js"></script>
</head>
<body>
  <div class="examples">
    <div class="english example">
      Nor again is there anyone who loves or pursues or desires
      to obtain pain of itself, because it is pain, but occasionally
      circumstances occur in which toil and pain can procure him some
      great pleasure.
    </div>

    <div class="latin example">
      Lorem ipsum dolor sit amet, consectetur adipisicing elit, sed
      do eiusmod tempor incididunt ut labore et dolore magna aliqua.
      Ut enim ad minim veniam, quis nostrud exercitation ullamco
      laboris nisi ut aliquip ex ea commodo consequat.
    </div>
  </div>
</body>
</html>
```

We've set up the basic structure of our elements. There's an examples <div> that'll hold each of the sections we want to display. Inside that are our example <div>s that contain the actual content we want users to switch between.

Now, let's get some JavaScript pulled together to create a tabbed interface so our users can toggle between these two examples. We'll use the jQuery library to give us some helper methods and shortcuts.

Creating the Tabbed Interface

First, we need to create a function that will manage calling the different pieces of our JavaScript puzzle. We'll call it styleExamples().

∖⫽   **Joe asks:**
⧘ᥫ   # Couldn't We Use jQuery UI Tabs to Do This?

Yes, we definitely could, but there's a lot in the UI Tabs that we won't be using, such as event hooks. Creating our own tabs lets us focus on keeping things light and gives us greater insight into how things work.

swapping/swapping.js
```
function styleExamples(){
  $("div.examples").each(function(){
    createTabs(this);
    activateTabs(this);
    displayTab($(this).children("ul.tabs").children().first());
  });
}
```

We locate all of the <div> tags that have a class of examples, which will be our containers, and pass each container to a function called createTabs(), which creates the tabbed interface our visitors will use to toggle between examples. We'll just cover createTabs() right now, and we'll talk about the rest of the functions soon.

swapping/swapping.js
```
function createTabs(container){
  $(container).prepend("<ul class='tabs'></ul>");
  $(container).children("div.example").each(function(){
    var exampleTitle = $(this).attr('class').replace('example','');
    $(container).children("ul.tabs").append(
      "<li class='tab "+exampleTitle+"'>"+exampleTitle+"</li>"
    );
  });
}
```

First, we create an unordered list that will hold our tabs and prepend it to the container that holds the examples.

Then we fetch each of the examples in the container and loop over them. Our examples have two classes on them: the title of the example and the example class. We just want the title, so we grab the class with .attr('class'), and then replace example with nothing. This gives us the title of each example, which we'll display in each tab. We then place the title inside of <li> tags, which we append to the unordered list we created initially.

If we open this page in our browser now, nothing will happen because the styleExamples() function isn't being called yet, so none of the JavaScript is being executed. Let's take care of that next.

Switching Between Tabs

Our content is being converted to a tabbed interface, but we don't yet have a way to let our users switch between the different tabs. We'll fix that by first calling styleExamples() when the page loads, which converts the example <div>s into our tabbed interface:

swapping/swapping.js
```
$(function(){
  styleExamples();
});
```

If we load the page in the browser now, we'll see an unordered list with "english" and "latin" in it. That's great, but it doesn't do much for us yet. Let's write a function that displays between the content of our different examples. First we'll hide all of the examples, and then we'll display the one we want to see.

swapping/swapping.js
```
  function displayTab(element){
    tabTitle = $(element)
      .attr('class')
      .replace('tab','')
      .replace('selected','').trim();

    container = $(element).parent().parent();
    container.children("div.example").hide();
    container.children("ul.tabs").children("li").removeClass("selected");

    container.children("div."+tabTitle).slideDown('fast');
    $(element).addClass("selected");
  }
```

We take the class from tab selected english down to just english and assign it to the variable tabTitle, which we will soon use to find the right <div> to display. Now we want to remove everything from sight.

swapping/swapping.js
```
container = $(element).parent().parent();
container.children("div.example").hide();
container.children("ul.tabs").children("li").removeClass("selected");
```

We get the container and hide all of the example <div>s inside it. We also remove the selected class from every <li>, even if they don't have one. We do this because it's much simpler to just hit everything at once, rather than inspecting each element, and it increases the readability of the code. Now we're ready to display the requested example.

swapping/swapping.js

```
container.children("div."+tabTitle).slideDown('fast');
$(element).addClass("selected");
```

Now we'll access the example that we want to show by finding the <div> with a class that matches the class passed in to the function and display it using jQuery's slideDown() functions. We could also try using .show() or .fadeIn() or getting other animation functions from jQuery UI. Finally, we'll set a class of selected on our current <li> to let our CSS indicate which tab is currently displayed.

Now, we have our displayTab(), but nothing is using it. When a user clicks one of the example titles, we want to switch to that example, so we need to make clicking the <li>s actually call displayTab().

swapping/swapping.js

```
  function activateTabs(element){
   $(element).children("ul.tabs").children("li").click(function(){
     displayTab(this);
   });
  }
```

This simply takes in our container, locates the <li>s that we created in createTabs(), and sets them to call displayTab() when they're clicked.

Styling the Tabs

Finally, let's go back to styleExamples() where we'll see how all of the functions we've written are called when the page loads, building up our styled examples.

swapping/swapping.js

```
function styleExamples(){
   $("div.examples").each(function(){
     createTabs(this);
     activateTabs(this);
     displayTab($(this).children("ul.tabs").children().first());
   });
 }
```

The final call to displayTab() sets the first of the tabs as our default tab, hiding all the rest and displaying it when the page finishes loading.

Now that we have all of the behavior wired up, let's apply a little CSS to it to make it look more like the interface we want.

swapping/swapping.css

```
li.tab {
  color: #333;
  cursor: pointer;
  float: left;
  list-style: none outside none;
  margin: 0;
  padding: 0;
  text-align: center;
  text-transform: uppercase;
  width: 80px;
  font-size: 120%;
  line-height: 1.5;
  background-color: #DDD;
}

li.tab.selected {
  background-color: #AAA;
}

ul.tabs {
  font-size: 12px;
  line-height: 1;
  list-style: none outside none;
  margin: 0;
  padding: 0;
  position: absolute;
  right: 20;
  top: 0;
}

div.example {
  font-family: "Helvetica", "san-serif";
  font-size: 16px;

}
div.examples {
  border: 5px solid #DDD;
  font-size: 14px;
  margin-bottom: 20px;
  padding: 10px;
  padding-top: 30px;
  position: relative;
  background-color: #000;
  color: #DDD;
}
```

That's it. We now have some generic code we can use to build out our real site so we can easily switch the product descriptions between different languages.

This solution saves quite a bit of space, and it's something we often see used on sites where space is limited. Some sites use this technique to show product information, reviews, and related items as tabs, while still making that information viewable in a linear format when JavaScript is unavailable.

Further Exploration

What if we wanted to always load a specific tab on the page? For example, if we were displaying code examples in Ruby, Python, and Java and a user of our site wanted to see the Python examples, it'd be nice if they didn't have to click the Python tab every time they visited a new page. We'll leave that up to you to explore on your own.

Also See

- Recipe 8, *Accessible Expand and Collapse*, on page 52

Recipe 8

Accessible Expand and Collapse

Problem

When we need to present long, categorized lists on a website, the best way to do it is with nested, unordered lists. However, when users are presented with this kind of layout, it can be hard to quickly navigate, or even comprehend, such a large list. So, anything we can do to assist our users will be appreciated. Plus, we want to make sure that our list is accessible in case JavaScript is disabled or a user is visiting our site with a screen reader.

Ingredients

- jQuery

Solution

A relatively easy way to organize a nested list, without separating the categories into separate pages, is to make the list collapsible. This means that entire sections of the list can be hidden or displayed to better convey selective information. At the same time, the user can easily manipulate which content should be visible.

For our example, we'll start with an unordered list that displays our products grouped by subcategories.

collapsiblelist/index.html
```html
<h1>Categorized Products</h1>

<ul class='collapsible'>
  <li>
    Music Players

    <ul>
      <li>16 Gb MP3 player</li>
      <li>32 Gb MP3 player</li>
      <li>64 Gb MP3 player</li>
    </ul>
  </li>
  <li class='expanded'>
    Cameras & Camcorders
```

```
<ul>
  <li>
    SLR
    <ul>
      <li>D2000</li>
      <li>D2100</li>
    </ul>
  </li>
  <li class='expanded'>
    Point and Shoot
    <ul>
      <li>G6</li>
      <li>G12</li>
      <li>CS240</li>
      <li>L120</li>
    </ul>
  </li>
  <li>
    Camcorders
    <ul>
      <li>HD Cam</li>
      <li>HDR-150</li>
      <li>Standard Def Cam</li>
    </ul>
  </li>
  </ul>
  </li>
</ul>
```

We'll want to be able to indicate that some of the nodes should be collapsed or expanded from the start. It would be tempting to simply mark the collapsed nodes by setting the style to display: none. But that would break accessibility since screen readers ignore content hidden like this. Instead, we're going to rely on JavaScript to toggle each node's visibility at runtime. We did this by adding a CSS class of "expanded" to set the initial state of the list.

If we knew the user wanted to look at "Point and Shoot Cameras" when they first reached this page, for example, this markup wouldn't show the limited list yet. Right now it will show the full categorized product list, as shown in Figure 13, *Our full categorized list without collapsibility*, on page 54. But once the list is made collapsible, the user would see only the names of the products they were looking for, as shown in Figure 14, *Our collapsed list*, on page 55. Then, without navigating away from the page, they can still choose to look at any of our other product categories.

Next we need to write the JavaScript for adding our collapsible functionality, as well as some Expand all and Collapse all helper links at the top of the list. Notice

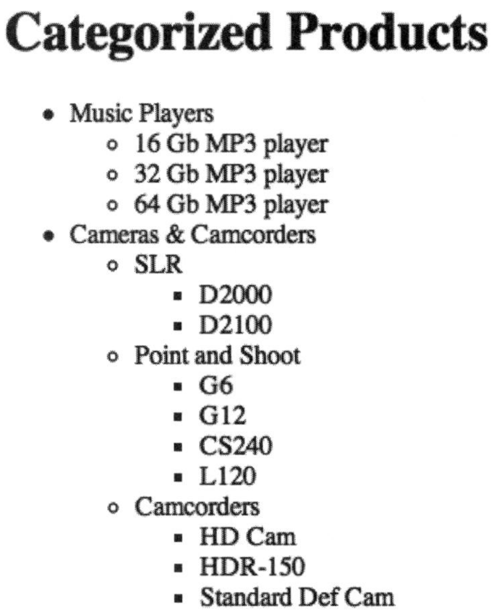

Categorized Products

- Music Players
  - 16 Gb MP3 player
  - 32 Gb MP3 player
  - 64 Gb MP3 player
- Cameras & Camcorders
  - SLR
    - D2000
    - D2100
  - Point and Shoot
    - G6
    - G12
    - CS240
    - L120
  - Camcorders
    - HD Cam
    - HDR-150
    - Standard Def Cam

Figure 13—Our full categorized list without collapsibility

that we're adding the links via the JavaScript code as well. Like the collapsible functionality itself, we don't want to change the markup unless we know this code is going to be used. This also gives us the advantage of being able to easily apply this behavior to any list on our site without having to change any markup beyond adding a .collapsible class to a <ul> element.

To start things off, we will write a function that toggles whether a node is expanded or collapsed. Since this is a function that will act on a DOM object, we will write it as a jQuery plug-in. That means we will assign the function definition to the jQuery.fn prototype. We can then trigger the function within the scope of the element that it was called against. The function definition should be wrapped within a self-executing function so we can use the $ helper without worrying about whether the $ helper has been overwritten by another framework. Finally, to make sure that our jQuery function is chainable and a responsible jQuery citizen, we return this. This is a good practice to follow when writing jQuery plug-ins; *our* plug-in functions will work the same way that we expect other jQuery plug-ins to work.

collapsiblelist/javascript.js
```
(function($) {
  $.fn.toggleExpandCollapse = function(event) {
    event.stopPropagation();
    if (this.find('ul').length > 0) {
```

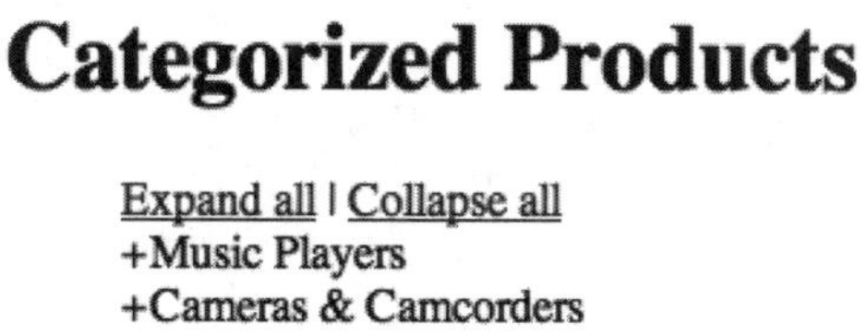

Categorized Products

<u>Expand all</u> | <u>Collapse all</u>
+Music Players
+Cameras & Camcorders

Figure 14—Our collapsed list

```
        event.preventDefault();
        this.toggleClass('collapsed').toggleClass('expanded').
          find('> ul').slideToggle('normal');
      }
      return this;
    }
})(jQuery);
```

We will bind the toggleExpandCollapse() to the click event for all <li> elements, including the elements with nothing underneath them, also known as *leaf nodes*. That's because we want the leaf nodes to do something crucial—absolutely nothing. Unhandled click events bubble up the DOM, so if we only attach a click observer to the <li> elements with .expanded or .collapsed classes, the click event for a leaf node would bubble up to the parent <li> element, which *is* one of our collapsible nodes. That means the code would trigger that node's click event, which would make it collapse suddenly and unexpectedly, and we'd be liable for causing undue harm to our users' fragile psyches. To prevent this Rube Goldberg–styled catastrophe from happening, we call event.stopPropagation(). Adding an event handler to all <li> elements ensures the click event will never bubble up and nothing will happen, just like we expect. For more details on event propagation, read *Why Not Just Return False?*, on page 56.

As mentioned at the beginning of the chapter, we want to give our users helper links that appear at the top of the list to toggle all of the nodes. We can create these links within jQuery and prepend them to our collapsible list. Because building HTML in jQuery can become verbose, we're better off moving the click event logic into separate helpers to prevent the prependToggleAllLinks() functions from becoming unreadable.

collapsiblelist/javascript.js
```
function prependToggleAllLinks() {
  var container = $('<div>').attr('class', 'expand_or_collapse_all');
  container.append(
      $('<a>').attr('href', '#').
      html('Expand all').click(handleExpandAll)
    ).
```

> \\\//   **Joe asks:**
>
> ⌣ **Why Not Just Return False?**
>
> In a jQuery function, `return false` works double duty by telling the event not to bubble up the DOM tree and not to do whatever the element's default action is. This works for most events, but sometimes we want to make the distinction between stopping event propagation and preventing a default action from triggering. Or we may be in a situation where we always want prevent the default action, even if the code in our function somehow breaks. That's why at times it may make more sense to call `event.stopPropagation()` or `event.preventDefault()` explicitly rather than waiting until the end of the function to return false.[a]
>
> ───────────
>
> a.   http://api.jquery.com/category/events/event-object/

```
    append(' | ').
    append(
      $('<a>').attr('href', '#').
      html('Collapse all').click(handleCollapseAll)
    );
  $('ul.collapsible').prepend(container);
}

function handleExpandAll(event) {
  $('ul.collapsible li.collapsed').toggleExpandCollapse(event);
}

function handleCollapseAll(event) {
  $('ul.collapsible li.expanded').toggleExpandCollapse(event);
}
```

We can quickly create a DOM object by wrapping a string representing the element type we want, in this case an <a> tag, in a jQuery element. Then we set the attributes and HTML through jQuery's API. For simplicity's sake, we're going to create two links that say "Expand all" and "Collapse all" that are separated by a pipe symbol. The two links will trigger their corresponding helper functions when they're clicked.

Finally, we will write an initialize function that gets called once the page is ready. This function will also hide any nodes that were not marked as .expanded and add the .collapsed class to the rest of the <li> elements.

collapsiblelist/javascript.js
```
function initializeCollapsibleList() {
  $('ul.collapsible li').click(function(event) {
    $(this).toggleExpandCollapse(event);
  });
```

```
$('ul.collapsible li:not(.expanded) > ul').hide();
$('ul.collapsible li ul').
  parent(':not(.expanded)').
  addClass('collapsed');
}
```

We bind the click event to all of the <li> elements that are in a .collapsible list. We also added the expand/collapse classes to all of the <li> elements, except the products themselves. These classes will help us when it comes time to style our list.

When the DOM is ready, we'll tie it all together by initializing the list and adding the "Expand all" | "Collapse all" links to the page.

```
collapsiblelist/javascript.js
$(document).ready(function() {
  initializeCollapsibleList();
  prependToggleAllLinks();
})
```

Since this is a jQuery plug-in, we can easily add this functionality to any list on our site by adding a .collapsible class to an unordered list. This makes the code easily reusable so that any long and cluttered list can be made easy to navigate and understand.

Further Exploration

If we start out by building a solid, working foundation without JavaScript, we can build upon that foundation to add in extra behavior. And if we write the JavaScript and connect the behavior into the page using CSS classes rather than adding the JavaScript directly to the HTML itself, everything is completely decoupled. This also keeps our sites from becoming too JavaScript dependent, which means more people can use your sites when JavaScript isn't available. We call this *progressive enhancement*, and it's an approach we strongly recommend.

When building photo galleries, make each thumbnail link to a larger version of the image that opens on its own page. Then use JavaScript to intercept the click event on the image and display the full-sized image in a lightbox, and then use JavaScript to add any additional controls that are useful only when JavaScript is enabled, just like we did in this recipe.

When you're building a form that inserts records and updates the values on the screen, create the form with a regular HTTP POST request first, and then intercept the form's submit event with JavaScript and do the post via Ajax. This sounds like more work, but you end up saving a lot of time; you get to leverage the form's semantic markup and use things like jQuery's serialize() method to prepare the form data, rather than reading each input field and constructing your own POST request.

Techniques like this are well-supported by jQuery and other modern libraries because they make it easy to build simple, accessible solutions for your audience.

Also See

- Recipe 9, *Interacting with Web Pages Using Keyboard Shortcuts*, on page 59
- Recipe 11, *Displaying Information with Endless Pagination*, on page 73

Recipe 9

Interacting with Web Pages Using Keyboard Shortcuts

Problem

Website visitors expect to use their mouse to interact with a website, but using the mouse isn't always the most efficient way. Keyboard shortcuts are becoming increasingly common on sites such as Gmail and Tumblr as a way to improve accessibility and allow users to quickly and comfortably perform common tasks. We want to bring this functionality to our site, but we need to make sure we don't interfere with the normal expected behavior of our application, like our search box.

Ingredients

* jQuery

Solution

Keyboard shortcuts use JavaScript to monitor the page for certain keys being pressed; they do this by binding a function to the document's keydown event. When a key is pressed, we check whether it's one of the keys we are using for a shortcut and then call the specified function for that key.

We have a site with a large number of blog entries on it about a variety of topics. After some usability testing, we saw that users decide whether they want to read the entry by scanning the title and part of the first sentence. If they're not interested, they scroll on to the next article. Because some entries are very long, users end up doing a lot of scrolling to get to the next article. We'd like to create some basic shortcuts that will let users move easily between the entries on the page, navigate between pages, and quickly use the search box. We'll work with an interface that looks like the one in Figure 15, *A basic page with a search box and multiple entries*, on page 60.

Getting Set Up

First we will add the ability to scroll between entries on the current page. We'll start by creating a page containing several items that all share a class of entry and use the j key to go to the previous record and k to go to the next one. These letters are commonly used for previous and next records on many

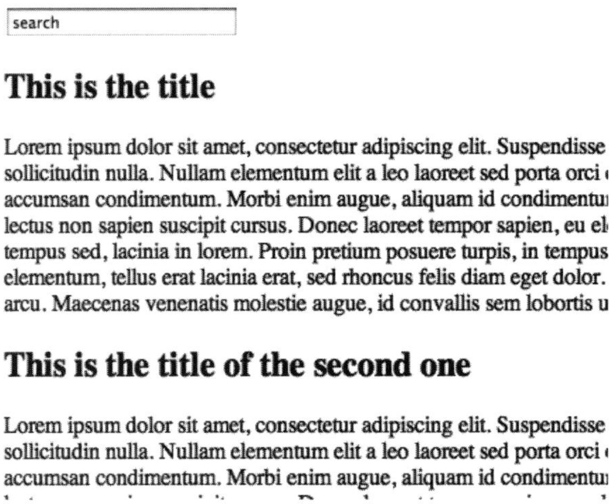

Figure 15—A basic page with a search box and multiple entries

applications, including Vim, which we cover in Recipe 38, *Changing Web Server Configuration Files with Vim*, on page 277, so it's not a bad idea to follow the convention. After that, we'll handle navigating between pages using the right and left arrows, followed by creating a shortcut to use the search box.

Let's start by creating a prototype that has a search box and a few search results so we have something we can test our keyboard navigation on.

keyboardnavigation/index.html
```html
<!DOCTYPE html>
<html>
  <head>
    <script type="text/javascript"
      src="http://ajax.googleapis.com/ajax/libs/jquery/1.7/jquery.min.js">
    </script>
    <script type="text/javascript"
      src='keyboard_navigation.js'></script>
  </head>
  <body>
    <p>Make this page longer so you can tell that we're scrolling!</p>
    <form>
      <input id="search" type="text"size="28" value="search">
    </form>
    <div id="entry_1" class="entry">
      <h2>This is the title</h2>
      <p>Lorem ipsum dolor sit amet...</p>
    </div>
    <div id="entry_2" class="entry">
      <h2>This is the title of the second one</h2>
      <p>In hac habitasse platea dictumst...</p>
```

```
    </div>
  </body>
</html>
```

Because of size constraints, this example page is very short. To see the full effect as we scroll between elements on the page, add a few more of the <div id="entry_x" class="entry"> sections. Make sure the content is longer than your browser can display at once so that you can see the effect of scrolling between entries.

Catching Key Presses

We'll use jQuery to set up a few event handlers when the page loads. When someone presses one of our navigation keys, we'll call the functions that navigate through the page. The $(document).keydown() method allows us to specify exactly what to call for different keys by using a case statement. Each case we define represents a different key by its key code.[7]

```
keyboardnavigation/keyboard_navigation.js
$(document).keydown(function(e) {
  if($(document.activeElement)[0] == $(document.body)[0]){
    switch(e.keyCode){
    // In Page Navigation
    case 74: // j
      scrollToNext();
      break;
    case 75: // k
      scrollToPrevious();
      break;
    // Between Page Navigation
    case 39: // right arrow
      loadNextPage();
      break;
    case 37: // left arrow
      loadPreviousPage();
      break;
    // Search
    case 191: // / (and ? with shift)
      if(e.shiftKey){
        $('#search').focus().val('');
        return false;
      }
      break;
    }
  }
});
```

---

7. To find other key codes, check out the list at http://www.cambiaresearch.com/c4/702b8cd1-e5b0-42e6-83ac-25f0306e3e25/javascript-char-codes-key-codes.aspx.

Before we check whether one of our keys is pressed, it's important to make sure we're not interrupting normal user activity. The first line of our keydown function is if($(document.activeElement)[0] == $(document.body)[0]), which makes sure that the active element on the page is the body of the page itself. By doing this, we avoid catching key presses when our user is typing in to a search box or a text area.

Scrolling

Scrolling between entries on our page involves getting a list of the current entries and knowing which one we last scrolled to. First we want to set everything so that when we first scroll on the page, we go to the first entry on the page.

keyboardnavigation/keyboard_navigation.js
```
$(function(){
  current_entry = -1;
});
```

When the page loads, we set a variable called current_entry to -1, meaning that we haven't scrolled anywhere yet. We use -1 because we are going to figure out which entry to display by loading all objects on the page with a class of .entry and picking the correct one based on its index in the resulting array. JavaScript arrays are zero-based, so the first entry will be at the 0 position.

In the "Catching Key Presses" section, we defined the functions to call when certain keys were pressed. When the j key is pressed, we want to scroll to the next entry on the page, so we call the scrollToNext() function.

keyboardnavigation/keyboard_navigation.js
```
function scrollToNext(){
  if($('.entry').size() > current_entry+1){
    current_entry++;
    scrollToEntry(current_entry);
  }
}
```

In scrollToNext(), we first check that we're not trying to scroll to an entry that doesn't exist by ensuring that incrementing the current_entry counter won't be larger than the number of entries on the page. If there's an entry to scroll to, we increase the current_entry by 1 and call scrollToEntry().

keyboardnavigation/keyboard_navigation.js
```
function scrollToEntry(entry_index){
  $('html,body').animate(
    {scrollTop: $("#"+$('.entry')[entry_index].id).offset().top},'slow');
}
```

scrollToEntry() uses the jQuery animation libraries to scroll our view to the ID of the specified entry. Since the current_entry represents the index of the entry we want to display, we grab the ID of that entry and tell jQuery to scroll there.

When the user presses the k key, we call a similar function called scrollToPrevious(), like this:

keyboardnavigation/keyboard_navigation.js
```
function scrollToPrevious(){
  if(current_entry > 0){
    current_entry--;
    scrollToEntry(current_entry);
  }
}
```

scrollToPrevious() makes sure we aren't trying to load a smaller entry than 0, since that will always be the first entry on the page. If we're not on the first entry, then we reduce the current_entry by 1 and once again call scrollToEntry().

Now that our users have the ability to scroll between entries on the page, it can be very easy to quickly review the content of the page. But once they get to the end of the page, they'll need to be able to move to the next page of records. Let's work on that next.

Pagination

Navigating between pages can happen in a variety of ways. For this example, we'll assume that the desired page is indicated by the page=1 querystring in the URL; however, this could easily be changed to work with p=1, entries/2, or anything else you might encounter.

To keep our code nice and clean, let's write a function called getQueryString() that pulls the page number out of the URL.

keyboardnavigation/keyboard_navigation.js
```
function getQueryString(name){
  var reg = new RegExp("(^|&)"+ name +"=([^&]*)(&|$)");
  var r = window.location.search.substr(1).match(reg);
  if (r!=null) return unescape(r[2]); return null;
}
```

Now, let's build a getCurrentPageNumber() function that uses the getQueryString() function to check whether page exists. If it does, we get it and turn it from a string to an integer and then return it. If it doesn't exist, that means that no page is currently set. If this is the case, we'll assume we're on the first page and return 1. It's important that we return an integer and not a string, because we're going to need to do math with the page number.

```
keyboardnavigation/keyboard_navigation.js
function getCurrentPageNumber(){
  return (getQueryString('page') != null) ?
    parseInt(getQueryString('page')) : 1;
}
```

Our keycode watcher is listening for the LEFT and RIGHT arrows. When the user presses the right arrow, we call the loadNextPage() function, which figures out what page number we're on and directs the browser to the next one.

```
keyboardnavigation/keyboard_navigation.js
function loadNextPage(){
  page_number = getCurrentPageNumber()+1;
  url = window.location.href;
  if (url.indexOf('page=') != -1){
    window.location.href = replacePageNumber(page_number);
  } else if(url.indexOf('?') != -1){
    window.location.href += "&page="+page_number;
  } else {
    window.location.href += "?page="+page_number;
  }
}
```

We first determine our current page number, and then we increase page_number by 1 since we're going to the next page. Then we grab the current URL so we can update it and load the next page. This is the most involved part of the process because there are several ways the URL could be structured. First we check whether the URL contains page=. If it does, as in http://example.com?page=4, then we just need to replace the current number using a regular expression and the replace() function. Since we'll need to replace the page number when going to the previous page, we have a replacePageNumber() function so if our URL structure changes, we only have to update our code in one place.

```
keyboardnavigation/keyboard_navigation.js
function replacePageNumber(page_number){
  return window.location.href.replace(/page=(\d)/,'page='+page_number);
}
```

If the URL doesn't contain page=, then we need to add the entire parameter to the querystring. Next, we check whether the URL contains other parameters. If it does, they'll be listed after the ? in the URL, so we check for ?. If it exists, as in http://example.com?foo=bar, then the page number will be added to the end. Otherwise, we need to create the querystring ourselves, which is done in the final else of the if... else block.

We use a similar, though simpler, technique to load the previous page. After figuring out the current page number and reducing it by 1, we just need to make sure we're not trying to load a page number that is less than 1. So, we check whether the new page_number is greater than 0. If it is, we update page= with the new number, and we're on our way.

```
keyboardnavigation/keyboard_navigation.js
function loadPreviousPage(){
  page_number = getCurrentPageNumber()-1;
  if(page_number > 0){
    window.location.href = replacePageNumber(page_number);
  }
}
```

Now that we can move between pages and among entries, let's create a way for users to quickly get access to the search box.

Navigating to the Search Box

The keyboard shortcut that makes the most sense for this is the ? key, but that's done by pressing two keys together, so we need to do things a little bit differently than our other shortcuts. First, we watch for the keycode of 191, which represents the / key. When this is pressed, we call the shiftKey property on the event, which will return true if the SHIFT key is down.

```
keyboardnavigation/keyboard_navigation.js
case 191: // / (and ? with shift)
  if(e.shiftKey){
    $('#search').focus().val('');
    return false;
  }
  break;
}
```

If the SHIFT key was pressed, we retrieve the search box by using its DOM ID and call the focus() method to place the cursor inside the search box. We then erase any content current in it by calling val(''). Finally, we call return false;, which prevents the ? that was typed from being placed in to the search box.

Further Exploration

We've added some quick keyboard shortcuts that let our users navigate throughout our site without having to take their hands off of their keyboards. Once the framework is in place, adding new keyboard shortcuts is a breeze. You could use keyboard shortcuts to display a lightbox on a page that opens when the user presses the spacebar. You could use keyboard shortcuts to pop up a console with information about ongoing tasks or use them to reveal further content in a blog post.

Many of the other JavaScript-based chapters in this book could have keyboard shortcuts added to them, such as browsing through the images in Recipe 4, *Creating Interactive Slideshows with jQuery*, on page 18 or using the keyboard or scanning and expanding items in Recipe 8, *Accessible Expand and Collapse*, on page 52.

Also See

- Recipe 4, *Creating Interactive Slideshows with jQuery*, on page 18
- Recipe 8, *Accessible Expand and Collapse*, on page 52
- Recipe 29, *Cleaner JavaScript with CoffeeScript*, on page 209
- Recipe 38, *Changing Web Server Configuration Files with Vim*, on page 277

Recipe 10

Building HTML with Mustache

Problem

Amazing interfaces require creating lots of dynamic and asynchronous HTML. Thanks to Ajax and JavaScript libraries like jQuery, we can change the user interface without reloading the page by generating HTML with JavaScript. We typically use methods like string concatenation to add new elements to our interfaces, but these are hard to manage and are prone to error. We have to dance around mixing single and double quotes and often are left to use jQuery's `append()` method endlessly.

Ingredients

- jQuery
- Mustache.js

Solution

Thankfully, new tools such as Mustache allow us to write *real* HTML, render data with it, and insert it into the document. Mustache is an HTML templating tool that is available in several common languages. The JavaScript implementation lets us write client-side views with clean HTML that are abstracted away from the JavaScript code. It allows for conditional logic as well as iteration.

With Mustache, we can simplify HTML creation when generating new content. We will explore the Mustache syntax by working with a JavaScript-driven product management application.

The existing application lets us manage products by adding new ones to a list. The example uses our standard development server since the requests are all handled by JavaScript and Ajax. When the user fills in the form to add a new product, it asks the server to save the product and then renders a new product in the list. To add the product to the list, we have to use string concatenation, which becomes awkward and hard to read, like this:

mustache/submit.html

```
var newProduct = $('<li></li>');
newProduct.append('<span class="product-name">' +
  product.name + '</span>');
newProduct.append('<em class="product-price">' +
  product.price + '</em>');
newProduct.append('<div class="product-description">' +
  product.description + '</div>');

productsList.append(newProduct);
```

Using Mustache.js is as easy as loading the script on the page. You can find a version of the file in this book's code repository, or you can download the most recent version on the Mustache.js GitHub page.[8]

Rendering a Template

To refactor our existing application, we first need to learn how to render a template using Mustache. The simplest way is to make a call to the to_html() function.

```
Mustache.to_html(templateString, data);
```

The function accepts two arguments; the first argument is a string of template HTML to be rendered against, and the second argument is the data to be injected into the HTML. The data variable is an object whose keys become the local variables in the template. Examine the following code:

```
var artist = {name: "John Coltrane"};
var rendered = Mustache.to_html('<span class="artist name">{{ name }}</span>',
  artist);
$('body').append(rendered);
```

The rendered variable contains our final HTML that has been spit back out from the to_html method. To place the name property in our HTML, Mustache uses a style of tags with double curly braces. Inside the curly braces, we place the name of a property. The last line appends the rendered HTML to the <body>.

This is the simplest method for rendering a template with Mustache. In our application, there will be more code related to sending a request to a server to retrieve the data, but the process for creating the template will be the same.

---

8. https://github.com/janl/mustache.js

Replacing an Existing System

Now that we understand how to render a template, we can remove the old method of string concatenation from the existing application. Let's examine the old code to see what can be removed and what needs replacing.

mustache/submit.html

```
function renderNewProduct() {
  var productsList = $('#products-list');

  var newProductForm = $('#new-product-form');

  var product = {};
  product.name = newProductForm.find('input[name*=name]').val();
  product.price = newProductForm.find('input[name*=price]').val();
  product.description =
    newProductForm.find('textarea[name*=description]').val();

  var newProduct = $('<li></li>');
  newProduct.append('<span class="product-name">' +
    product.name + '</span>');
  newProduct.append('<em class="product-price">' +
    product.price + '</em>');
  newProduct.append('<div class="product-description">' +
    product.description + '</div>');

  productsList.append(newProduct);

  productsList.find('input[type=text], textarea').each(function(input) {
    input.attr('value', '');
  });
}
```

That messy code is a headache to read and even worse to maintain. Instead of using jQuery's append method to build up the HTML, let's use Mustache to render the HTML. We can write real HTML and render the data using Mustache! Our first step to reducing the JavaScript madness is to build our template. Then, we'll render it with our product data in one simple step.

If we create a <script> element with a content type of text/template, then we can place Mustache HTML inside of that element and pull it out for our template. We'll give it an ID so that we can reference it in our JavaScript code with jQuery.

```
<script type="text/template" id="product-template">
  <!-- template HTML -->
</script>
```

Next, let's write the HTML for our template. We already have the product in object form, so we can use its properties as the variable names in our template, like this:

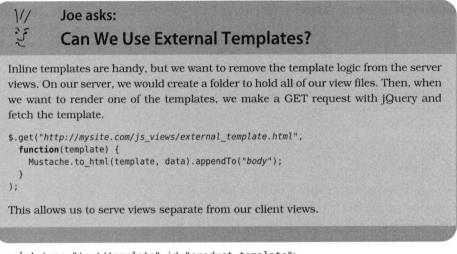

```
<script type="text/template" id="product-template">
  <li>
    <span class="product-name">{{ name }}</span>
    <em class="product-price">{{ price }}</em>
    <div class="product-description">{{ description }}</div>
  </li>
</script>
```

With our template in place, we can go back to our previous code and rewrite how we're inserting the HTML. We can grab a reference to the template with jQuery and use the html() to grab the inner content. Then, all we need to do is pass the HTML and the data to Mustache.

```
var newProduct = Mustache.to_html( $('#product-template').html(), product);
```

When we look at the results, things look pretty good, but we don't really need to show the description field if there's no description coming back from the server. We don't want to render the corresponding <div> if the description isn't present. Thankfully, Mustache allows for conditional statements. We can check whether the description is there and conditionally render the <div>.

```
{{#description}}
  <div class="product-description">{{ description }}</div>
{{/description}}
```

Using the same operator, Mustache will iterate over an array for you. It checks the property to see whether it's an array and will automatically iterate.

Using Iteration

Since we have been able to replace much of the existing code for building a new product, we have decided to make more of the application work using

JavaScript. We want to replace the index page that shows products and their notes with some JavaScript code that does the same rendering. We will create an array of products on one of the data object's properties, and each product in that array will have a notes property. The notes is an array that will be iterated over inside the template.

First, let's get the products and render them, assuming our server returns a JSON array that looks like this:

mustache/index.html
```
$.getJSON('/products.json', function(products) {
  var data = {products: products};
  var rendered = Mustache.to_html($('#products-template').html(), data);
  $('body').append(rendered);
});
```

Now, we need to build a template to render the products. With Mustache, we iterate by passing our array to the hash operator, as in {{#variable}}. Inside of our iteration, any properties we call are in the context of the objects in the array.

mustache/index.html
```
<script type="text/template" id="products-template">
  {{#products}}
    <li>
      <span class="product-name">{{ name }}</span>
      <em class="product-price">{{ price }}</em>
      <div class="product-description">{{ description }}</div>
      <ul class="product-notes">
        {{#notes}}
          <li>{{ text }}</li>
        {{/notes}}
      </ul>
    </li>
  {{/products}}
</script>
```

Now, we can allow our index page to be fully generated in the browser, using templates and Mustache.

JavaScript templates are a nice way to improve the organization of a JavaScript application. We learned how to render templates, use conditional logic, and build with iteration. Mustache.js is a simple way to remove string concatenation and build HTML in a semantic and readable way.

Further Exploration

Mustache templates let us keep our client-side code clean, but we can also use them in server-side languages. There are implementations of Mustache in Ruby, Java, Python, ColdFusion, and many more. You can find more on these implementations at the official site.[9]

This means you could use Mustache as the templating engine on both the backend and frontend of a project. For example, if you had a Mustache template that represented a row of an HTML table and you used that template inside a loop to construct the initial table when you initially render the page, you could reuse that same template to append a row to the table after a successful Ajax request.

Also See

- Recipe 11, *Displaying Information with Endless Pagination*, on page 73
- Recipe 13, *Snappier Client-Side Interfaces with Knockout.js*, on page 84
- Recipe 14, *Organizing Code with Backbone.js*, on page 93
- Recipe 20, *Building a Status Site with JavaScript and CouchDB*, on page 144

---

9.   http://mustache.github.com/

Recipe 11

Displaying Information with Endless Pagination

Problem

To prevent information overload for our users and to keep our servers from grinding to a halt, it's important to limit how much data is shown at once on our list pages. This is traditionally handled by adding pagination to these pages. That is, we show only a small subset of data to start with, while allowing the users to jump between the pages of information at their own discretion. What they see is a small part of all of the information that is potentially available to them.

As websites have evolved, web developers have learned that the majority of the time users go through these pages sequentially. They would actually be happy to scroll through an entire list of data until they found what they were looking for or they reached the end of the dataset. We need to provide that type of experience for our users without taxing our servers.

Ingredients

- jQuery
- Mustache.js[10]
- QEDServer

Solution

By implementing endless pagination, we can provide an efficient way of managing our resources, while at the same time improving the end-user experience. Instead of forcing users to choose the next page of results and then reloading the entire interface, we load the next page of results in the background and add those results to the current page as the user scrolls toward the end of the page.

We want to add a list of our product line to our site, but our inventory is much too big to reasonably load all at once. This means that we're going to have to add pagination for this list and limit the user to seeing ten products

---

10. http://github.com/documentcloud/underscore/blob/master/underscore.js

at a time. To make our users' lives even easier, we're going to ditch the Next Page button and automatically load the following page when we think they're ready for it. From the user's perspective, it will seem as if the entire product list has been available to them since they first loaded the page.

We'll use QEDServer and its product catalog to build a working prototype. We'll place all of our code in the public folder in QEDServer's workspace. Start up QEDServer and then create a new file called products.html in the public folder that QEDServer creates. You can look at *QEDServer*, on page xiv for details on how QEDServer works.

To keep our code clean, we'll use the Mustache Template library, which we discuss in Recipe 10, *Building HTML with Mustache*, on page 67, so we'll download that and place it in the public folder as well.

We'll start out by creating a simple HTML5 skeleton in index.html that includes jQuery, the Mustache Template library, and endless_pagination.js, which we'll create to hold our pagination code.

endlesspagination/products.html

```html
<!DOCTYPE html>
<html>
  <head>
    <meta charset='utf-8'>
    <title>AwesomeCo Products</title>
    <link rel='stylesheet' href='endless_pagination.css'>
    <script type="text/javascript"
      src="http://ajax.googleapis.com/ajax/libs/jquery/1.7/jquery.min.js">
    </script>
    <script type="text/javascript" src="mustache.js"></script>
    <script src="endless_pagination.js"></script>
  </head>
  <body>
    <div id="wrap">
      <header>
        <h1>Products</h1>
      </header>
    </div>
  </body>
</html>
```

For the body of this initial page, we add a content placeholder and a spinner image, which is shown in Figure 16, *Reaching the bottom of the page*, on page 76. The spinner is there so if the user ever *does* reach the end of the current page, it will appear as if the next page is already loading, which it should be.

endlesspagination/products.html
```
<div id='content'>
</div>
<img src='spinner.gif' id='next_page_spinner' />
```

QEDServer's API is set up to return paginated results and responds to JSON requests. We can see this by navigating to http://localhost:8080/products.json?page=2.

Now that we know what information we're getting from the server, we can start building the code that will update the interface by writing a function that takes in a JSON array, marks it up using a Mustache template, and appends it to the end of the page. We'll put this code into a file named endless_pagination.js. We'll start by writing the functions that will do the heavy lifting. First we'll need a function that renders the JSON response into HTML.

endlesspagination/endless_pagination.js
```
function loadData(data) {
  $('#content').append(Mustache.to_html("{{#products}} \
    <div class='product'> \
      <a href='/products/{{id}}'>{{name}}</a> \
      <br> \
      <span class='description'>{{description}}</span> \
    </div>{{/products}}", { products: data }));
}
```

As we loop through each product, our template will create a <div> where the content is the name of the product as a link. Then the new items are appended to the end of the product list so they appear on the page.

Next, since we're going to request the next page when we reach the end of the current page, we're going to need a way to determine what the next page is. We can do this by storing the current page as a global variable. Then when we're ready, we can build the URL for the next page.

endlesspagination/endless_pagination.js
```
var currentPage = 0;
function nextPageWithJSON() {
  currentPage += 1;
  var newURL = 'http://localhost:8080/products.json?page=' + currentPage;

  var splitHref = document.URL.split('?');
  var parameters = splitHref[1];
  if (parameters) {
    parameters = parameters.replace(/[?&]page=[^&]*/, '');
    newURL += '&' + parameters;
  }
  return newURL;
}
```

Figure 16—Reaching the bottom of the page

The nextPageWithJSON() function increments the currentPage variable and appends it to the current URL as a page= parameter. We also want to remember any other parameters that were in the current URL. At the same time, we want to make sure that the old page parameter, if it exists, gets overridden. This way we'll get the desired response from the server.

Now that we have functions in place to show new content and determine what the URL is for the next page, let's add the function that actually requests that content from our server. At its core, this function is just an Ajax call to the server. However, we do need to implement a rudimentary way to prevent extra, unwanted calls to the server. We'll add a global variable called loadingPage() that we initialize to 0. We'll increment it before we make the Ajax call and set it back when we're done. This creates something called a *mutex* or a locking mechanism. Without this lock in place, we could potentially make dozens of calls to the server for the next page, which the server would obligingly deliver, even if it's not really what we want.

endlesspagination/endless_pagination.js

```
var loadingPage = 0;
function getNextPage() {
  if (loadingPage != 0) return;
```

```
    loadingPage++;
    $.getJSON(nextPageWithJSON(), {}, updateContent).
      complete(function() { loadingPage-- });
}

function updateContent(response) {
  loadData(response);
}
```

After the Ajax call has finished, we hand off the response to the loadData() function we defined in the code, on page 75. After loadData() adds the new content, we update the URL stored in the nextPage variable. This way, we're all set up to make the *next* Ajax call.

With the function to request the next page in place, we need a way to determine whether the user is ready to load that page. Normally this is where the user would just click the Next Page link, but instead we want a function that returns true when the bottom of the browser's screen is within a given distance from the bottom of the page. With the function to request the next page in place, we need a way to determine whether the user is ready to load that page. Normally this is where the user would just click the Next Page link, but instead we want a function that returns true when the bottom of the browser's screen is within a given distance from the bottom of the page.

endlesspagination/endless_pagination.js

```
function readyForNextPage() {
  if (!$('#next_page_spinner').is(':visible')) return;

  var threshold = 200;
  var bottomPosition = $(window).scrollTop() + $(window).height();
  var distanceFromBottom = $(document).height() - bottomPosition;

  return distanceFromBottom <= threshold;
}
```

Finally, we apply a scroll event handler that calls the observeScroll() function. That way, every time the user scrolls through the page, we call the newly created readyForNextPage() helper function. When the helper function returns true, we'll call getNextPage() to make our Ajax request.

endlesspagination/endless_pagination.js

```
function observeScroll(event) {
  if (readyForNextPage()) getNextPage();
}

$(document).scroll(observeScroll);
```

Functionality in IE8

When testing this code in IE8, it will not work out of the box. Unfortunately, IE8 expects request headers for JSON to be in a very specific format, such as sending a charset of "utf8" when it's expecting "UTF-8." Without proper headers, the Ajax request will silently fail, leaving the page empty except for the spinner. Keep this in mind when dealing with JSON on the server and in IE on the client.

We've taken care of the endless part, but in reality there *will* be an actual end to our content. After the user has seen the last product, we want to hide the spinner since seeing it will only confuse them and make them think that either their Internet connection has slowed or that our site is broken. To remove the spinner, we add a final check to hide it when the server has returned an empty list.

endlesspagination/endless_pagination.js
```
function loadData(data) {
  $('#content').append(Mustache.to_html("{{#products}} \
    <div class='product'> \
      <a href='/products/{{id}}'>{{name}}</a> \
      <br> \
      <span class='description'>{{description}}</span> \
    </div>{{/products}}", { products: data }));
  if (data.length == 0) $('#next_page_spinner').hide();
}
```

And that's it. When we reach the bottom of our list, the spinner disappears.

Further Exploration

This technique is excellent for displaying long lists of information and is a behavior users are going to come to expect. Since we've separated our functionality into separate functions, it will be easy to adapt this solution to other scenarios. We can change the code to load the content earlier or later by changing the threshold variable or to render an HTML or XML response instead of one from JSON by modifying the loadData() function. And best of all, we can rest easy knowing that our site will still be accessible even if jQuery somehow goes missing, which we can test by disabling JavaScript.

In the next recipe, we'll explore how we can make this code more user-friendly by adding support for URL changes and the Back button.

Also See

- Recipe 12, *State-Aware Ajax*, on page 79
- Recipe 10, *Building HTML with Mustache*, on page 67

Recipe 12

State-Aware Ajax

Problem

One of the things that makes the Internet great is that we can easily share links with each other. But with the advent of Ajax-enabled sites, this is no longer the case by default; clicking an Ajax link no longer guaranteed that the browser's URL would be updated. Not only does this prevent the sharing of links, but it breaks the Back button. These types of sites don't act like Good Net Citizens™ because once your session is over, there's no way to pick up where you last left off.

Unfortunately, the endless pagination we wrote in Recipe 11, *Displaying Information with Endless Pagination*, on page 73 isn't being a very Good Net Citizen. As we scroll through the pagination and request new pages via Ajax, the browser's URL never changes. Yet, we're in a different state, and the site is displaying different information than when the page was loaded. For example, if we liked a product on page 5 and sent the link in an email to a friend, they wouldn't necessarily know what we were talking about since they wouldn't see the same list as us.

That's not all. When a user clicks the browser's Back button on an all-Ajax site, they often end up at whatever page led them to our site instead of where they expected to go. Then they get frustrated, click the Forward button, and have completely lost their place. Thankfully, we have a great solution to these interface problems.

Ingredients

- jQuery
- Mustache.js[11]
- QEDServer

---

11. http://github.com/documentcloud/underscore/blob/master/underscore.js

Solution

We're going to go back and finish implementing Recipe 11, *Displaying Information with Endless Pagination*, on page 73. While the old method works, we can't easily share links with anyone. To keep our web karma in alignment and prevent user frustration, the right thing to do is to make this list page state-aware. When we change the page that we're looking at, we want to change the current URL. The HTML5 specification introduced a JavaScript function called pushState(), which, in most browsers, lets us alter the URL without leaving the page. This is great news for us web developers! We can make an entire Ajax web application that never goes through the traditional request/reload life cycle. At the same time, we get the advantages that come with that workflow. This means there's no need to reload resources like the extraneous header and footer HTML or repeated requests for images, style sheets, or JavaScript files every time we move to the next screen. And users can quickly share the current URL with others or refresh the page and retain their spot in their workflow. Best of all, the Back button can work as expected too.

Using the pushState Function

The details for pushState() are still being ironed out. Most old browser versions don't support pushState(), but there are fallback solutions that use the hash portion of the URL. The solution works, but it is ugly. It's not only the issue of having pretty-looking URLs. The Internet has a very good long-term memory. It was not only built to send links of funny, talking kittens to your grandmother but also to find pages you linked to years ago that may have moved to a different server (assuming the original content creators were also Good Net Citizens and set up the old URL to return the appropriate 301 HTTP status code). If we use the URL hash as a stopgap for important information, we could be stuck supporting those deprecated links until the end of time.[12] Since URL hashes are never sent to the server, our application would have to continue redirecting traffic after pushState() becomes standard.

With that said, let's see what it takes to make our endless products page state-aware.

Parameters to Track

Because we don't know which page a user will load on the first request, we will keep track of the starting page as well as the current page. If a user went directly to page 3, we want them to be able to get back to page 3 on subsequent

---

12. http://danwebb.net/2011/5/28/it-is-about-the-hashbangs

visits. If they start scrolling down from page 3 and load multiple pages, for instance to page 7, we want to know that too. We need a way to keep track of the start and end pages so that a hard refresh won't require the user to scroll through the site again.

Next, we need a way to send the start and end pages from the client. The most direct way would be to set these params in the URL during a get request. When a page is first loaded, we'll set the page parameter of the URL to be the current page and assume the user wants to see only that page. If the client also passes in a start_page parameter, we'll know that the user wants to see a range of pages, from start_page through page. So, following our earlier example, if we were on page 7 but started browsing from page 3, our URL would look like http://localhost:8080/products?start_page=3&page=7.

This set of parameters should be enough information for us to re-create a list of products from the server and subsequently show the user the same page they saw when they first visited this URL.

statefulpagination/stateful_pagination.js

```
function getParameterByName(name) {
  var match = RegExp('[?&]' + name + '=([^&]*)')
    .exec(window.location.search);

  return match && decodeURIComponent(match[1].replace(/\+/g, ' '));
}

var currentPage = 0;
var startPage = 0;

$(function() {
  startPage = parseInt(getParameterByName('start_page'));
  if (isNaN(startPage)) {
    startPage = parseInt(getParameterByName('page'));
  }
  if (isNaN(startPage)) {
    startPage = 1;
  }
  currentPage = startPage - 1;

  if (getParameterByName('page')) {
    endPage = parseInt(getParameterByName('page'));
    for (i = currentPage; i < endPage; i++) {
      getNextPage(true);
    }
  }

  observeScroll();
});
```

All we're doing here is figuring out the start_page and current_page and then requesting those pages from the server. We use mostly the same function from the previous chapter, getNextPage(), but it's been slightly modified to allow multiple requests at a time. Unlike when the user is scrolling and we want to prevent multiple, overlapping requests, right now it's all right since we know exactly which pages should be requested.

Just as we tracked the currentPage in the code, on page 75, we want to track the startPage. We'll grab this parameter from the URL so we can make the requests for the pages that haven't been loaded yet. This number will never change, but we do want to make sure that it gets added to the URL and stays there every time a new page is requested.

Updating the Browser's URL

To update the URL, let's write a function called updateBrowserUrl() that will call pushState() and set the parameters for the start_page and page. It's important to remember that not every browser supports pushState(), so we need to check that it's defined before we call it. For those browsers, this solution simply will not work, but that shouldn't stop us from future-proofing our site.

```
statefulpagination/stateful_pagination.js
function updateBrowserUrl() {
  if (window.history.pushState == undefined) return;

  var newURL = '?start_page=' + startPage + '&page=' + currentPage;
  window.history.pushState({}, '', newURL);
}
```

The pushState() function takes three parameters. The first is a state object that is generally a JSON object. This argument could potentially be a storage point for that information since we get JSON back from the server as we scroll. But, since our data is relatively lightweight and easy to get from the server, this strategy is overkill. For now, we'll pass in an empty hash. The second argument is a string that will update the title of the browser. This feature isn't widely implemented yet, and for our purposes, even if it was implemented, we don't really have a reason to update the browser's title. We pass in a filler argument again, this time an empty string.

Finally, we get to the meat, or if you're vegetarian, the tofu, of the pushState() function. The third parameter is how we want the URL to change. This method is flexible and can be either an absolute path or just the parameters to be updated at the end of the URL. For security reasons, we can't change the domain of the URL, but we can change everything after the top-level domain with relative ease. Since we're worried only about updating the parameters of the URL, we prepend the pushState()'s third parameter with a ?. Finally, we set the start_page and page parameters, and if they already exist, pushState() is smart enough to update them for us.

statefulpagination/stateful_pagination.js
```
function updateContent(response) {
  loadData(response);
  updateBrowserUrl();
}
```

Lastly, we add a call to updateBrowserUrl() from the updateContent() function in order to make our endless pagination code state-aware. With this added, our users can now use the Back button to leave our page and return with the Forward button without losing their spot. They can also hit the Refresh button with impunity and get the same results. Most importantly, our links our now sharable across the Web. We've been able to make our index page a Good Net Citizen with minimal effort thanks to the hard work of modern browser developers.

Further Exploration

As we add more JavaScript and Ajax to our pages, we have to be aware of how the interfaces behave. HTML5's pushState() method and the History API give us the tools we need to provide support for the regular controls in the browser that people already know how to use. Abstraction layers like History.js[13] make it even easier by providing graceful fallbacks for old browsers that don't yet support the History API.

The approaches we discussed here are also making their way into JavaScript frameworks like Backbone.js, which means even better Back button support for the most complex single-page applications.

Also See

- Recipe 10, *Building HTML with Mustache*, on page 67
- Recipe 12, *State-Aware Ajax*, on page 79
- Recipe 14, *Organizing Code with Backbone.js*, on page 93

---

13. http://plugins.jquery.com/plugin-tags/pushstate

Recipe 13

Snappier Client-Side Interfaces with Knockout.js

Problem

When developing modern web applications, we often try to update only part of the interface in response to user interaction instead of refreshing the entire page. Calls to the server are often expensive, and refreshing the entire page can cause people to lose their place.

Unfortunately, the JavaScript code for this can very quickly become difficult to manage. We start out watching only a couple of events, but suddenly we have several callbacks updating several regions of the page, and it becomes a maintenance nightmare.

Knockout is a simple yet powerful framework that lets us bind objects to our interface and can automatically update one part of the interface when another part changes, without lots of nested event handlers.

Ingredients

- Knockout.js[14]

Solution

Knockout.js uses *view models*, which encapsulate much of the view logic associated with interface changes. We can then bind properties of these models to elements in our interface.

We want our customers to be able to modify the quantity of items in their shopping cart and see the updated total in real time. We can use Knockout's view models and data bindings to build the update screen for our shopping cart. We'll have a line for each item, a field for the customer to update the quantity, and a button to remove the item from the cart. We'll update the subtotal for each line when the quantity changes, and we'll update the grand total whenever anything on the line changes. When we're done, we'll have an interface that looks like Figure 17, *Our cart interface*, on page 85.

---

14. http://knockoutjs.com

Product	Price	Quantity	Total	
Macbook Pro 15 inch	1699	1	1699	(Remove)
Mini Display Port to VGA Adapter	29	1	29	(Remove)
Magic Trackpad	69	1	69	(Remove)
Apple Wireless Keyboard	69	1	69	(Remove)
Total			1866	

Figure 17—Our cart interface

Knockout Basics

Knockout's "view models" are simply regular JavaScript objects with properties and methods with a few special keywords. Here's a simple Person object with methods for first name, last name, and full name.

knockout/binding.html
```
var Person = function(){
  this.firstname = ko.observable("John");
  this.lastname = ko.observable("Smith");
  this.fullname = ko.dependentObservable(function(){
    return(
      this.firstname() + " " + this.lastname()
    );
  }, this);
};

ko.applyBindings( new Person );
```

We use HTML5's data- attributes to bind this object's methods and logic to elements on our interface.

knockout/binding.html
```
<p>First name: <input type="text" data-bind="value: firstname"></p>
<p>Last name: <input type="text" data-bind="value: lastname"></p>
<p>Full name:
   <span aria-live="polite" data-bind="text: fullname"></span>
</p>
```

When we update either the first name or the last name text boxes, the full name shows up on the page. Since the update happens dynamically, this can cause troubles for blind users with screen readers. To solve that issue, we use the aria-live attribute to give the screen readers a hint that this part changes dynamically.

That's a relatively trivial example, so let's dig into Knockout a little more by building a single line of our cart, getting the total to change when we update the quantity. Then we'll refactor it so we can build the entire shopping cart. We'll start with the data model.

We'll represent the line item using a simple JavaScript object called LineItem with properties for name and price. Create a new HTML page and include the Knockout.js library in the page's <head> section:

knockout/item.html
```
<!DOCTYPE html>
<html>
  <head>
    <title>Update Quantities</title>
    <script type="text/javascript" src="knockout-1.3.0.js"></script>
  </head>

  <body>
  </body>

</html>
```

Add a new <script> block at the bottom of the page, above the closing <body> tag, and add this code:

knockout/item.html
```
var LineItem = function(product_name, product_price){
    this.name = product_name;
    this.price = product_price;
};
```

In JavaScript, functions are object constructors, so we can use a function to mimic a class. In this case, the class's constructor accepts the name and the price when we create a new LineItem instance.

Now we need to tell Knockout that we want to use this lineItem class as our view model so its properties are visible to our HTML markup. We do that by adding this call to our script block.

knockout/item.html
```
var item = new LineItem("Macbook Pro 15", 1699.00);
ko.applyBindings(item);
```

We're creating a new instance of our LineItem to Knockout's applyBindings() method, and we're setting the product name and price. We will make this more dynamic later, but for now we'll hard-code these values.

With the object in place, we can build our interface and pull data from the object. We'll use an HTML table to mark up our cart, and we'll use <thead> and <tbody> tags to give us a little more structure.

```
knockout/item.html
<div role="application">
  <table>
    <thead>
      <tr>
        <th>Product</th>
        <th>Price</th>
        <th>Quantity</th>
        <th>Total</th>
      </tr>
    </thead>
    <tbody>
      <tr aria-live="polite">
        <td data-bind="text: name"></td>
        <td data-bind="text: price"></td>
      </tr>
    </tbody>
  </table>
</div>
```

Since our table row updates based on user input, we use the aria-live attribute on the table row so screen readers know to watch that row for changes. We also wrap the whole cart within a <div> with the HTML5-ARIA role of application, which tells screen readers that this is an interactive application. You can learn about these in the HTML5 specification.[15]

Pay special attention to these two lines:

```
knockout/item.html
<td data-bind="text: name"></td>
<td data-bind="text: price"></td>
```

Our LineItem instance is now a global, visible object on our page, and its name and price properties are visible as well. So, with these two lines, we're saying that we want the "text" of this element to get its value from the property we specify.

When we load the page in our browser, we see the row of our table start to take shape, and the name and price are filled in!

Let's add a text field to the table so that the user can update the quantity.

```
knockout/item.html
<td><input type="text" name="quantity"
    data-bind='value: quantity, valueUpdate: "keyup"'>
</td>
```

---

15. http://www.w3.org/TR/html5-author/wai-aria.html

In Knockout, we reference data fields within regular HTML elements with text, but HTML form elements like <input> have value attributes. This time we bind the value attribute to a quantity property in our view model, which we need to define next.

The quantity property isn't just for displaying data; it's going to set data as well, and when we set data, we need events to fire. We do that by using Knockout's ko.observable() function as the value of our quantity property in our class.

```
this.quantity = ko.observable(1);
```

We're passing a default value to ko.observable() so the text field has a value when we bring the page up for the first time.

Now we can enter the quantity, but we need to show the row's subtotal. Let's add a table column to print out the subtotal:

```
<td data-bind="text: subtotal "></td>
```

Just like our name and price columns, we set the text of the table cell to the value of our view model's subtotal property.

This brings us to one of the more powerful features of Knockout.js, the dependentObservable() method. We defined our quantity property as observable, which means that other things notice when that field changes. We declare a dependentObservable(), which executes code whenever our observed field changes, and we assign that dependentObservable() to a property on our object so it can be bound to our user interface.

```
this.subtotal = ko.dependentObservable(function() {
  return(
    this.price * parseInt("0"+this.quantity(), 10)
  ); //<label id="code.subtotal" />
}, this);
```

But how does the dependentObservable() know what fields to watch? It actually looks at the observable properties we access in the function we define! Since we're adding the price and quantity together, Knockout tracks them both and runs this code when either one changes.

The dependentObservable() takes a second parameter that specifies the context for the properties. This is because of how JavaScript's functions and objects work, and you can read more on this in the Knockout.js documentation.

And that's it for a single row. When we change the quantity, our price updates in real time. Now let's take what we learned here and turn this into a multiple-line shopping cart with line totals and a grand total.

Using Control Flow Bindings

Binding objects to HTML is quite handy, but it's likely that we'll have more than one item in our cart, and duplicating all that code is going to get a little tedious, not to mention more difficult since we'll have more than one LineItem object to bind. We need to rethink the interface a bit.

Instead of working with a LineItem as the view model, let's create another object that represents the shopping cart. This Cart object will hold all of the LineItem objects. Using what we know about Knockout's dependentObservables, this new Cart object can have a property that computes the total when any of the items in the cart changes.

But what about the HTML for the line item? Well, we can reduce duplication by using a *control-flow binding* and tell Knockout to render our line-item HTML once for each item in our cart. Let's get started.

First, let's define an array of items we'll use to populate the cart.

```
knockout/update_cart.html
var products = [
  {name: "Macbook Pro 15 inch", price: 1699.00},
  {name: "Mini Display Port to VGA Adapter", price: 29.00},
  {name: "Magic Trackpad", price: 69.00},
  {name: "Apple Wireless Keyboard", price: 69.00}
];
```

In a real-world situation, we would get this data from a web service or Ajax call or by generating this array on the server side when we serve up the page.

Now, let's create a Cart object that holds the items. We define it the same way we defined our LineItem.

```
knockout/update_cart.html
var Cart = function(items){
  this.items = ko.observableArray();

  for(var i in items){
    var item = new LineItem(items[i].name, items[i].price);
    this.items.push(item);
  }
}
```

and we need to change our binding from using the LineItem class to the Cart class.

> ### Joe asks:
> ## What About Knockout and Accessibility?
>
> Interfaces that rely heavily on JavaScript often raise a red flag when it comes to accessibility, but the use of JavaScript alone doesn't make a site inaccessible to the disabled.
>
> In this recipe, we made use of the HTML5 ARIA roles and attributes to help screen readers understand the application we're developing, but accessibility is about much more than screen readers; it's about making our applications usable by the widest audience possible.
>
> Knockout is a JavaScript solution and will work only when JavaScript is enabled or available, so you need to take that under consideration. We recommend that you build applications to work without JavaScript and then use Knockout to *enhance* your application. Our example uses Knockout to render the cart's contents, but if we were using a server-side framework we could render the HTML for the cart and use Knockout's binding features on top of the rendered HTML. The accessibility of a site depends much more on the implementation than on the library or technology used.

knockout/update_cart.html

```
var cartViewModel = new Cart(products);
ko.applyBindings(cartViewModel);
```

The items are stored in the cart using an observableArray(), which works just like an observable() but has the properties of an array. When we created a new instance of our cart, we passed in the array of data. Our object iterates over the items of data and creates new LineItem instances that get stored in the items array. Since this array is observable, our user interface will change whenever the array's contents change. Of course, now that we're dealing with more than one item, we'll need to modify that user interface.

Then we modify our HTML page and tell Knockout to repeat the table rows by using a Knockout data-bind call on the <tbody> tag.

knockout/update_cart.html

```
<tbody data-bind="foreach: items">
  <tr aria=live="polite">
    <td data-bind="text: name"></td>
    <td data-bind="text: price"></td>
    <td><input type="text" name="quantity" data-bind='value: quantity'></td>
    <td data-bind="text: subtotal "></td>
  </tr>
</tbody>
```

We tell Knockout to render the contents of the <tbody> for each entry in the items array. We don't have to change anything else in that row.

At this point, we have multiple lines displaying on the page, each subtotaling correctly. Now let's handle computing the grand total and removal of items.

The Grand Total

We've already seen how Knockout's dependentObservable() method works when we used it to calculate the subtotal for each item. We can use the same approach to calculate the total for the entire cart by adding a dependentObservable() to the Cart itself.

knockout/update_cart.html
```
this.total = ko.dependentObservable(function(){
  var total = 0;
  for (item in this.items()){
    total += this.items()[item].subtotal();
  }
  return total;
}, this);
```

Any time any of the items in our array changes, this code will fire. To display the grand total on the form, we simply need to add the appropriate table row. Since it's the total for the cart and not for a line item, it doesn't go in the <tbody>. Instead, we'll place it in a <tfoot> tag, which we place right above the closing <thead> tag. Placing the footer *above* the table body can help some browsers and assistive devices more quickly identify the table structure.

knockout/update_cart.html
```
<tfoot>
  <tr>
    <td colspan="4">Total</td>
    <td aria-live="polite" data-bind="text: total()"></td>
  </tr>
</tfoot>
```

When we refresh our page, we can change any quantity and update both the line total and the cart total simultaneously. Now, about that Remove button...

Removing Items

To wrap this project up, we need to add a Remove button to the end of each row that removes the item from the row. Thanks to all the work we've done, this is a very simple task. First, we modify the table to add the Remove button.

knockout/update_cart.html
```
<td>
  <button
    data-bind="click: function() { cartViewModel.remove(this) }">Remove
  </button>
</td>
```

Be Sure to Reconcile with the Server!

Building a shopping cart update screen entirely on the client side is becoming more popular. In some cases, it's just not possible to send Ajax requests back and forth every time a user makes a change to the interface.

When you use an approach like this, you'll want to synchronize the data in the cart on the client side with data on the server. After all, you wouldn't want someone changing prices on you!

When the user checks out, submit the updated quantities to the server and recompute the totals on the server side before checking out.

This time, instead of binding data to the interface, we bind an event and a function. In this case, we pass the item (this) to the remove() method on our cartViewModel instance. Since we haven't defined the remove() method yet, this button won't work. So, let's fix that by adding this method to our Cart object:

knockout/update_cart.html
```
this.remove = function(item){ this.items.remove(item); }
```

That's it! Since the items array is an observableArray, our entire interface gets updated. Even our grand total changes!

Further Exploration

Knockout is great for situations where we need to build a dynamic single-page interface, and because it's not tied to a specific web framework, we can use it anywhere.

More importantly, the view models Knockout uses are just ordinary JavaScript, which means we can use Knockout to implement many commonly requested user interface features. For example, we could very easily implement an Ajax-based live search, build in-place editing controls that persist the data back to the server, or even update the contents of one drop-down field based on the selected value of another field.

Also See

- Recipe 14, *Organizing Code with Backbone.js*, on page 93

Recipe 14

Organizing Code with Backbone.js

Problem

As users demand more robust and responsive client-side applications, developers respond with amazing JavaScript libraries. But as applications get more complex, the client-side code starts to look like your basic kitchen junk drawer, with libraries strewn about, all crammed together in a disorganized pile of event bindings, jQuery Ajax calls, and JSON parsing functions.

We need a way to develop our client-side applications using the same approach we've been using for years in our server-side code—a framework. With a robust JavaScript framework, we'll be able to keep things organized, reduce duplication, and standardize on something other developers understand.

Because Backbone is a complex library, this is a much longer and more complex recipe.

Ingredients

- Backbone.js[16]
- Underscore.js[17]
- JSON2.js[18]
- Mustache[19]
- jQuery
- QEDServer

Solution

We can use a number of frameworks to make this work, but Backbone.js is one of the most popular because of its flexibility, robustness, and code quality, despite being relatively new at the time of writing. We can use Backbone to do event binding similar to what we did with Knockout in Recipe 13, *Snappier Client-Side Interfaces with Knockout.js*, on page 84, but with Backbone, we

---

16. http://documentcloud.github.com/backbone
17. http://documentcloud.github.com/underscore/
18. https://github.com/douglascrockford/JSON-js
19. http://mustache.github.com/

get models that interact with our server, and we get a request routing system that can monitor changes in the URL. With Backbone, we get a more robust framework that handles more complex client-server applications well but might be overkill for simpler applications.

Let's use Backbone to improve the responsiveness of our online store's interface. Data from our logs and user studies shows that page refreshes are taking too long, and a lot of the stuff we're going to the server for could be done on the client. Our manager suggested that we take our product management interface and turn it into a single-page interface where we can add and delete products without page refreshes.

Before we get into building our interface, let's dig a little deeper into what Backbone is and how we can use it to solve our problem.

Backbone Basics

Backbone is a client-side implementation of the Model-View-Controller pattern, and it's heavily influenced by server-side frameworks like ASP.NET MVC and Ruby on Rails. Backbone has several components that help us keep things organized as we communicate with our server-side code.

Models represent the data and can interact with our backend via Ajax. Models are also a great place to do any business logic or data validations.

Views in Backbone are a little different from views in other frameworks. Instead of being the presentation layer, Backbone's views are more like "view controllers." We may have lots of events in a typical client-side interface, and the code these events trigger lives in these views. They can then render templates and modify our user interface.

Routers watch changes in the URL and can tie models and views together. When we want to show different "pages" or tabs on an interface, we can use routers to handle requests and display different views. In Backbone, they also provide support for the browser's Back button.

Finally, Backbone introduces collections, which give us an easy way to fetch and work with multiple model instances. Figure 18, *Backbone's components*, on page 95 shows how these components work together and how we'll use them to build our product management interface.

By default, Backbone's models use jQuery's ajax() method to communicate with a RESTful server-side application using JSON. The backend needs to accept GET, POST, PUT, and DELETE requests and be able to look for JSON in the body of the request. These are merely defaults, though, and the Backbone

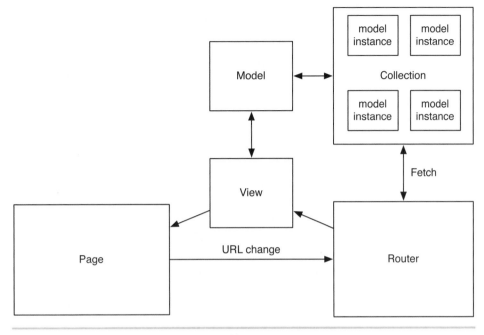

Figure 18—Backbone's components

documentation explains how to modify your client-side code to work with different kinds of backends.

The backend we'll be working with supports Backbone's default behavior, so we'll simply be able to call some methods on our Backbone models, and Backbone will seamlessly serialize and deserialize our product information.

One last note—as we mentioned in *What About Knockout and Accessibility?*, on page 90, it's best to use frameworks like Backbone *on top of* an existing website, to provide an enhanced user experience. If your client-side code builds on a solid foundation, it's easier to provide a solution that works without JavaScript. In this recipe, we assume we're building an interface that already has a working non-JavaScript alternative.

Building Our Interface

We're going to build a simple, single-page interface to manage products in our store, like the one in Figure 19, *Our product interface*, on page 96. We'll have a form at the top of the page for adding products, and below that, we'll display a list of the products. We'll use Backbone to talk to our backend to retrieve or modify our product inventory, using its REST-like interface:

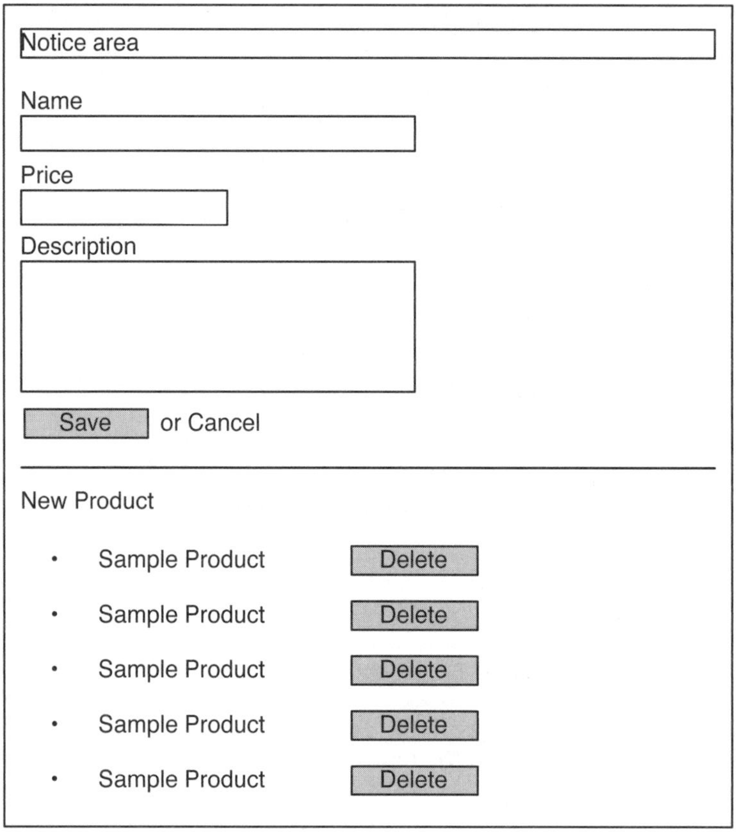

Figure 19—Our product interface

- A GET() request to http://example.com/products.json retrieves the list of products.

- A GET request to /products/1.json retrieves a JSON representation of the product with the ID of 1.

- A POST request to /products.json with a JSON representation of a product in the request body creates a new product.

- A PUT request to http://example.com/products/1.json with a JSON representation of a product in the request body updates the product with the ID of 1.

- A DELETE request to /products/1.json deletes the product with the ID of 1.

Because Ajax requests have to be done against the same domain, we'll be using QEDServer for our development server and using its product management API. We'll place all of our files in the public folder that QEDServer creates in our workspace so our development server will serve them properly.

To build our interface, we'll create a model to represent our product and a collection to hold multiple product models. We'll use a router to handle requests for displaying the product list and showing the form to add a new product. In addition, we'll have views for the product list and the product form.

First, let's create a lib folder to hold the Backbone library and its dependencies.

```
$ mkdir javascripts
$ mkdir javascripts/lib
```

Next, we need to get Backbone.js and its components from the Backbone.js website.[20] In this recipe, we're using Backbone 0.5.3. Backbone requires the Underscore.js library, which provides some JavaScript functions Backbone uses behind the scenes so we can write less code. We also need the JSON2 library, which provides broader support for parsing JSON across browsers. And since we're already familiar with Mustache templates, we need that library as well so we can use it for our templating language.[21] Download these files and place them in the javascripts/lib folder.

Finally, let's create a single app.js file in the javascripts folder. This file will contain all of our Backbone components and custom code. Although it might make sense to split these into separate files, we'd end up with an additional call to the server for each file when we load the page.

Now that we have everything we need, let's create a very simple HTML skeleton in index.html to hold our user interface elements and include the rest of our files. First, we'll declare the usual boilerplate pieces and create empty <div>s for our messages to the user, our form, and a <ul> for the product list.

backbone/public/index.html
```
<!DOCTYPE html>
<html>
  <head>
    <title>Product Management</title>
  </head>
  <body role="application">
    <h1>Products</h1>
    <div aria-live="polite" id="notice">
    </div>
    <div aria-live="polite" id="form">
    </div>
    <p><a href="#new">New Product</a></p>
```

---

20. http://documentcloud.github.com/backbone/
21. To save time, you can find all of these files in the book's source code.

```
  <ul aria-live="polite" id="list">
  </ul>
 </body>
</html>
```

We'll be updating these regions without refreshing the page, so we're adding in the HTML5 ARIA attributes to tell screen readers how to handle these events.[22]

Below those regions and right *above* the closing <body> tag, we include jQuery, the Backbone library, its prerequisites, and our app.js file:

backbone/public/index.html
```
<script type="text/javascript"
  src="http://ajax.googleapis.com/ajax/libs/jquery/1.7/jquery.min.js">
</script>
<script type="text/javascript"
        src="javascripts/lib/json2.js"></script>
<script type="text/javascript"
        src="javascripts/lib/underscore-min.js"></script>
<script type="text/javascript"
        src="javascripts/lib/backbone-min.js"></script>
<script type="text/javascript"
        src="javascripts/lib/mustache.js"></script>
<script type="text/javascript"
        src="javascripts/app.js"></script>
```

Now, let's get to work building the product list.

Listing Products

To list products, we'll fetch the products from our Ajax backend. To do this, we need a model and a collection. The model will represent a single product, and the collection will represent a group of products. When we create and delete a product, we'll be using the model directly, but when we want to grab a list of products from our server, we can use the collection to fetch records and give us a group of Backbone models we can work with.

First, let's create the model. In javascripts/app.js, we'll define our Product like this:

backbone/public/javascripts/app.js
```
var Product = Backbone.Model.extend({

  defaults: {
    name: "",
    description: "",
    price: ""
  },
```

---

22. http://www.w3.org/TR/html5-author/wai-aria.html

```
  url : function() {
    return(this.isNew() ? "/products.json" : "/products/" + this.id + ".json");
  }
});
```

We're setting up some default values for situations where there's no data, like when we create a new instance. Next, we're telling the model where it should get its data. Backbone uses a model's url() method to figure this out, and we have to fill it in.

With a model defined, we can now create a collection, which we'll use to grab all of the products for our list page.

```
backbone/public/javascripts/app.js
var ProductsCollection = Backbone.Collection.extend({
  model: Product,
  url: '/products.json'
});
```

Like a model, a collection also has a url() method we have to implement, but since we're interested only in fetching all of the products, we can just hard-code the URL to /products.json.

We'll access this collection in several places in our application, so let's create an instance of our Products collection. At the very top of javascripts/app.js, we'll create the object.

```
backbone/public/javascripts/app.js
$(function(){
  window.products = new ProductsCollection();
```

We attach this product collection object to the window object. This will let us easily access the collection of products from multiple views later.

With our model and collection defined, we can turn our attention to the view.

The List Template and View

Backbone views encapsulate all of the logic associated with changing the interface in response to events. We'll use two views to render our list of products. We'll create one view to represent a single product, which will render a Mustache template and handle any events related to that product. We'll then use a second view that will iterate over our collection of products and then render the first view for each object, placing the results onto our page. This way, we'll have more fine-grained control over each component.

First, we create a simple Mustache template that our Backbone views will use to iterate over a collection of products. We need to add this template to our index.html page, *above* the <script> tags that include our libraries:

backbone/public/index.html

```
<script type="text/html" id="product_template">
  <li>
    <h3>
      {{name}} - {{price}}
      <button class="delete">Delete</button>
    </h3>
    <p>{{description}}</p>
  </li>
</script>
```

We display the product name, price, and description, as well as a button to delete the product.

Next, we create a new view called ProductView by extending Backbone's View class and defining a few key pieces:

backbone/public/javascripts/app.js

```
ProductView = Backbone.View.extend({
  template: $("#product_template"),
  initialize: function(){
    this.render();
  },
  render: function(){
  }
});
```

First, we use jQuery to pull our Mustache template off of the index page by its ID and store in a property called template. This way, we're not continuously pulling the template off the page every time we want to render a product.

Then we define an initialize() function, which will fire when we create a new instance of our ListView, and we'll tell it to fire the view's render() function.

Every view has a default render() function, but we need to override it so it actually does something. We'll have it render our Mustache template, which we grab from our template variable. Since the object we stored in the template variable is a jQuery object, we call the html() method to get the template contents out of the object.

backbone/public/javascripts/app.js

```
render: function(){
  var html = Mustache.to_html(this.template.html(), this.model.toJSON() );
  $(this.el).html(html);
  return this;
}
```

We're referencing this.model in this method, which will contain the products we want to list. When we create a new instance of our view, we can assign a model or a collection to the view so we can easily reference the model or collection in the view's methods without having to pass it around, just like we're doing with the Mustache template. We call toJSON() on our model that we pass to the template so that the model's data is easily available to the template.

The render() method places the rendered HTML from the Mustache template into a property on the view called el and then returns this instance of the ProductView. When we call this method, we'll take the results out of that property and append it to the page.

To do that, we'll create a view called ListView, which has nearly the same structure as our ProductView view, but instead of rendering a Mustache template, it's going to iterate over our products collection and render our ProductView for each one.

backbone/public/javascripts/app.js

```
ListView = Backbone.View.extend({
  el: $("#list"),

  initialize: function() {
    this.render();
  },

  renderProduct: function(product){
    var productView = new ProductView({model: product});
    this.el.append(productView.render().el);
  },

  render: function() {
    if(this.collection.length > 0) {
      this.collection.each(this.renderProduct, this);
    } else {
      $("#notice").html("There are no products to display.");
    }
  }
});
```

We need to update the contents of the list region on our page with the list of products. We're storing a reference to this region in a property called el. This gives us convenient access to it from our render() method, similar to how we referenced our Mustache template in ProductView.

Backbone uses Underscore.js to give us some helpful functions that make working with collections very easy. In our render() method, we're iterating over the collection using the each() method and calling our renderProduct method. The each() method automatically passes the product. We pass this as a second parameter to specify that we want the view to be the scope for the renderProduct().

Without that, the each() method would look for our renderProduct() method on the collection, and it wouldn't work.

So far, we've declared a model, a collection, and a couple of views, and we've added a template, but we still don't have anything to show for it. We need to tie this all together when we load our page in our browser. We'll do that with a router.

Handling URL Changes with Routers

When we bring up our page, we'll want to fire some code to fetch our collection of products from the Ajax API. Then we'll need to pass the collection of products to a new instance of our ListView so we can display the products. Backbone's routers let us respond to changes we make in the URL and respond by executing functions.

Let's create a new router called ProductsRouter. Inside this file, we'll extend Backbone's router and then define a *route* that maps the part of the URL that appears after the hash mark to a function in our router. To handle the default case where there is no hash in the URL, we define a route that's empty and map it to a function called index(). When we load the page index.html, this default route will fire.

```
backbone/public/javascripts/app.js
ProductsRouter = Backbone.Router.extend({
    routes: {
      "": "index"
    },
    index: function() {
    }
});
```

Inside of the index() action, we call the fetch() method of our Products collection to retrieve the data from our server.

```
backbone/public/javascripts/app.js
index: function() {
  window.products.fetch({
    success: function(){
      new ListView({ collection: window.products });
    },
    error: function(){
      $("#notice").html("Could not load the products.");
    }
  });
}
```

The fetch() method takes in success and error callbacks. When we get an error from our backend, we display a notice to the users in the notice region of the page. When the backend returns data to the collection, the success() callback fires, and we create a new instance of our view. Since our list view automatically renders thanks to the code we placed in the initialize() method of the view, we don't have anything else to do except create a new instance of the router to kick everything off.

In javascripts/app.js, we create the Router instance right below our definition for window.productCollection. Then we have to tell Backbone to start tracking URL changes.

backbone/public/javascripts/app.js
```
window.products = new ProductsCollection();
// START_HIGHLIGHTING
$.ajaxSetup({ cache: false });
window.router = new ProductsRouter();
Backbone.history.start();
// END_HIGHLIGHTING
```

The Backbone.history.start(); line makes Backbone start watching changes in the URL. If we forget this, the router won't work, and we won't see anything happen.

This line prevents some browsers from caching Ajax responses from our server:

```
$.ajaxSetup({ cache: false });
```

When we visit http://localhost:8080/index.html, we finally see a list of our products.

To review our progress so far, we have a router that looks at the URL and fires a method that uses our collection to fetch some models from our web service. This collection is then passed to a view, which renders a template and outputs the template onto our user interface. You can see a diagram of these interactions in Figure 20, *Listing products with Backbone*, on page 104. That may seem like lot of steps and a lot of code for something that's fairly trivial, but it will add up to huge time savings as we evolve our code. We've laid the groundwork for adding, updating, and deleting products, and we won't have to struggle with where these pieces go. Let's go a little further by adding the ability to add products.

Creating a New Product

To create a product, we'll need to add a form to the page when the user clicks the New Product link. When the user fills out the form, we'll take the form data, submit it to our backend, and then redisplay the list.

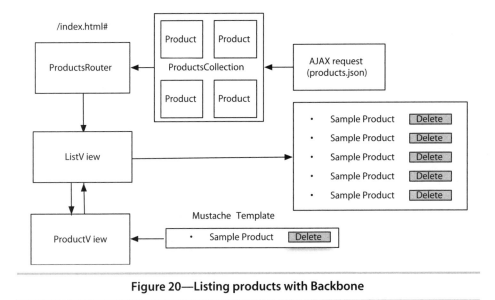

Figure 20—Listing products with Backbone

First, let's add a Mustache template for the form to our index.html page, *right below* the product template but still *above* the <script> tags that include our libraries:

backbone/public/index.html

```html
<script type="text/html" id="product_form_template">
  <form>
    <div class="row">
      <label>Name<br>
        <input id="product_name" type="text" name="name"
               value="{{name}}">
      </label>
    </div>
    <div class="row">
      <label>Description<br>
        <textarea id="product_description"
                  name="description">{{description}}</textarea>
      </label>
    </div>
    <div class="row">
      <label>Price<br>
        <input id="product_price" type="text" name="price"
               value="{{price}}">
      </label>
    </div>
    <button>Save</button>
  </form>
  <p><a id="cancel" href="#">Cancel</a></p>
</script>
```

The Mustache template tags will pull values out of the model into the form fields. This is why we set default values in our Backbone model. We could also reuse this template for editing records later.

Now we need a view to render this template from a model. Let's create a new view called FormView in javascripts/app.js similar to the one we created for our list. This time, we'll set the el variable to the form region of our page, and we have the render() function grab our form template, rendering the result into that region.

```
backbone/public/javascripts/app.js
FormView = Backbone.View.extend({
  el: $("#form"),
  template: $("#product_form_template"),
  initialize: function(){
    this.render();
  },
  render: function(){
    var html = Mustache.to_html(this.template.html(), this.model.toJSON() );
    this.el.html(html);
  }
});
```

When our user clicks the New Product link, we want this view to render the form onto the page. Since the link changes the URL by adding #new, we can use the router to respond to that change. First, we need to modify the routes section so we have a route for #new, which is where our New Products link points.

```
backbone/public/javascripts/app.js
routes: {
  "new": "newProduct",
  "": "index"
},
```

And then we need to define the function that grabs a new model and passes it to a new instance of a Form view so that view can render on the page. We'll place this method above our index() method, and since these method declarations are actually defined as properties on the this object, we need to ensure we place a comma between each of these declarations.

```
backbone/public/javascripts/app.js
newProduct: function() {
  new FormView( {model: new Product()});
},
```

When we reload our page and click the New Product link, our form displays. With Backbone's History tracking, we can press the Back button in our browser, and the URL will change. But we can't save new records yet. We need to add the logic for that next.

Responding to Events in the View

We've used our router to display the form, but routers can only respond to changes in the URL. We need to respond to click events on the Save button and the Cancel link. We'll do that in the Form view we created.

First, let's define events for the view to watch. We add this to our view, above the initialize() function:

```
backbone/public/javascripts/app.js
events: {
  "click .delete": "destroy"
 },
events: {
    "click #cancel": "close",
    "submit form": "save",
},
```

The syntax here is a little different than typical JavaScript event monitoring; the key of the hash defines the event we're watching followed by the CSS selector for the element we want to watch. The value specifies the function on the view we want to invoke. In our case, we're watching the click event on our cancel button and the submit event on our form.

The code for the "close" link is easy—we simply remove the contents of the HTML element that contains this view:

```
backbone/public/javascripts/app.js
close: function(){
  this.el.unbind();
  this.el.empty();
},
```

The save() method is a little more complex. We first prevent the form from submitting, and then we grab the values from each form field, placing those values into a new array. Then we set the model's attributes and call the model's save() method.

```
backbone/public/javascripts/app.js
save: function(e){
  e.preventDefault();
  data = {
    name: $("#product_name").val(),
    description: $("#product_description").val(),
    price: $("#product_price").val()
  };
  var self = this;
```

```
    this.model.save(data, {
      success: function(model, resp) {
        $("#notice").html("Product saved.");
        window.products.add(self.model);
        window.router.navigate("#");
        self.close();
      },
      error: function(model, resp){
        $("#notice").html("Errors prevented the product from being created.");
      }
    });
  },
```

The save() method expects us to use the same approach we used with the fetch() method on collections, in which we define the behavior for success and for errors. Since those callbacks have a different scope, we create a temporary variable called self that we assign the current scope to so we can reference that scope in the success callback. Unlike the each() method we used when we rendered the list of products, Backbone doesn't support passing the scope to the callbacks.[23]

When the save is successful, we add this new model to our collection, and we use the router to alter the URL. This doesn't actually fire the associated function in the router, though, which means we won't see our new product in the list. But that's an easy fix thanks to Backbone's event binding.

When we add a model to a collection, the collection fires off an add event that we can watch. Remember the renderProduct() method in our List view? We can have our List view execute that method any time we add a model to our collection. All we have to do is add this line to the initialize() method of our ListView:

backbone/public/javascripts/app.js
```
this.collection.bind("add", this.renderProduct, this);
```

The bind() method lets us bind to specific events, specifying the event, the function, and the scope. We pass this as the third parameter to specify that we want the *view* to be the scope, and not the collection, just like we did in the List view's render() method with collection.each.

Since we reused the renderProduct() when we added a new record, the new record is appended to the bottom of the list. To make it appear at the top of the list, we could instead make a new addProduct(), which would use jQuery's prepend() method instead, but we'll leave that up to you to try.

---

23. At least, not at the time this was written.

Now that we can create products and see the list of products update all on the same page without refreshing, let's turn our attention to removing products. That's where a lot of this up-front work and code organization really pays off.

Deleting a Product

To delete a product, we use what we learned from working in the FormView and implement a destroy() function in our ProductView that fires when we press the Delete button.

First, we define the event to watch for clicks on the buttons with the class of "delete."

backbone/public/javascripts/app.js

```
events: {
  "click .delete": "destroy"
 },
events: {
    "click #cancel": "close",
    "submit form": "save",
},
```

Then we define the destroy() method that the event will call. Inside this method we call the destroy() method on our model that's bound to this view. This uses the same success and error callback strategy we've used previously. We use the self trick we used when creating records to get around the scope issues, just like we did when we saved records in the Form view.

backbone/public/javascripts/app.js

```
destroy: function(){
  var self = this;
  this.model.destroy({
    success: function(){
      self.remove();
    },
    error: function(){
      $("#notice").html("There was a problem deleting the product.");
    }
  });
},
```

When the model is successfully deleted by the server, our success callback fires, calling the remove() method of this view, making the record disappear from the screen. If something goes wrong, we display a message on the screen instead.

And that's it! We now have a simple, well-organized prototype that we can show off or continue to evolve.

Further Exploration

This application is a good start, but there are a few things you can explore on your own.

First, we're using jQuery to update the notice in several places, like this:

```
$("#notice").html("Product saved.");
```

You could create a wrapper function for that to decouple it from the markup or even use another Backbone view and Mustache template to display those messages.

When we save records, we're explicitly pulling the values off the form with jQuery selectors. You could instead place the data right into the model instance by using onchange events on the form fields.

We built support for adding and removing records in this recipe, but you could go one step further and add support for editing records. You could use the router to display the form and even reuse the same form view we used for creating products.

Backbone provides a great system for working with backend data, but that's just the beginning. You're not required to use Backbone with an Ajax backend; you could just as easily use it to persist data to HTML5's client-side storage mechanism.

For more robust integration with server-side applications, Backbone supports HTML5's History pushState(), which means we can use real URLs instead of hash-based ones. We can then have graceful fallbacks that serve pages from our server when JavaScript is disabled but work with Backbone when Java-Script is available.

With its numerous options and excellent support for Ajax backends, Backbone is an incredibly flexible framework that works well for those client-side situations where we need an organized structure.

Also See

- Recipe 10, *Building HTML with Mustache*, on page 67
- Recipe 13, *Snappier Client-Side Interfaces with Knockout.js*, on page 84

CHAPTER 3

Data Recipes

Web developers work with data in many forms. Sometimes we're pulling in a widget from another service, and other times we're taking data from our users. In these recipes, we spend some time consuming, manipulating, and presenting data.

Recipe 15

Adding an Inline Google Map

Problem

Users want simple methods to locate their destination, and they want that information quickly in an easy and accessible manner. While addresses and written directions work, the simplest way is to glance at a map, memorize the street number, and grab your keys and go. By including a map on our site, we immediately give users a sense of where things are located and how they can get there.

Ingredients

- The Google Maps API

Solution

Using the Google Maps API, we can bring the power and functionality of Google Maps into our own application. We can render maps of two types: static and interactive. The static map is an image that we can insert into our page, whereas the interactive map allows for zooming and panning. The Google Maps API supports any programming language that can make a request to Google's servers. The documentation includes a lot of JavaScript examples, which is perfect for our needs.[1]

We can use the API to accomplish any task that a user could accomplish in the full application. We can render maps of two types: static and interactive. The static map is an image that we can insert into our page, whereas the interactive map allows for zooming and panning.

Along with rendering maps, the JavaScript API lets us insert other elements on the maps. We can place markers and bind mouse events to the markers. We can also create pop-out dialogs that show information directly within the map. We can show street views, geolocate the user, create routes and

---

1. http://code.google.com/apis/maps/documentation/javascript/reference.html

directions, and draw custom models on the map. The sky is in fact the limit until Google launches its space program and takes over NASA.[2]

We're working with a local university to develop a map for their web page for new visitors. The Admissions office wants to show these visitors where they can find places to eat as well as where to park. We'll create an interactive map that contains markers and information by using the JavaScript Google Maps API.

Let's start off by creating a basic HTML document. We will declare the <DOCTYPE> as HTML5 as a recommendation from Google; however, if you can't use <DOCTYPE html> in your application, you're not explicitly required to do so.

googlemaps/map_example.html

```
<!DOCTYPE html>
<html lang="en">
  <head>
    <meta charset="utf-8">
    <title>Freshman Landing Page</title>
    <style>
    </style>
    <script type="text/javascript">
    </script>
  </head>
  <body>
  </body>
</html>
```

Next, we'll include the Google Maps JavaScript API in our document. To make this request, we need to define whether our application is using a sensor to determine our user's location. Since this is not within the scope of the tutorial, we will set it to false.

googlemaps/map_example.html

```
<script type="text/javascript"
  src="http://maps.google.com/maps/api/js?sensor=false">
</script>
```

The API requires a <div> to act as a container for the map, so we'll add that to our page.

googlemaps/map_example.html

```
<div id="map_canvas"></div>
```

---

2. http://www.google.com/space

The map will scale to the size of this container, so let's set dimensions on this <div> with CSS, by adding it to a new <style> section in our page's <head> region like this:

googlemaps/map_example.html
```
#map_canvas {
  width: 600px;
  height: 400px;
}
```

This container is now ready to hold a map that is 600x400 pixels. Let's go fetch some data.

Loading the Map with JavaScript

At the bottom of our <head> region, let's add a <script> block to hold the code that will initialize our map. We'll create a function called loadMap() to load the map based on our latitude and longitude, and we'll make this happen when the browser window loads. If you're using a framework such as jQuery in your project, you can do the loading of the map inside of your DOM-ready call, but we'll do this with vanilla JavaScript for our example.

googlemaps/map_example.html
```
window.onload = loadMap;
```

Next, we'll create the loadMap() function. Since we're not using a sensor, we'll hard-code our latitude and longitude. These coordinates define the center point of the map. To find these values, we have a few options. We could navigate to Google Maps, find what we want to center our map on, right-click a pin, and select "What's here?" The values for latitude and longitude appear in the search box. Alternatively, we can use Google Maps Lat/Long Popup.[3] This application allows us to click a location to find our values.

googlemaps/map_example.html
```
function loadMap() {
  var latLong = new google.maps.LatLng(44.798609, -91.504912);

  var mapOptions = {
    zoom: 15,
    mapTypeId: google.maps.MapTypeId.ROADMAP,
    center: latLong
  };

  var map = new google.maps.Map(document.getElementById("map_canvas"),
        mapOptions);
}
```

---

3. http://www.gorissen.info/Pierre/maps/googleMapLocationv3.php

Within this function, we create an object to hold some options for our map. We can define the type of map we want, a zoom value, and more. The zoom requires some experimentation; the higher the number, the further in it zooms. A value of 15 works well for street-level maps.

We can change how the map appears by setting a different mapTypeId. Note that zoom values along with maximum ranges for zoom change when changing map type. You can find a reference for map types in the Google Maps API documentation.[4]

Finally, we create the map. The Map constructor requires that we pass the DOM element that will hold the map along with our object containing the options. When we load this page in our browser, as shown in Figure 21, *The initial map*, on page 116, we see a map centered on our desired location.

Creating Marker Points

To show incoming freshman where they can go to get a bite to eat or otherwise be social, we will create markers on the map. A marker in Google Maps is one of many overlays that we can add. Overlays respond to a click event, and we will use this to show an info window when the marker is clicked.

Since we already have our map, creating the marker is as simple as invoking the constructor and passing some options.

googlemaps/map_example.html

```
mogiesLatLong = new google.maps.LatLng(44.802293, -91.509376);
var marker = new google.maps.Marker({
  position: mogiesLatLong,
  map: map,
  title: "Mogies Pub"
});
```

To define a marker, we pass the latitude and longitude coordinates, the map that will hold the marker, and a title that appears when we hover over the marker.

Next, let's create the info window that appears when this marker is clicked. To create an info window, invoke the constructor.

googlemaps/map_example.html

```
var mogiesDescription = "<h4>Mogies Pub</h4>" +
  "<p>Excellent local restaurant with top of the line burgers and sandwiches.</p>";
var infoPopup = new google.maps.InfoWindow({
  content: mogiesDescription
});
```

---

4. http://code.google.com/apis/maps/documentation/javascript/reference.html#MapTypeId

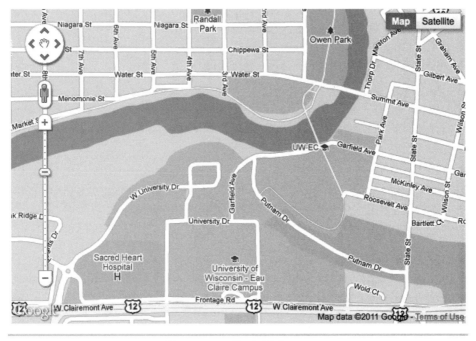

Figure 21—The initial map

Finally, we need to add an event handler to the marker. Using the Google Maps event object, we add a listener to open the info window.

googlemaps/map_example.html
```
google.maps.event.addListener(marker, "click", function() {
  infoPopup.open(map,marker);
});
```

When we click the marker, a new window shows up that gives us information about the location, as you can see in Figure 22, *A clicked marker*, on page 117.

We can add any amount of HTML that we wish to the window. This gives us the freedom to show large amounts of information. From here, we can gather the coordinates of other points of interest and build the rest of the map.

Further Exploration

We have only scratched the surface of what can be accomplished with the Google Maps API. Along with markers, there are other layers of interaction that make the map more usable for your customers. You can create directions, map routes, use geolocation, and even add street views. Each of these features

Figure 22—A clicked marker

is well explained in the Google Maps API documentation,[5] and there are a number of working examples to follow along with.

Google Maps is just one component of the Google APIs. To see a full list of Google APIs, take a look at the Google APIs and Developer Products Page.[6]

Also See

- Recipe 17, *Building a Simple Contact Form*, on page 126
- Recipe 18, *Accessing Cross-site Data with JSONP*, on page 134
- Recipe 19, *Creating a Widget to Embed on Other Sites*, on page 138

---

5. http://code.google.com/apis/maps/documentation/javascript/reference.html
6. http://code.google.com/more/table

Recipe 16

Creating Charts and Graphs with Highcharts

Problem

As the old cliché goes, "A picture is worth a thousand words," and charts are no exception. With a chart or graph, we can present data to our customers and clients in a meaningful and often more attractive way.

There are many options for creating charts, from server-side solutions that generate images to systems that that run with Adobe Flash. We need a simple and effective way to create charts and graphs that doesn't require Flash, since it doesn't work on iOS devices, but we also don't want to use resources on our server to generate images.

Ingredients

- jQuery
- Highcharts[7]
- QEDServer

Solution

The Highcharts JavaScript library lets us easily create interactive and readable charts and graphs. It works across platforms, and since it runs on the client's machine, it doesn't require any special configuration on our servers. The interface built into Highcharts is highly interactive and customizable, letting us present data in a number of ways. In this recipe, we'll build and customize a simple chart and then build a more complex one using some remote data.

Our sales team has developed an affiliate program for our company's shopping site. We've been tasked to develop an interface for our affiliates, and we want to show their data in a visual way with graphs and charts. We'll use Highcharts to build these. But first, let's look at what it takes to get a simple chart displayed on our page.

---

7. http://www.highcharts.com/

Building a Simple Chart

Let's build a simple pie chart so we can get acquainted with Highcharts and its various options. First, let's build a simple HTML document and include the necessary JavaScript files. We'll need highcharts.js, which we can get from the Highcharts website, and we'll need the jQuery library, since Highcharts relies on it. Although other sections of this book use jQuery 1.7, Highcharts requires jQuery version 1.6.2.

highcharts/example_chart.html

```
<script type="text/javascript"
  src="/jquery.js">
</script>
<script type="text/javascript" src="/highcharts.js"></script>
```

Now that we have Highcharts loaded, let's build a chart. Highcharts requires us to create a <div>, which it will use to hold the chart, so let's create one in the <body>. We'll give the <div> an id so we can reference it with our JavaScript code, like this:

highcharts/example_chart.html

```
<body>
  <div id="pie-chart"></div>
</body>
```

All the magic is done by creating a new instance of the Highcharts.Chart class and passing it some options. Highcharts has many options for configuring a chart, and this configuration can very quickly get long and unwieldy. To keep it simple, we'll create a variable called chartOptions and set some values on it that will be expected by Highcharts.

highcharts/example_chart.html

```
$(function() {
  var chartOptions = {};

  chartOptions.chart = {
    renderTo: "pie-chart"
  };
  chartOptions.title = {text: "A sample pie chart"};
  chartOptions.series = [{
    type: "pie",
    name: "Sample chart",
    data: [
      ["Section 1", 30],
      ["Section 2", 50],
      ["Section 3", 20]
    ]
  }];
  var chart = new Highcharts.Chart(chartOptions);
});
```

The first value we set is a chart property that contains information about the chart. This is where we pass the ID of the <div> we created earlier. We set a title for the chart with some sample text. Finally, the series property is an array that contains an object for each type of chart you want to render. Highcharts allows us to pass any number of objects that will be rendered on top of each other. Each object defines a chart type, a name, and a dataset. The format of this data changes depending on the type of chart we're using. For the pie chart, the data is a two-dimensional array where the inner arrays are pairs of X and Y data.

With just a few lines of code, we have a chart that looks like Figure 23, *Our simple pie chart*, on page 121. Let's go a little further now and explore some additional options.

Customizing Our Chart's Appearance

Highcharts supports pie graphs, line graphs, area graphs, and scatter plots, and the extensibility of the graph types lets us create any number of more interesting graphs.

Consider our chartOptions variable from before. We can define a property on it called plotOptions, which is an object containing a number of settings for modifying how the graph is drawn. Let's define some options on our pie chart from earlier.

We can set options for all charts by defining them in the series property on our chartOptions object, but we can also define options for each chart type. Let's customize our pie chart by changing the appearance of the labels that point to each section of the chart.

highcharts/example_chart.html
```
var pieChartOptions = {
  dataLabels: {
    style: {
      fontSize: 20
    },
    connectorWidth: 3,
    formatter: function() {
      var label = this.point.name + " : " + this.percentage + "%";
      return label;
    }
  }
};

chartOptions.plotOptions = {
  pie: pieChartOptions
};
```

A sample pie chart

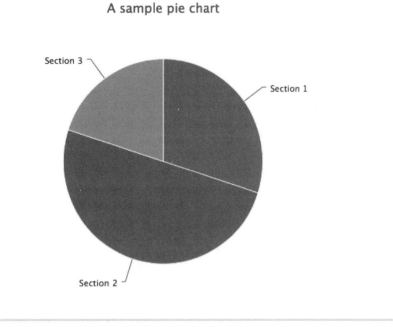

Figure 23—Our simple pie chart

We first increase the font size to make them more visible. Then we increase the connector width to match the font size. Lastly, we create a function that returns a newly formatted label with our desired information. The default labels showed only the point name, so we changed it to show the percentage as well. Our finished graph looks like the one in Figure 24, *Our finished pie chart*, on page 122.

The plotOptions property has a ton of options; refer to the Highcharts documentation on the plotOptions property to see them all.[8]

Now that we know how to create and configure a simple chart, let's use Highcharts to model our affiliate data.

Modeling the Affiliate Data Sets

Our affiliate program tracks quite a bit of data. In most cases, data sets are best represented by a varying types of graphs. To explore another type of graph, we're going to model some customer data that comes through. The customer data includes information such as names, locations of the customer, and age. This kind of information is useful for profiling customers and making

---

8.   http://www.highcharts.com/ref/#plotOptions

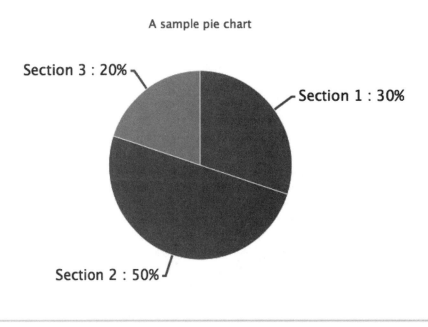

Figure 24—Our finished pie chart

assumptions on how to market products. It's our job to transform this raw data into a graph that our marketing folks can quickly analyze before they dig into the hard data.

We want to be able to glance at the data and understand how old the customers are. Let's use a bar graph so that it's easily to see the mean and the most frequent value. We'll create something that looks like Figure 25, *Our customer data bar graph*, on page 123.

To get started, let's create a new HTML document with jQuery and Highcharts included in it. We'll be working with JSON data and Ajax requests, so place this new HTML file in the public directory of your QEDServer installation.

```
highcharts/affiliates.html
<!DOCTYPE html>
<html lang="en">
<head>
  <meta charset="utf-8">
  <title>Affiliate Customer Data</title>
  <script type="text/javascript"
    src="/jquery.js">
  </script>
  <script type="text/javascript" src="/highcharts.js"></script>
</head>
```

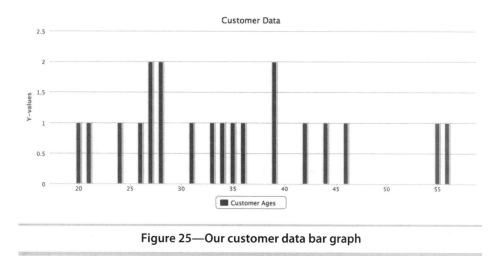

Figure 25—Our customer data bar graph

```
<body>
  <div id="customer-data"></div>
</body>

</html>
```

Within this file, we'll create a <script> and set up our new instance of the Highcharts.Chart class. Let's set a few simple options, including the chart's title and the target element on our page where the chart will go.

```
highcharts/affiliates.html
var options = {
  chart: {
    renderTo: "customer-data"
  },
  title: {
    text: "Customer Data"
  },
  credits: {
    enabled: false
  }
};
```

Now that our document is ready to go, let's do some work with our data.

Showing the Customer Data

Normally, we'd get our customer data from a backend system, but for the purpose of this recipe, we've created some sample data you can use. You can find it in the book's source code, which you can download from the book's website.

Remember that we can't just pull in regular JSON data from a remote server because of the security restrictions of the web browser. Our index.html page and our data file have to be hosted on the same web server. Place this sample data file in a folder called sample_data within the public folder that QEDServer uses. This way, QEDServer can serve it from http://localhost:8080/sample_data/customer_data.json, and our page can consume it properly.

To show the ages in a bar graph, we need to pair an age with the number of times it has occurred. Right now, we have only a list of ages. Let's write some JavaScript to collect the ages and sum up the frequencies. We will make a request to get our customer data and do all our work inside of the success callback, which gets invoked when we get data back from our Ajax request.

highcharts/affiliates.html
```
$.getJSON('/sample_data/customer_data.json', function(data) {

  var ages = [];

  $.each(data.customers, function(i, customer) {
    if (typeof ages[customer.age] === "undefined") {
      ages[customer.age] = 1;
    } else {
      ages[customer.age] += 1;
    }
  });

  var age_data = [];

  $.each(ages, function(i, e) {
    if (typeof e !== "undefined") {
      age_data.push([i, e]);
    }
  });
});
```

Here, we used an array to store some intermediate data. The ages array uses ages as indexes and stores the number of occurrences for that age. Then, we look through and collect ages that exist in the array to map them to the two-dimensional array that Highcharts needs. Now that we have our data in the correct format, let's render our chart.

highcharts/affiliates.html
```
options.series = [{
  type: "column",
  name: "Customer Ages",
  data: age_data
}];

var chart = new Highcharts.Chart(options);
```

Now with our final chart rendered, we can easily glance at the chart and see the most occurring ages for our customers.

Further Exploration

Highcharts is a powerful JavaScript library. In this recipe, we built simple to complex charts that only begin to take advantage of the number of options that are available. The Highcharts reference[9] is a great way to learn about just how much Highcharts is capable of. We recommend taking a look at the documentation and considering what options you would like to use on future projects. Also, the documentation includes a link to an example of most of the available options on JSFiddle.net.[10]

Also See

- Recipe 18, *Accessing Cross-site Data with JSONP*, on page 134
- Recipe 15, *Adding an Inline Google Map*, on page 112
- Recipe 9, *Interacting with Web Pages Using Keyboard Shortcuts*, on page 59
- Recipe 23, *Mobile Drag and Drop*, on page 162

---

9. http://highcharts.com/ref
10. A JavaScript-sharing site: http://jsfiddle.net

Recipe 17

Building a Simple Contact Form

Problem

Websites, even mostly static websites, need to provide a way to contact the site's owner. Simply placing an email address on the page isn't always good enough, because it's not as inviting or engaging, and it's harder for the site owner to sort and organize messages that come from the website. We need an easy, intuitive way for visitors to get in touch.

Ingredients

- A server running PHP

Solution

A contact form allows us to remove a lot of work for visitors, making it more likely that they will send us an email. We can create an HTML form to handle the data entry, write some scripts to handle sending the email, and give user feedback for errors and successful emails.

There is no way to contact us through our current website, and we're concerned that we've been missing out on potential business opportunities. Our manager wants us to create a simple form that sends us an email.

There are many server-side languages we can choose from, but the PHP scripting language is perfect for this situation. There's not much heavy lifting, and the script that processes the data from our contact form will be easy to build because of PHP's simple syntax. In addition to its simple approach, it is readily available on most shared hosting solutions, easy to install on servers where it's not already there, and is a very handy tool for simple backend functions like this where heavier frameworks would be overkill.

To create our contact form, we'll create both HTML and PHP components. We'll use HTML to build the form to ask for the data, and then we'll use PHP to handle the data and send the email. We will also add a few important interface features such as error feedback. We'll use our virtual machine to test this form. If you haven't already, refer to Recipe 37, *Setting Up a Virtual Machine*, on page 272 recipe to create your own PHP development server.

Creating the HTML

Let's start by creating the HTML for the form. The form will ask the user for four things: a name, an email address, a subject, and a message. We will require that the email address be provided; otherwise, we'll be unable to easily get back to the user. We will also set a default value for the subject to get them started. Now that we know what we're collecting, let's create the file contact.php and create the form.

contact/contact.php
```
<form id="contact-form" action="contact.php" method="post">

    <label for="name">Name</label>
    <input class="full-width" type="text" name="name">

    <label for="email">Your Email</label>
    <input class="full-width" type="text" name="email">

    <label for="subject">Subject</label>
    <input class="full-width" type="text" name="subject"
           value="Web Consulting Inquiry">

    <label for="body">Body</label>
    <textarea class="full-width" name="body"></textarea>

    <input type="submit" name="send" value="Send">

</form>
```

The form's action points to itself, and it uses the post method. This allows us to do all of the scripting for sending the email on the same page as the contact form. We create a field for each part of the email the user needs to fill out as well as a submit button. At this point, the form is on the page but looks like a jumble of words and boxes. Let's add some styling to arrange the labels and inputs.

contact/contact.php
```
body {
  font-size: 12px;
  font-family: Verdana;
}

#contact-form {
  width: 320px;
}

#contact-form label {
  display: block;
  margin: 10px 0px;
}

#contact-form input, #contact-form textarea {
  padding: 4px;
}
```

```css
#contact-form .full-width {
  width: 100%;
}

#contact-form textarea {
  height: 100px;
}
```

We changed some font properties, added a good amount of padding and margin, and moved form items to read well. The form is much more readable and usable, as shown in Figure 26, *The form with styles*, on page 129. Now we are ready to create the functionality for the form and write some backend code.

Sending the Email

When the page is processed by PHP, we want to catch any POST requests and send an email. We have already set our page to post to itself, so we just need to add some PHP to the top of the page. If the submit button has been clicked, we need to grab data from the $_POST variable, validate the data, and send it through PHP's mail() function. All of our code for the preprocessing will be in a PHP block above the <html> tag.

contact/contact.php
```php
<?php
if (isset($_POST["send"])) {
}
?>
```

The preprocessing should run only if the Send button has been clicked. Since we gave the button a name attribute in our HTML, we check it in the $_POST array. Now, let's get the data that the user has entered. We can use the same $_POST array to get the data, so let's store them in variables so that they are easier to work with.

contact/contact.php
```php
$name = $_POST["name"];
$email = $_POST["email"];
$subject = $_POST["subject"];
$body = $_POST["body"];
```

Now that we have the data in a few variables, we should make sure that the email the user is giving us is a real email. Let's compare the email against a regular expression to check its validity. Also, we want to let the user know if the email field is incorrect.

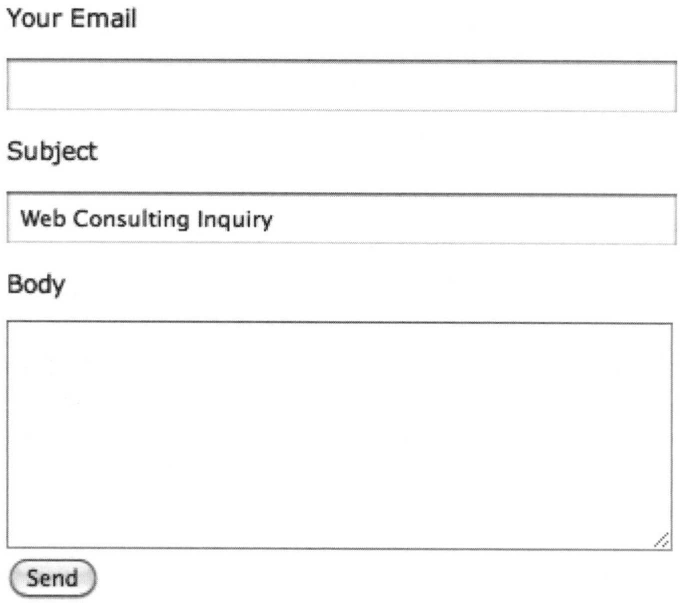

Your Email

Subject

Web Consulting Inquiry

Body

Send

Figure 26—The form with styles

contact/contact.php
```php
$errors = array();

$email_matcher = "/^[_a-z0-9-]+(\.[_a-z0-9-]+)*" .
"@" .
"[a-z0-9-]+" .
"(\.[a-z0-9-]+)*(\.[a-z]{2,3})$/";

if (preg_match($email_matcher, $email) == 0) {
  array_push($errors, "You did not enter a valid email address");
}
```

We store any form errors in an array so we can check it later to output a message for each error we find. We define the $errors array here so that it's available for the rest of the HTML page.

Time to send the email! We will make a call to PHP's mail() function. It accepts a number of arguments: an email address to send to, a subject, a message, and any headers we want to send. Let's set some variables to store these components based on the data we already have and make the call to mail().

contact/contact.php

```php
if (count($errors) == 0) {
  $to = "joe@awesomeco.com"; // your email
  $subject = "[Generated from awesomeco.com] " . $subject;

  $from = $name . " <" . $email . ">";
  $headers = "From: " . $from;

  if (!mail($to, $subject, $body, $headers)) {
    array_push($errors, "Mail failed to send.");
  }
}
```

When we call the mail() function, we ensure that there were no errors in sending it. The function returns true if the email was successful, so we can use that value as a flag. We save a new string in the $errors array so we can let the user know something went wrong. With the functionality for our email form in place, let's test it and make sure it works.

Testing Our Contact Form

To test our contact form, we need a PHP–enabled folder on our development server. For this recipe, we'll use a virtual machine running on our own network at http://192.168.1.100. If you don't have a virtual machine for development, refer to Recipe 37, *Setting Up a Virtual Machine*, on page 272 to set up a server for testing purposes.

With our development server running, let's send up a copy of the file we have been working on. We can use the scp command to send the file or an SFTP program such as FileZilla for Windows users.

```
$ scp contact.php webdev@192.168.1.100:/var/www/
```

When we navigate to http://192.168.1.100/contact.php, we can enter in our data in the fields and press send. To see your received email, check your email. You should receive an email similar to the one shown in Figure 27, *A sent email*, on page 131.

Showing the Form Errors

In our PHP code, we validated that the email the user entered is a real email address. However, if an invalid address is entered, there's currently no feedback. To fix this, we need to head back to our HTML and render the errors.

contact/contact.php

```php
<?php if (count($errors) > 0) : ?>
  <h3>There were errors that prevented the email from sending</h3>

  <ul class="errors">
    <?php foreach($errors as $error) : ?>
```

[Generated from awesomeco.com] Web Consulting Inquiry Inbox | X

John Smith john@smith.com   show details 11:40 AM (0 minutes ago)

Hello Sir,

I would like a website. Let's talk!

↩ Reply   → Forward

Figure 27—A sent email

```
    <li><?php echo $error; ?></li>
  <?php endforeach; ?>
  </ul>
<?php endif; ?>
```

At the top of our form, we'll make sure that the $errors array is not empty. If it contains anything, we know we need to iterate through the array and echo out the messages. The syntax for the if and for blocks are an alternative syntax. It allows us to write normal HTML instead of using the echo statement and dancing around single and double quotes. Using this code, we'll have a list of errors that we can style. Let's make the header and list items red so they stand out a bit more.

contact/contact.php
```css
.errors h3, .errors li {
  color: #FF0000;
}

.errors li {
  margin: 5px 0px;
}
```

With the errors in place, the user experience is improving. However, there's one more annoyance with the error system in our contact form. When the user has an error in the form, they lose any of the data that they previously entered. Since we have the post data in variables from earlier, it's an easy fix. We need to add value properties to each <input> field and text into the <textarea>. Our new form fields change to this:

```html
<label for="name">Name</label>
<input class="full-width" type="text" name="name"
       value="<?php echo $name; ?>" />

<label for="email">Your Email</label>
<input class="full-width" type="text" name="email"
       value="<?php echo $email; ?>" />
```

```
<label for="subject">Subject</label>
<input class="full-width" type="text" name="subject"
  value="<?php echo isset($subject) ?
    $subject : 'Web Consulting Inquiry'; ?>" />

<label for="body">Body</label>
<textarea class="full-width" name="body"><?php echo $body; ?></textarea>
```

Now, the user experience for the errors section of our contact form is complete. When users enter incorrect data, they see their existing data as expected as well as feedback regarding the errors. Figure 28, *Showing form errors*, on page 133 gives an example of a user entering an invalid email address.

With our contact form complete, we will see more users email us, improving our business.

Further Exploration

A contact form is only one example of what can be done with a PHP-powered form. Using this concept and focusing on the idea of a web consulting firm, we could also build a form that helps the user find a quote for a service. It's also a good idea to improve the form's usability across platforms. The HTML5 specification defines a number of additional input types, such as the email type. This gives a different touch keyboard on iOS, Android, and other mobile platforms. To learn more about these new features available in the HTML5 spec, take a look at *HTML5 and CSS3: Develop with Tomorrow's Standards Today* [Hog10].

Also See

- Recipe 19, *Creating a Widget to Embed on Other Sites*, on page 138
- Recipe 27, *Creating a Simple Blog with Jekyll*, on page 193
- Recipe 37, *Setting Up a Virtual Machine*, on page 272
- Recipe 36, *Using Dropbox to Host a Static Site*, on page 268
- Recipe 42, *Automate Static Site Deployment with Jammit and Rake*, on page 296

**There were errors that prevented the
email from sending**

- You did not enter a valid email address

Name

```
John Smith
```

Your Email

```
bademail@website
```

Figure 28—Showing form errors

Recipe 18

Accessing Cross-site Data with JSONP

Problem

We need to access data from a site on another domain but are unable to do it using a server-side language, either because of restrictions on our web server or because we want to push the load on to the user's browser. Regular API calls to external sites are not an option because of the same-origin policy,[11] which prevents client-side programming languages like JavaScript from accessing pages on different domains.

Ingredients

- jQuery
- A remote server returning JSONP
- Flickr API Key[12]

Solution

We can use JSONP to load remote data from a server at another domain. JSONP, or JSON with Padding, returns data in the JSON format but wraps it in a call to a function. When the browser loads the script from the remote server, it tries to run the function if it exists on the page, with the JSON data passed in as a variable. All we have to do is write the function that will be called and tell it how to process the JSON, and we will be able to work with data from a remote site.

We'll use the Flickr API to load the twelve most interesting photos of the moment. Some APIs let you set the function name that wraps the content when you load the page on their server, but the Flickr API always returns data wrapped in a call to jsonFlickrApi(). This is the function we'll need to write on our page once we have the data loaded from Flickr.

We'll start with a blank page with no content in the <body>; everything that ends up being displayed on the page will be loaded dynamically.

---

11. https://developer.mozilla.org/en/Same_origin_policy_for_JavaScript
12. http://www.flickr.com/services/api/keys/

First we'll create a function to load photos from Flickr. In loadPhotos(), we set our API key, the method from Flickr we want to use, and the number of photos we want Flickr to return to us. Other methods available from Flickr are in the API documentation.[13]

jsonp/index.html

```
function loadPhotos(){
  var apiKey = '98956b44cd9ee04132c7f3595b2fa59e';
  var flickrMethod = 'flickr.interestingness.getList';
  var photoCount = '12';
  var extras = 'url_s';
  $.ajax({
    url:'http://www.flickr.com/services/rest/?method='+flickrMethod+
      '&format=json&api_key='+apiKey+
      '&extras='+extras+
      '&per_page='+photoCount,
    dataType: "jsonp"
  });
}
```

We define a few variables to make it easier to change what we're requesting from Flickr without having to dig through the URL. We also add an extra attribute, url_s, to the request so that the data we get back contains the URL of a small version of the photos. Next, jQuery's ajax() function makes a call to Flickr. We set the dataType to "jsonp" so that jQuery knows this request will be across domains.

Now we'll create the function that loads the data returned to us from Flickr's API. The data returned from Flickr contains several things, including how many other pages are available if we want to get more photos, but this time we'll just use the twelve photos we requested.

jsonp/flickr_response.html

```
jsonFlickrApi({
  "photos": {
    "page": 1,
    "pages": 250,
    "perpage": 2,
    "total": 500,
    "photo": [
      {
        "id": "5889925003",
        "owner": "12386438@N04",
        "secret": "51c74e7c3e",
        "server": "6034",
        "farm": 7,
```

---

13. http://www.flickr.com/services/api/

```
        "title": "",
        "ispublic": 1,
        "isfriend": 0,
        "isfamily": 0,
        "url_s": "http:\/\/farm7.static.flickr.com\/1\/image_m.jpg",
        "height_s": "160",
        "width_s": "240"
      },
      ...
    ]
  },
  "stat": "ok"
})
```

The data we get from Flickr includes the photos in an array appropriately called photos, so we'll want to loop over each of those and build out the image tags to add to the page.

jsonp/index.html
```
function jsonFlickrApi(data){
  $.each(data.photos.photo, function(i,photo){
    var imageTag = $('<img>');
    imageTag.attr('src', photo.url_s);
    $('body').append(imageTag);
  });
}
```

We call $.each(data.photos.photo, function(i,photo){...} to go over the array of photos. Inside our loop we'll work with each photo to build an <img> tag and set its src attribute to the URL of the small photo that we requested with url_s in the extras param of the querystring. Now that the <img> is built, append it to the body of the page, and we have our own gallery of the twelve most interesting pictures on Flickr at this moment.

With all the pieces in place, we just need to call loadPhotos() when the DOM is ready, and then we'll have a page full of photos.

jsonp/index.html
```
$(function(){
  loadPhotos();
});
```

JSONP gives us a way to load dynamic content from external sites without needing to resort to server-side languages. It's a pretty easy way to pull content in to our pages.

Further Exploration

What if we were relying on an external site to provide functionality for our site and they made the current status of their system available via JSONP? We could refresh the current status at a regular interval, like every 60 seconds, and update the page when there is an update.

Since this all happens on the client side, we don't have to worry about any additional load on our server, but it could be something that our user doesn't want to happen. To avoid making unwanted requests, we could add a checkbox to the page that, when checked, activates the timer and the updater.

Also See

- Recipe 19, *Creating a Widget to Embed on Other Sites*, on page 138
- Recipe 14, *Organizing Code with Backbone.js*, on page 93

Recipe 19

Creating a Widget to Embed on Other Sites

Problem

Widgets are a combination of HTML, JavaScript, and CSS that allow owners of other sites to embed code in their site that will display content from another site. From general information about our site to tailored content around a user's activities, widgets let us expand the reach of our site and allow users to share that they use our site. It's a simple concept, but developing a widget requires us to do a few things that may be unfamiliar, like ensuring our JavaScript doesn't conflict with existing JavaScript on our user's site and loading data from a remote site. Properly encapsulating our code will ensure that the functions we introduce don't inadvertently overwrite existing code or other widgets, which could break a page that was working fine before our widget was added to the page.

Ingredients

- jQuery
- JSONP

Solution

Widgets are small chunks of code that users can add to their own web pages that will load content from another site. Using JavaScript and CSS, we can load content from our server and insert it in to the page, and all the user has to do is load a JavaScript file from our server. Additionally, because none of the actual code is on the user's server, we can make adjustments and add new features, and the end users will see those changes as we make them available.

We'll create a widget that lets users include the commit logs from the official Ruby on Rails repository[14] on their website. We'll use JavaScript to create an anonymous function to avoid conflicting with any JavaScript that is already on the page. Next we'll check to see whether jQuery is already loaded so that we have access to its shortcuts and helper methods. If it's not or if it's not

---

14. https://github.com/rails/rails

the right version, we'll load our own copy. Then we'll execute and create our actual widget by loading data remotely with JSONP, which lets us access information from a remote server via JavaScript, without issues because of getting that data from a different domain. After loading the content with JavaScript, we will generate HTML and insert it on the page, as shown in Figure 29, *Our widget on a simple page*, on page 140.

A widget should be simple to add, so we'll design our widget so our user has to add only two lines of code on their site: a link to the JavaScript and a <div> where the content will be inserted once it has loaded.

widget/index.html

```html
<!DOCTYPE html>
<html>
  <head>
    <title>Widget Examples</title>
  </head>
  <body>
    <div style="width:350px; float:left;">
      <h2>AwesomeCo</h2>
      <p>
        Lorem ipsum dolor sit amet, consectetuer adipiscing elit, sed diam
        nonummy nibh euismod tincidunt ut laoreet dolore magna aliquam erat
        volutpat. Ut wisi enim ad minim veniam, quis nostrud exerci tation
        ullamcorper suscipit lobortis nisl ut aliquip ex ea commodo consequat.
        Duis autem vel eum iriure dolor in hendrerit in vulputate velit esse
        molestie consequat, vel illum dolore eu feugiat nulla facilisis at
        vero eros et accumsan et iusto odio dignissim qui blandit praesent
        luptatum zzril delenit augue duis dolore te feugait nulla facilisi.
      </p>
    </div>
    <script src="widget.js"></script>
    <div id="widget"></div>
  </body>
</html>
```

First, we create an anonymous function that keeps our code from affecting the user's existing code. This is a common and critical practice that isolates our code from other JavaScript code. When we give our users some code to place on their site, we want to make sure we don't cause their existing code to stop working, and we need to ensure their code doesn't break our widget. This function will automatically run once the script has been loaded on the page, which will then populate our widget.

```javascript
(function() {...})();
```

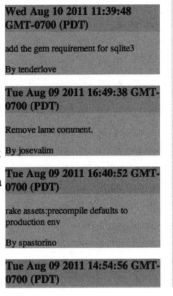

AwesomeCo

Lorem ipsum dolor sit amet, consectetuer adipiscing elit, sed diam nonummy nibh euismod tincidunt ut laoreet dolore magna aliquam erat volutpat. Ut wisi enim ad minim veniam, quis nostrud exerci tation ullamcorper suscipit lobortis nisl ut aliquip ex ea commodo consequat. Duis autem vel eum iriure dolor in hendrerit in vulputate velit esse molestie consequat, vel illum dolore eu feugiat nulla facilisis at vero eros et accumsan et iusto odio dignissim qui blandit praesent luptatum zzril delenit augue duis dolore te feugait nulla facilisi. Nam liber tempor cum soluta nobis eleifend option congue nihil imperdiet doming id quod mazim placerat facer possim assum. Typi non habent claritatem insitam; est usus legentis in iis qui facit eorum claritatem. Investigationes demonstraverunt lectores legere me lius quod ii legunt saepius. Claritas est etiam processus dynamicus, qui sequitur mutationem consuetudium lectorum. Mirum est notare.

Figure 29—Our widget on a simple page

Since our widget is going use jQuery, we want to make sure that it is scoped to run only within the widget, again ensuring that our widget stays completely isolated from any other client-side code.

```
widget/widget.js
var jQuery;
if (window.jQuery === undefined || window.jQuery.fn.jquery !== '1.7') {
    var jquery_script = document.createElement('script');
    jquery_script.setAttribute("src",
        "http://ajax.googleapis.com/ajax/libs/jquery/1.7/jquery.min.js");
    jquery_script.setAttribute("type","text/javascript");
    jquery_script.onload = loadjQuery; // All browser loading, except IE
    jquery_script.onreadystatechange = function () { // IE loading
        if (this.readyState == 'complete' || this.readyState == 'loaded') {
            loadjQuery();
        }
    };
    // Insert jQuery to the head of the page or to the documentElement
    (document.getElementsByTagName("head")[0] ||
      document.documentElement).appendChild(jquery_script);
} else {
    // The jQuery version on the window is the one we want to use
    jQuery = window.jQuery;
    widget();
}
```

```
function loadjQuery() {
    // load jQuery in noConflict mode to avoid issues with other libraries
    jQuery = window.jQuery.noConflict(true);
    widget();
}
```

When we load jQuery, we assign it to a variable that is scoped to our function using var. By using var for all of our variables, we ensure that they are scoped to only our function, again ensuring that we don't affect the user's existing code. If the jQuery version we want is already loaded, we'll use the existing library; otherwise, we build a script tag and insert it in to the document. We also call jQuery's noConflict() method when we load our local instance of jQuery to avoid conflicts with other versions of jQuery or other libraries like Prototype that use $() as a top-level function name.

Now that we've gotten jQuery in place, we can load our widget's data using JSONP and insert it in to the page. We'll use GitHub's API to load the latest commits to Rails.

widget/widget.js
```
function widget() {
  jQuery(document).ready(function($) {
    // Load Data
    var account = 'rails';
    var project = 'rails';
    var branch = 'master';

    $.ajax({
      url: 'http://github.com/api/v2/json/commits/list/'+
        account+
        '/'+project+
        '/'+branch,
      dataType: "jsonp",
      success: function(data){
        $.each(data.commits, function(i,commit){
          var commit_div = document.createElement('div');
          commit_div.setAttribute("class", "commit");
          commit_div.setAttribute("id","commit_"+commit.id);
          $('#widget').append(commit_div);
          $('#commit_'+commit.id).append("<h3>"+
            new Date(commit.committed_date)+
            "</h3><p>"+commit.message+"</p>"+
            "<p>By "+commit.committer.login+"</p>");
        });
      }
    });
```

```
    var css = $("<link>", {
      rel: "stylesheet",
      type: "text/css",
      href: "widget.css"
    });
    css.appendTo('head');
  });
}
```

In widget(), we first load our data using JSONP and get ready to display it. We use jQuery's ajax() function to request the data and then use the success call to create a new <div> for each commit that contains the date of the commit, its author, and its message. As we create each <div>, we append it to the #widget <div> that we had the user add to their page alongside the <script> tag.

After we've loaded the data, we can build the HTML to display the data in the widget and insert it into the widget <div> that we had the user add alongside the <script> tag. We also load a style sheet and apply it to the widget.

widget/widget.css
```
#widget {
  width:230px;
  display:block;
  font-size: 12px;
  height: 370px;
  overflow-y: scroll;
}

.commit {
  background-color: #95B4D9;
  width:200px;
}

.commit h3 {
  display:block;
  background-color: #7DA7D9;
}
```

The style sheet we load sets a height and width for the element and sets its overflow-y attribute to scroll. This lets us include large amounts of data without worrying about overwhelming the page that our widget is embedded on.

Now we have a simple chunk of code we can give to anyone who wants to include information from our site on their own. Whether it's information tailored to their specific account or general news about what's happening on our site, widgets make it easy to extend the reach of our content and potentially increase our users' interaction with our site.

Further Exploration

The widget we created loads content only once, when the page it is embedded on loads, but doesn't offer any information specific to one user or their account. If we wanted our widget to include information to identify a user so that the remote server could return more relevant data, how might we do that? This could be done with a variable in the URL of the <script> tag that we use to dynamically generate the JavaScript on the server. You could also use a different JavaScript file for each user's content.

Widgets can also offer much more interaction and go beyond just displaying content from JSON or XML. You could use jQuery to create a widget that users can click through multiple records, rather than having to scroll as they do in our example. You could load this data when the page loads or make a request to the remote server every time a new record is requested. Or you could have the widget that automatically refreshes itself every 60 seconds with the latest content.

You could also create an interactive widget that requests data from visitors on our user's site and allows them to submit information to us, whether via email or submitting to our site.

There are many possibilities for widgets. Any time there is information that users want to share or when you want to make it easy for a user to collect data for your site, giving them a widget to use is a great option.

Also See
- Recipe 18, *Accessing Cross-site Data with JSONP*, on page 134
- Recipe 29, *Cleaner JavaScript with CoffeeScript*, on page 209

Recipe 20

Building a Status Site with JavaScript and CouchDB

Problem

Database-driven applications can be somewhat complex. A typical database-driven application usually consists of a mix of HTML, JavaScript, SQL queries, and a server-side programming language, as well as a database server. Developers need to know enough about each of these components to make them work together. We need an alternative that's simple and lets us leverage some of the web development skills we already have, while still giving us the flexibility we need to get more complex as our needs change.

Ingredients

- CouchDB[15]
- A Cloudant.com account[16]
- CouchApp[17]
- jQuery
- Mustache[18]

Solution

CouchDB is a document database and web server combined into one small but powerful package. We can build database-driven applications using only HTML and JavaScript and upload them right to the CouchDB server so it can serve them to our end users directly. We'll even use JavaScript to query our data, so we don't need to learn yet another language. And it just so happens we have a good excuse to play with CouchDB.

Despite our best efforts, we've been experiencing some network problems with our web servers recently. It's important to communicate this downtime to our end users, so we can keep some of the angry support calls at bay. We'll use CouchDB to develop and host a very simple site that will alert our end users

---

15. http://couchdb.apache.org/
16. http://cloudant.com
17. http://couchapp.org
18. http://mustache.github.com/

to issues with our network. Since we could be experiencing trouble with our network, we need to host the status site on a separate network, so we'll use a service called Cloudant instead of setting up our own CouchDB server. Cloudant is a CouchDB hosting provider that gives us a small free CouchDB instance we can use for testing.

To speed up the process, we'll use CouchApp, a framework for building and deploying HTML and JavaScript applications for CouchDB. CouchApp gives us tools to create projects and push files up to our CouchDB database. But before we start hacking on our status site, let's dig into how CouchDB works.

Understanding CouchDB

CouchDB is a "document database." Instead of storing "rows" in "tables," we store "documents" in "collections." This is different from relational databases like MySQL and Oracle. Relational databases use a *relational model*, where we divide the data into multiple entities and relate things together to reduce data duplication. We then use queries to pull this data together into something we can use. In a relational model, a person and her address would be in separate tables. This is a fine, trusted solution, but it's not always a good fit.

In a document database, we're more concerned with storing the data as a document so we can reuse it later, and we're not all that interested in how one document relates to another. While some folks like to pit traditional relational databases and document database against each other, you'll often find that they serve completely different needs or can actually complement each other.

For our status update system, each status update will be a CouchDB document, and we'll create a simple interface that displays these documents. Let's start by defining our database and our status document.

Creating the Database

We'll use the web interface Cloudant provides to create a new database. When we log into our Cloudant account for the first time, we'll be prompted to create our first database. We'll call our database statuses.

We can also use the Cloudant interface to create a couple of status documents. Once we've selected our database, we'll see a list of documents in the database. The New Document button gives us a simple interface to add status messages.

Documents are just a collection of keys and values represented as JSON data. Each of our status notifications needs a title and a description, and so a JSON representation looks like this:

Manipulating CouchDB with cURL

Since CouchDB uses a RESTful JSON API, we can create databases, update documents, and run queries from the command line instead of a GUI tool. We can use cURL, a command-line tool for making HTTP requests to do just that. The cURL program is available on most operating systems and might even be installed for you if you're on OS X or Linux.

For example, instead of creating our statuses database with the GUI, we can use cURL to send a PUT request like this:

```
curl -X PUT http://awesomeco:****@awesomeco.cloudant.com/statuses
```

and we can push some data like this:

```
curl -X POST http://awesomeco:****@awesomeco.cloudant.com/statuses \
  -H "Content-Type: application/json" \
  -d '{"title":"Unplanned Downtime","description":"Someone tripped over the cord."}'
```

The -H flag sets the content type, and the -d flag lets us pass a string of data to send.

With cURL, we can set up and seed our database in much less time that we could by going through a web console. We could even script it so we can do it over and over again.

```
{
  "title": "Unplanned Downtime",
  "description": "Someone tripped over the power cord!"
}
```

We can either add each field to the document using the wizard or choose the View Source button and insert the JSON directly. We could also use cURL, as discussed in *Manipulating CouchDB with cURL*, on page 146.

Let's use the GUI to add a couple of documents so we'll have something to display. We first create a new document and set a title and description for a status message. We can leave the _id field blank, as shown in Figure 30, *Adding a new document with the Cloudant Wizard*, on page 147.

Now that we have some data in our database, let's build an interface to display it.

Creating a Simple CouchApp

CouchApps are applications that we can host from CouchDB itself. The CouchApp command-line application gives us some tools to create and manage these applications. With CouchApp, we can even push our files directly to our remove database.

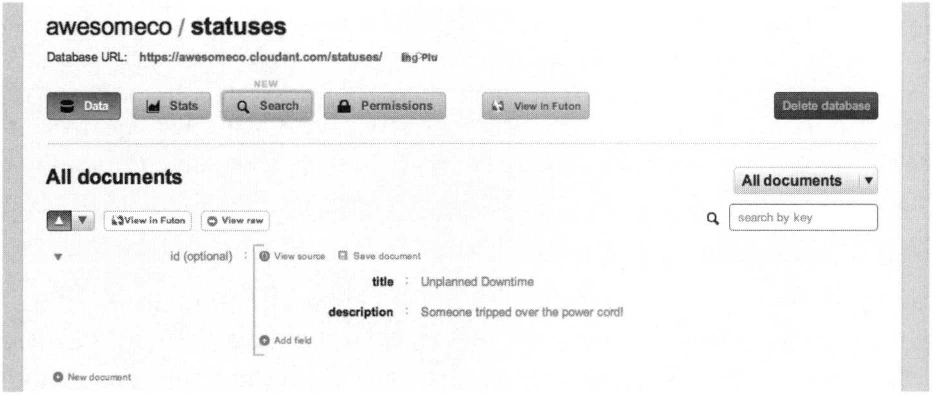

Figure 30—Adding a new document with the Cloudant Wizard

CouchApp is written in Python, but there are installers for Windows and OS X we can use that don't require us to have Python on our system. Visit the installation page, get the package for your system, and install it.[19]

With CouchApp installed, we can create our first application from our shell like this:

```
$ couchapp generate app statuses
```

This creates a new folder called statuses, which contains a new CouchApp. There are several subfolders within this app, each with a different purpose.

The _attachments folder is where we'll put our HTML and JavaScript code for our interface. When we push our CouchApp to our CouchDB server, the contents of this folder will be uploaded as a design document.

The views folder holds CouchDB "views," which are different representations of our documents. For example, a document may contain thirty fields, but we can use views to show only the two or three fields we're interested in for a particular purpose. Views are a common component in many types of databases, even relational ones.

We can then push this app right to our CouchDB database from the command line:

```
$ couchapp push statuses \
http://awesomeco:****@awesomeco.cloudant.com/statuses

2011-07-20 14:24:28 [INFO] Visit your CouchApp here:
http://awesomeco.cloudant.com/statuses/_design/statuses/index.html
```

---

19. http://couchapp.org/page/installing

We're pushing the statuses folder, which contains our entire app, into the statuses database, where it will be stored as a "Design document." We can look at our app in the browser at http://awesomeco.cloudant.com/statuses/_design/statuses/index.html, although it will simply show us a boilerplate "Welcome" page. Let's get to work building our actual status application now that we know how to push our files to the server.

Creating a View to Query Date

We use views in CouchDB to optimize the results we want to return, rather than just querying our documents directly. When we access a view, CouchDB executes a JavaScript function we define to pare down the results and manipulate them into a data structure that works for us.

The couchapp command can create the files for our view. Since we want to display the status messages, we'll create a messages view, like this:

```
$ couchapp generate view statuses messages
```

This creates a new folder called views/messages, which contains two files: map.js and reduce.js. The map.js file is where we specify the fields we want to display.

Each status message has a title and description, but they also contain a unique identifier and a revision number. For our status page, we only need the title and description, so we'll alter the map.js to look like this:

couchapps/statuses/views/messages/map.js
```
function(doc) {
➤   emit( "messages", {
➤     title: doc.title,
➤     description: doc.description
➤   } )
}
```

The file reduce.js can be used to simplify or summarize the results of the query we're building. Since we don't need to do that here, we simply delete reduce.js entirely.

We can verify that our view works by pushing the application to our remote CouchDB instance at Cloudant again:

```
$ couchapp push statuses \
http://awesomeco:****@awesomeco.cloudant.com/statuses
```

and then pulling up http://awesomeco.cloudant.com/statuses/_design/statuses/_view/messages in our browser. We should see something that looks like this:

```
{"total_rows":2,"offset":0,"rows":[
  {"id":"02abeecc98362b3a26f85ea047bfaf5d","key":"messages","value":
    {"title":"Unscheduled Downtime",
    "description":"Someone tripped over the power cord!"}
  }
]}
```

With the view in place, let's whip up some HTML and jQuery code to display the status messages on our site.

Displaying the Messages

To build our simple interface, we can replace most of what's in the default page in _attachments/index.html with this:

couchapps/statuses/_attachments/index.html
```
<body>
  <h1>AwesomeCo Status updates</h1>

  <div id="statuses">
    <p>Waiting...</p>
  </div>

  <script src="vendor/couchapp/loader.js"></script>
</body>
</html>
```

We'll then update the contents of the statuses region with the data we pull from our database.

As we learned in Recipe 10, *Building HTML with Mustache*, on page 67, we can use templates when we're going to be building up HTML we want to add to the page. Our page includes a JavaScript file called loader.js that loads up several JavaScript libraries we need to make a basic CouchApp run, including jQuery and the jQuery Couch library. We simply copy the mustachejs.js file into vendor/couchapps/_attachments and add it to the list of scripts, like this:

couchapps/statuses/vendor/couchapp/_attachments/loader.js
```
couchapp_load([
  "/_utils/script/sha1.js",
  "/_utils/script/json2.js",
  "/_utils/script/jquery.js",
➤ "vendor/couchapp/mustache.js",
  "/_utils/script/jquery.couch.js",
  "vendor/couchapp/jquery.couch.app.js",
  "vendor/couchapp/jquery.couch.app.util.js",
  "vendor/couchapp/jquery.mustache.js",
  "vendor/couchapp/jquery.evently.js"
]);
```

With that in place, we can now add a simple Mustache template to our index.html page that represents the status message. The jQuery CouchDB plug-in will return a data structure that looks like this:

```
data = {
  rows: [
    {
      id: "9e227166d51569f2713728da59ff9d6b",
      key: "messages",
      value: {
        title: "Unplanned Downtime",
        description: "Someone tripped over the power cord."
      }
    }
  ]
};
```

So, when we want to pull the title and description for each status message into our template, we use Mustache's iterator to loop over the rows array and then prefix the fields with value, since they're nested under that key in the object. Let's add this template to index.html:

couchapps/statuses/_attachments/index.html
```html
<script type="text/html" id="template">
  {{#rows}}
  <div class="status">
    <h2>{{ value.title }}</h2>
    <p>{{ value.description }}</p>
  </div>
  {{/rows}}
</script>
```

With the template in place, we need to make a connection to CouchDB and fetch our status messages so we can feed this data into our Mustache template. We'll define this as a function inside of a new <script> block on our index.html page.

couchapps/statuses/_attachments/index.html
```javascript
$db = $.couch.db("statuses");
var loadStatusMessages = function(){
  $db.view("statuses/messages",{
    success: function( data ) {
      var template = Mustache.to_html(
        $("#template").html(), data
      );
      $("#statuses").html(template);
    }
  });
}
```

AwesomeCo Status updates

Unplanned Downtime

Someone tripped over the power cord!

Figure 31—Our status site

We're using the same "success" callback pattern we've used in Recipe 14, *Organizing Code with Backbone.js*, on page 93. There's an error callback you could define yourself, but the CouchDB plug-in throws up an error message for us by default.

Finally, we just need to call this function when our page loads, like this:

```
couchapps/statuses/_attachments/index.html
$(function(){
  loadStatusMessages();
});
```

All that's left is to push the CouchApp to our database one last time. When we visit our page in the browser again, we see our status messages, nicely rendered, just like in Figure 31, *Our status site*, on page 151. From here, we can continue to build out this application, making changes to the code and pushing it up to the server.

Further Exploration

We've built a very trivial, but functional, web application using only HTML and JavaScript, all hosted with a CouchDB database, but there's more we could do. We could use JavaScript frameworks like Backbone to organize our code as things get more complex. CouchApp actually includes a framework called Evently that simplifies some of the event delegation stuff you might find in a more complex user interface.[20] While we didn't need it in our simple example, you might find that it works for you.

The URL for our application is quite long and ugly, but CouchDB has its own URL-rewriting features, so we can shorten http://awesomeco.cloudant.com/statuses/_design/statuses/index.html to something less clunky, like http://status.awesomeco.com.

---

20. http://couchapp.org/page/evently

CouchDB isn't just a client-side data store, though. We could also integrate CouchDB into server-side applications. It's a good, solid document store that's easy to use and extend. While it may not fit every need, it certainly has its place, especially when working with data that isn't necessarily relational.

Also See

- Recipe 10, *Building HTML with Mustache*, on page 67
- Recipe 13, *Snappier Client-Side Interfaces with Knockout.js*, on page 84
- Recipe 14, *Organizing Code with Backbone.js*, on page 93

## CHAPTER 4

Mobile Recipes

More and more people access websites and applications from mobile devices, and we need to develop with these users in mind. Limited bandwidth, smaller screens, and new user interface interactions create interesting problems for us to solve. With these recipes, you'll learn how to save bandwidth with CSS sprites, work with multitouch interfaces, and build a mobile interface with transitions.

Recipe 21

Targeting Mobile Devices

Problem

As web developers, we're used to accounting for a lot of factors when designing a site. Different browsers and different screen resolutions have always affected how our content looks, and making a site look as good on a 13" laptop as on a 30" monitor takes time. We may have considered how our sites looked on PDAs in the past, but with the recent explosion of smartphones and tablets, we now need to be increasingly aware of how our sites look on screens that are not only smaller but whose orientation can change.

Ingredients

- jQuery
- CSS Media Queries

Solution

We can use *CSS Media Queries*, which let us load specific style sheets based on conditions of a particular browser. Media Queries have been around since HTML4 and CSS2, but in CSS3 they have been extended, adding attributes like device-width and device-height. Knowing that we can target different style sheets for specific widths and heights gives us a huge advantage.

In Recipe 8, *Accessible Expand and Collapse*, on page 52, we created a products list that can expand and collapse. Lately, our analytics team has seen a spike in traffic from mobile users, and 90 percent of those mobile users have iPhones. Currently, our site looks like Figure 32, *Current version of our products list*, on page 155. Its small fonts make it hard to navigate on a mobile device.

We'll use the code we completed in Recipe 8, *Accessible Expand and Collapse*, on page 52 as a starting point. Since most of our traffic comes from iPhone users, we'll target those users first. In the <head> section of our page, we'll add a few new tags to load CSS styles designed for the iPhone. We'll keep these styles in a file named iPhone.css and put it in the same directory as style.css from Recipe 8, *Accessible Expand and Collapse*, on page 52.

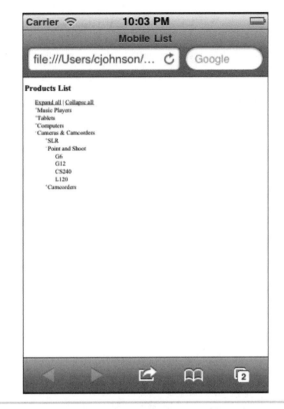

Figure 32—Current version of our products list

targeting_mobile/index.html
```
<link rel="stylesheet" type="text/css" href="iPhone.css"
media="only screen and (max-device-width: 480px)">
    <meta name="viewport"
      content="width=device-width;
                height=device-height;
                maximum-scale=1.4;
                initial-scale=1.0;
                user-scalable=yes"/>
```

When referencing iPhone.css, we use a normal style sheet link, but we also add the media attribute. By setting the media attribute to "only screen and (max-device-width: 480px)," we know that it will get used only by mobile devices with a max screen width of 480 pixels. This way, desktop browsers will ignore it, and any other mobile devices with the same resolution will pick it up as well.

We also added a viewport meta tag to control how the content is viewed in mobile browsers. This is because mobile browsers don't automatically fit everything inside of the screen but rather try to lay out the content as it would appear on a desktop computer. Since the browser tries to show us everything at once, the site looks small until we zoom in. When the viewport meta tag is set, mobile devices will automatically fit the content to the device's width.

Now let's take a look at some of the design changes we can make to optimize this list for the iPhone. We'll start by setting the font-weight to be bold on the <body> tag, which makes the text easier to read.

targeting_mobile/iPhone.css
```
body{
  font-weight: bold;
}
```

We'll make sure our <ul> uses a significant portion of the page without over-flowing. We also want it to hug the left side of the screen more to use all of our screen's real estate.

targeting_mobile/iPhone.css
```
ul.collapsible {
  width:430px;
  margin-left:-10px;
}
```

Next we declare that the <ul> tag should not be wider than 430 pixels so that it will fit within the confines of the display. We also add a margin-left to move the list closer to the left side of the screen.

Beyond simple appearance, we also have to think about how users will interact with the site on a mobile device. Since the iPhone is manipulated by fingers, rather than a pixel precise mouse, we'll want to space out the <li> elements so users are less likely to tap the wrong link.

targeting_mobile/iPhone.css
```
ul li{
  padding-top:10px;
}
```

Lastly, let's add some extra space to the "+" and "-" symbols used to show which parts of the list are collapsed. Otherwise, they'll crowd the text, making the list hard to read.

targeting_mobile/iPhone.css
```
ul.collapsible li:before {
  width: 20px;
}
```

Now when we look at our site on the iPhone (Figure 33, *Our list on an iPhone*, on page 157), we see that the page appears better suited to its new mobile

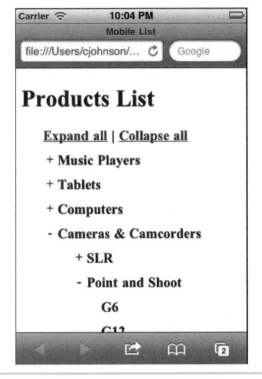

Figure 33—Our list on an iPhone

home. We can also look at this on an Android phone with a similar screen resolution (Figure 34, *Our list on an Android phone*, on page 158).

Media Queries gives us control over how our site looks for multiple devices and orientations. And since mobile users tend to interact with sites differently than desktop users, we can even use Media Queries to tailor the user experience per device type.

Further Exploration

You can take this further and show specific navigation for mobile users. You can even accentuate things like addresses and phone numbers, which are helpful to mobile users. You can reference styles like Tait Brown's "iOS Inspired jQuery Mobile Theme"[1] with Media Queries to give a site an iOS native feel with relative ease.

---

1. https://github.com/taitems/iOS-Inspired-jQuery-Mobile-Theme

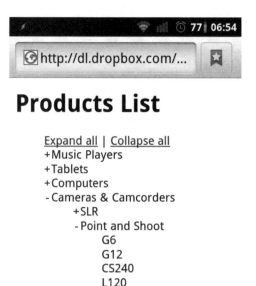

Figure 34—Our list on an Android phone

You can also use frameworks like Skeleton[2] that provide media query support out of the box. We discuss this further in Recipe 26, *Rapid, Responsive Design with Grid Systems*, on page 184.

Also See

- Recipe 36, *Using Dropbox to Host a Static Site*, on page 268
- Recipe 25, *Using Sprites with CSS*, on page 178
- Recipe 24, *Creating Interfaces with jQuery Mobile*, on page 169
- Recipe 26, *Rapid, Responsive Design with Grid Systems*, on page 184
- *HTML5 and CSS3: Develop with Tomorrow's Standards Today* [Hog10]

Recipe 22

Touch-Responsive Drop-Down Menus

Problem

Drop-down navigation is a common element on modern websites, and the pattern for implementing it is well-established. On desktop browsers these menus work just fine and only require some CSS magic. But just like Recipe 23, *Mobile Drag and Drop*, on page 162, a user on a mobile device doesn't have a mouse and therefore can't trigger :hover events, at least not in a consistent way. We need to be aware of this limitation for our mobile users so we can give them the same experience as our desktop users.

Ingredients

* jQuery

Solution

Our first step is to make our website accessible and confirm that it can be navigated without the drop-down menus. We can do this making the top-level links point to pages that include links to all of the appropriate subcategories. This way, any user can reach the subcategories even if the drop-down links are unavailable. At this point, we could say we've handled *mobile* navigation since users can navigate our site, which looks like Figure 35, *Our top-level links without hovering*, on page 160. But now it's time to add the drop-down menus since we want to give our mobile users the same user experience as our desktop users.

On the desktop our drop-down lists are controlled by the CSS :hover event. But without a mouse there's no way to "hover" over a link. On iOS devices, tapping a :hover link will activate the hover effect while a second tap will follow the link, so this is a good alternative. Unfortunately in other mobile browsers, tapping down on a :hover link will also activate the hover command, but unless the user slides their finger away from the link before lifting up, the link will be followed. This completely defeats the purpose of having a drop-down menu since it would only flash on the screen for a second before the user ended up on another page.

Products

This is where the content for our site goes.

Figure 35—Our top-level links without hovering

To get around this inconsistent behavior, we're going to go ahead and make the iOS behavior the default for all browsers. This can be done by watching all of the clicks on the web page. When a click on the navigation header is detected, we'll prevent the default operation unless the same link is clicked twice in a row. This means we'll need to track a few separate click events: any click on the page, clicks on the top-level categories, and clicks on the subcategories.

mobiledropdown/mobiledropdown.js
```
var lastTouchedElement;
$('html').live('click', function(event) {
  lastTouchedElement = event.target;
});
```

To start, we'll add a global variable that will track the last element clicked anywhere on the page. Without this variable, we wouldn't know whether the user had tapped on a category or just tapped elsewhere on the screen to hide a drop-down list, or even follow a non-drop-down link.

Next we want to know when a category header link was tapped and if it's the same category that was tapped last. On the first tap we'll prevent the default action from occurring; namely, we don't want the user to follow the link just yet. The page will look like Figure 36, *Our drop-down menu after Entertainment has been tapped*, on page 161. If they click the same link again, *then* they'll be allowed to follow the link. The only exception is iOS devices. Since they already work correctly, there's no need to prevent the default action.

mobiledropdown/mobiledropdown.js
```
function doNotTrackClicks() {
  return navigator.userAgent.match(/iPhone|iPad/i);
}
$('navbar.dropdown > ul > li').live('click', function(event) {
  if (!(doNotTrackClicks() || lastTouchedElement == event.target)) {
    event.preventDefault();
  }
  lastTouchedElement = event.target;
});
```

Products

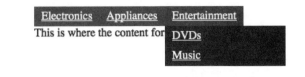

Figure 36—Our drop-down menu after Entertainment has been tapped

As long as the link being clicked is different from the last element clicked and the client isn't an iOS device, we prevent the browser from following the link. We also update lastTouchedElement to the clicked link. Normally this would be handled by the event handler attached to the <html> element, but there is one more click event we have to handle.

If we were to test the site right now, we would see that the subcategories have the same behavior as the categories. We have to click on a subcategory twice to follow the link. This is because the subcategory click events bubble up to the category click events and inherit the category link's behavior. To prevent this from happening, we'll need to call stopPropagation() when a subcategory is clicked. (We talked about event propagation in *Why Not Just Return False?*, on page 56.)

```
mobiledropdown/mobiledropdown.js
$('navbar.dropdown li').live('click', function(event) {
  event.stopPropagation();
});
```

With this code in place, our mobile users now have a consistent experience across platforms. And as long as the individual category pages list links to the subcategories, the site will continue to be accessible for users on non-smartphone devices.

Further Exploration

This approach also affects desktop browsers, which means that category links have to be double-clicked to be activated. Along with bypassing this code when an iPhone is detected, we could also skip it when the site is not being accessed by a mobile browser. The code for doing this can be found at http://detectmobilebrowsers.com and could easily be applied to our site via jQuery.

Also See

- Recipe 8, *Accessible Expand and Collapse*, on page 52

Recipe 23

Mobile Drag and Drop

Problem

Drag-and-drop functionality has been an easy feature to add to websites for the past decade. There are various plug-ins out in the wild that can add drag and drop with little effort, and it's not even that difficult to write from scratch. The problem is that most of these approaches don't work on mobile devices since they respond only to events triggered by the user's mouse. We need to make these interfaces work for our mobile users by using some new events.

Ingredients

- jQuery

Solution

Browsers on mobile devices like the iPad and various other touch interfaces have a new set of events they listen for instead of the normal mousedown and mouseup events. Two of these new events, touchstart and touchend, are perfect substitutes.

We have a pop-up window on our website that we use to display product details. This pop-up is draggable so users can move the detail window to the side of the screen. Unfortunately, we've received some feedback from users with iPads that they can't move the pop-up windows. As we dig into the code, we discover that it was in fact written to respond to the mousedown and mouseup events. It's time to give our mobile users the same attention we give our desktop users.

Layout and Style

We're going to be using JavaScript to handle these events, but first we need to create our markup. The page is an unordered list of products and a hidden <div> for the draggable window.

dragndrop/index.html
```
<header>
  <h1>Products list</h1>
</header>
```

```
<div id='content'>
  <ul>
    <li><a href="product1.html" class="popup">
      AirPort Express Base Station
    </a></li>
    <li><a href="product1.html" class="popup">
      DVI to VGA Adapter
    </a></li>
  </ul>
</div>
<div class="popup_window draggable" style="display: none;">
  <div class="header handle">
    <div class="header_text">Product description</div>
    <div class="close">X</div>
    <div class="clear"></div>
  </div>
  <div class="body"></div>
</div>
```

We also need to make sure that the pop-up window is absolutely positioned. Here are some basic styles that we'll need.

dragndrop/style.css

```
.clear {
  clear: both;
}
.popup_window {
  width: 500px;
  height: 300px;
  border: 1px solid #000;
  position: absolute;
  top: 50px;
  left: 50px;
  background: #EEE;
}
.popup_window .header {
  width: 100%;
  display: block;
}
.popup_window .header .close {
  float: right;
  padding: 2px 5px;
  border: 1px solid #999;
  background: red;
  color: #FFF;
  cursor: pointer;
  margin: 0;
}
.popup_window .header:after {
  clear: both;
}
```

In addition, we need to create an individual product page that the links will point to. Normally this page would be built on the server, but for demonstration purposes we'll just create a single page for all of the product links. We'll name this page product1.html. All of these files belong in the same directory.

dragndrop/product1.html
```
<h3>Product Name</h3>
<div class='product_details'>
  <missing>Need a real product page</missing>
  <p>This is a product description. Below is a list of features:</p>
  <ul>
    <li>Durable</li>
    <li>Fireproof</li>
    <li>Impenetrable</li>
    <li>Fuzzy</li>
  </ul>
</div>
```

Basic Drag and Drop

So far, our links will work just fine, but now we want them to load the pages that they reference into the pop-up window, rather than redirecting the browser. We added the popup classes to our product links so we know which links should be loaded into the pop-up when clicked.

dragndrop/dragndrop.js
```
$('.popup').live('click', updatePopup);
function updatePopup(event) {
  $.get($(event.target).attr('href'), [], updatePopupContent);
  return false;
}
function updatePopupContent(data) {
  var popupWindow = $('div.popup_window');
  popupWindow.find('.body').html($(data));
  popupWindow.fadeIn();
}
$('.popup_window .close').live('click', hidePopup);
function hidePopup() {
  $(this).parents('.popup_window').fadeOut();
  return false;
}
```

These functions give us a way to hide and show the pop-up window. Everything looks great; we can load it dynamically with new data and still see most of the page. The problem is that it's now in the way, as shown in Figure 37, *The pop-up window is blocking our content*, on page 165, and we have no way of moving it. Now it's time to make it draggable. We'll start by making it work in desktop browsers and then apply the same logic to the touch events.

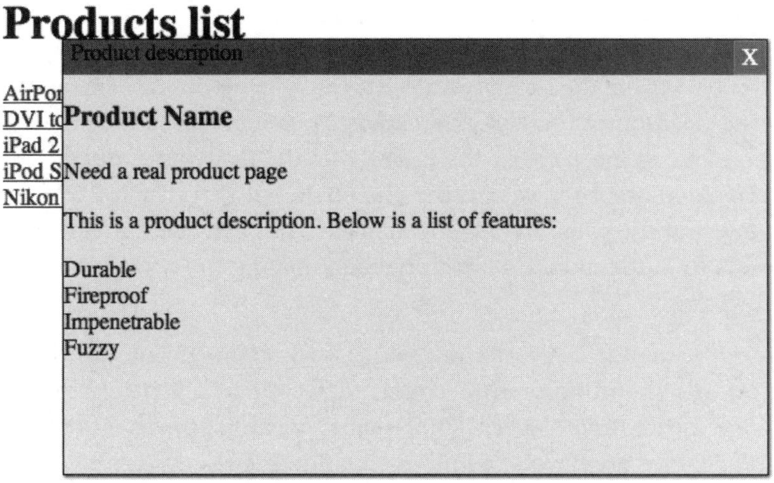

Products list

Figure 37—The pop-up window is blocking our content.

```
dragndrop/dragndrop.js
$('.draggable .handle').live('mousedown', dragPopup);
function dragPopup(event) {
  event.preventDefault();
  var handle = $(event.target);
  var draggableWindow = $(handle.parents('.draggable')[0]);
  draggableWindow.addClass('dragging');
  var cursor = event;
  var cursorOffset = {
    pageX: cursor.pageX - parseInt(draggableWindow.css('left')),
    pageY: cursor.pageY - parseInt(draggableWindow.css('top'))
  };
    $(document).mousemove(function(moveEvent) {
      observeMove(moveEvent, cursorOffset,
        moveEvent, draggableWindow)
    });
    $(document).mouseup(function(up_event) {
      unbindMovePopup(up_event, draggableWindow);
    });
}
function observeMove(event, cursorOffset, cursorPosition, draggableWindow) {
  event.preventDefault();
  var left = cursorPosition.pageX - cursorOffset.pageX;
  var top  = cursorPosition.pageY - cursorOffset.pageY;
  draggableWindow.css('left', left).css('top', top);
}
function unbindMovePopup(event, draggableWindow) {
  draggableWindow.removeClass('dragging');
}
```

We start by watching for any <div> elements with a handle class in a draggable element. When the mouse is pressed down, we call dragPopup(). This adds another observer for the mousemove event. Every time the mouse is moved, we update the position of the draggable_window. The event gives us the position of the mouse, but we need to set the position of the draggable <div>'s upper-left corner. To calculate this, we capture the offset between the initial position of the window and the position of the first click. That way, we can subtract those extra pixels from the mouse's position when moving the window in the observeMove() function.

Then so we can finish the move event, we add an event handler for the mouseup event. When this event is triggered, we clean up the changes that we made since the mousedown event. This means we stop observing the mousemove event and remove an extra style class we added to the draggable_window.

Add Mobile Functionality

Thankfully, with the hard part out of the way, it will be easy to adapt this approach for mobile devices. Other than the use of mouse-related events, the dragPopup() function does most of what we want. So, it should just be a matter of mimicking that mouse-related code and making it act on the touch events.

First we need a way to check that the touch events are supported. If we were to call a touch-related function on a desktop, our code would break. To prevent that, we'll wrap our touch code in isTouchSupported() if statements.

dragndrop/dragndrop.js
```
function isTouchSupported() {
  return 'ontouchmove' in document.documentElement;
}
```

Then we'll add an event handler for the touchstart event alongside our handler for the mousedown event. These will both trigger the dragPopup() function. Then we trigger the dragPopup function from the touchstart event.

dragndrop/dragndrop.js
```
$('.draggable .handle').live('mousedown', dragPopup);
if (isTouchSupported()) {
  $('.draggable .handle').live('touchstart', dragPopup);
}
```

Since a user can touch multiple spots, the touch event actually returns an array of touches. But we're focused on only one-finger movements for now, so we'll use the first touch in the array to determine the position of the user's finger. We'll then pass in this location as the cursorPosition.

```
dragndrop/dragndrop.js
function dragPopup(event) {
  event.preventDefault();
  var handle = $(event.target);
  var draggableWindow = $(handle.parents('.draggable')[0]);
  draggableWindow.addClass('dragging');
  var cursor = event;
  if (isTouchSupported()) {
    cursor = event.originalEvent.touches[0];
  }
  var cursorOffset = {
    pageX: cursor.pageX - parseInt(draggableWindow.css('left')),
    pageY: cursor.pageY - parseInt(draggableWindow.css('top'))
  };

  if (isTouchSupported()) {
    $(document).bind('touchmove', function(moveEvent) {
      var currentPosition = moveEvent.originalEvent.touches[0];
      observeMove(moveEvent, cursorOffset,
        currentPosition, draggableWindow);
    });
    $(document).bind('touchend', function(upEvent) {
      unbindMovePopup(upEvent, draggableWindow);
    });
  } else {
    $(document).mousemove(function(moveEvent) {
      observeMove(moveEvent, cursorOffset,
        moveEvent, draggableWindow)
    });
    $(document).mouseup(function(up_event) {
      unbindMovePopup(up_event, draggableWindow);
    });
  }
}
function unbindMovePopup(event, draggableWindow) {
  if (isTouchSupported()) {
    $(document).unbind('touchmove');
  } else {
    $(document).unbind('mousemove');
  }
  draggableWindow.removeClass('dragging');
}
```

Unfortunately jQuery 1.7 doesn't fully support observing touch events using the live() function, which means that we can't access the touches array from the jQuery event. Instead, we'll have to get the position of the user's finger from the original event. Now we can also mimic the mousemove behavior with the touchmove event by calling observeMove(), which will remain the same. The final difference is that on the touchend event, we unbind the touchmove event, just like we did with the mouseup and mousemove events, respectively.

Further Exploration

Now that we've seen how a single touch event can be handled, it should be easy to figure out how to start handling multifinger gesture commands. Since the touch events return an array of touch positions, we can determine when a user has multiple fingers on the screen and where each finger is. This means we can know when users are pinching the screen, swiping side to side, or using one of our own gestures that we invented. It's an exciting time for web developers now that we're finally getting this kind of control in a browser. For more about what we can do with this new API, check out HTML5 Rocks.[3]

Also See

- Recipe 31, *Debugging JavaScript*, on page 228
- Recipe 22, *Touch-Responsive Drop-Down Menus*, on page 159

---

3. http://www.html5rocks.com/en/mobile/touch.html

Recipe 24

Creating Interfaces with jQuery Mobile

Problem

We've been asked to build a mobile interface for an existing web application. A native application for the iOS and Android platforms would be ideal, but we don't have the time, resources, or knowledge to build them. To solve this problem, we can bring together the benefits of both web applications and native applications.

Ingredients

- jQuery
- jQuery Mobile[4]

Solution

Developing native applications for mobile devices is not a simple task, and the programming knowledge required creates a large barrier to entry. Android and iOS application development is typically done with Java and Objective-C, languages that many web developers don't have experience using. With *jQuery Mobile*, we can develop web applications that behave similarly to native applications for the iOS and Android platforms. jQuery mobile makes it easy to develop native-feeling applications using tools we're already familiar with—HTML, JavaScript, and CSS.

We're going to explore jQuery Mobile by creating a site to browse through our company's products. Our application will allow the user to view and search for products. When we're done, we'll have built a mobile interface that looks like Figure 38, *A jQuery Mobile home page*, on page 170.

Creating an application with jQuery Mobile relies on some semantic HTML and the data attributes available in HTML5. Using these attributes, we can build most of the application without writing any JavaScript.

---

4.   http://jquerymobile.com/

Figure 38—A jQuery Mobile home page

Building the Document

Let's set up an HTML file to use jQuery Mobile. Our application will run on QEDServer, so make sure it's running. In the public folder of the server, create a file called index.html. We'll use this boilerplate HTML to get started:

```
jquerymobile/index.html
<!DOCTYPE html>
<html lang="en">
  <head>
    <meta charset="utf-8">
    <title>Incredible Products from AwesomeCo</title>

    <link rel="stylesheet"
      href="http://code.jquery.com/mobile/1.0rc1/jquery.mobile-1.0rc1.min.css">
    <script type="text/javascript"
      src="http://ajax.googleapis.com/ajax/libs/jquery/1.6.4/jquery.min.js">
    </script>
    <script type="text/javascript"
      src="http://code.jquery.com/mobile/1.0rc1/jquery.mobile-1.0rc1.min.js">
    </script>
  </head>

  <body>
  </body>
</html>
```

The boilerplate includes three files: the jQuery Mobile CSS, the jQuery library, and the jQuery Mobile script itself. With this set up, we are ready to start adding pages and content to the application. The version of jQuery Mobile we are using still requires jQuery version 1.6.4.

Creating Pages

A jQuery Mobile application consists of a set of pages. These pages can link to each other, but we can show only one page on the screen at a time. To build pages in jQuery Mobile, we use a <div> that has a data attribute of role set to "page." When the application runs, it loads whichever page comes first in the body of our HTML. Let's create a page for our home screen.

```
jquerymobile/index.html
<div data-role="page">
  <div data-role="header">
    <h1>AwesomeCo</h1>
  </div>
  <div data-role="content">
  </div>
  <div data-role="footer">
    <h4>&copy; 2012 AwesomeCo</h4>
  </div>
</div>
```

Each page has three sections: the header, the content, and the footer. The header holds information about the current page in an <h1> tag. The header also can hold buttons for navigation within the application, as we'll see later. The content region can hold any number of paragraphs, links, lists, forms, and any other HTML element you would use on a normal web page. The footer is an optional section that can hold a copyright or any other information.

Now that our landing page is ready, let's create a few items to populate the content. We'll need some buttons to get to the other pages in our application.

```
jquerymobile/index.html
<p>Welcome to AwesomeCo, your number one source
  for all things awesome.</p>

<div data-role="controlgroup">
  <a href="#products" data-role="button">View All Products</a>
  <a href="#search" data-role="button">Search</a>
</div>
```

First we created a paragraph giving some information about the application. Then we made a <div> with a role of "controlgroup." This role removes the margin between the links so they appear as one set, as you can see in Figure 39, *Buttons without icons*, on page 172. We also gave the anchors a role of "button" so that they are styled accordingly. The two anchors link to other pages by setting the ID of the target page in the href attribute.

These buttons look great, but they could be enhanced to give some more feedback to the user. To add an icon to a button, we define the data-icon

Figure 39—Buttons without icons

attribute. The available icons can be found in the documentation,[5] but for our page we're going to use the right arrow icon and the search icon.

jquerymobile/index_icons.html
```
<div data-role="controlgroup">
  <a href="#products" data-role="button"
    data-icon="arrow-r">View All Products</a>
  <a href="#search" data-role="button"
    data-icon="search">Search</a>
</div>
```

With these buttons, our home page navigation is complete. We've created a button group that will bring us to the various parts of our application and added customization to give some more feedback to the user. Our home page now looks like our original example in Figure 38, *A jQuery Mobile home page*, on page 170.

The buttons we've added look good, but they don't actually go anywhere yet. We need to make another page so that we can be sure that they're working correctly.

jquerymobile/index.html
```
<div data-role="page" id="products">
  <div data-role="header">
    <h1>Products</h1>
  </div>
  <div data-role="content">
  </div>
```

---

5.   http://jquerymobile.com/demos/1.0rc1/#/demos/1.0rc1/docs/buttons/buttons-icons.html

Testing jQuery Mobile

When it comes to testing jQuery Mobile, the browser on a computer just doesn't cut it. It shows the application with odd dimensions and scale for a desktop setting. The browser can be fine for just a quick look to see whether we're on the right track, but to see the application more realistically, we use a browser emulator. The emulator acts like a normal browser but has the same dimensions as a mobile device. If you're on a Mac, the most common emulator is called iPhoney.[a] For Windows or Linux users, there's a free online option called testiphone.com.[b]

This works great for building web applications with jQuery Mobile. If you're using iPhoney, make sure that the Zoom to Fit option in the View menu is unchecked. This will allow the mobile application to scale correctly in the window.

a. http://marketcircle.com/iphoney/
b. http://testiphone.com/

```
<div data-role="footer">
  <h4>&copy; 2012 AwesomeCo</h4>
</div>
</div>
```

Now, when we load the page in our browser and click the product link, the application transitions to the products page.

Viewing Products

We can load the products page now, but it needs some content. Since QED-Server has this data for us, we'll use jQuery to load the products into a list. First let's make sure we have some products in the database by navigating to http://localhost:8080/products. If there aren't any records in your database, then create a few placeholder items.

Since we have already created the structure for the products page, let's create an empty <ul> in our content section to hold our list of products.

jquerymobile/index.html
```
<div data-role="content">
➤   <ul id="products-list" data-role="listview"></ul>
</div>
```

The <ul> we created has a role of listview so that jQuery Mobile can style it. We also set an ID so that we can easily reference it with JavaScript. If we reload the application and navigate to the products page, it's pretty empty. To load some products, we'll use the custom events in jQuery Mobile to load the content dynamically when the user requests the page.

jquerymobile/index.html

```
$(function() {
  var productsPage = $("#products");
  var productsList = $("#products-list");

  productsPage.bind("pagebeforeshow", function() {
    $.mobile.showPageLoadingMsg();
    $.getJSON("/products.json", function(products) {
      productsList.html("");

      $.each(products, function(i, product) {
        productsList.append("<li><a href='#product'>" +
          product.name + "</a></li>");
      });

      productsList.listview("refresh");
      $.mobile.hidePageLoadingMsg();
    });
  });
});
```

We used the page's pagebeforeshow event to break the flow of navigation and load the products. The first line inside the event handler turns on a loading screen to alert users that there is something working in the background. The getJSON() request queries the server, which returns an array of products. Those products are iterated over and added to the list. Since we created new HTML, we refreshed the listview, which tells jQuery Mobile to apply styles to newly inserted elements. Last, we removed the loading screen and let the new page load.

Now, when we navigate to our products page, as shown in Figure 40, *The products page*, on page 175, we're given a list of products to browse.

Our last goal for viewing the products is to create a show page for a specific product. When we tap a product, we want that product to show with any available information. Since we don't want to create a page for each product, we'll dynamically load the product and use a single-page template for all of our products. First we need to head back to where we generated the contents for the products listview. We'll need to add data to the anchors to keep track of the product ID we're navigating to. We'll place the product ID from our server into a custom data attributed called data-product-id like this:

jquerymobile/index_icons.html

```
$.each(products, function(i, product) {
  productsList.append("<li><a href='#product' data-product-id='" +
    product.id + "'>" + product.name + "</a></li>");
});
```

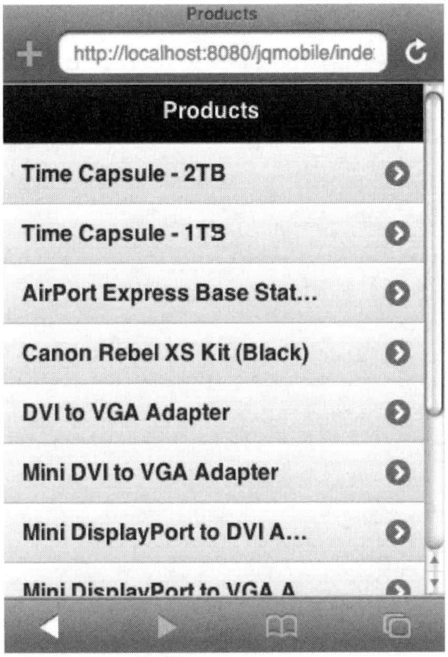

Figure 40—The products page

Now that we have the ID stored, we'll need to create a page to show the product. This will be fairly empty, because we are going to load the content dynamically when it's needed. Let's create header, footer, and content <div>s as we did before.

```
jquerymobile/index_icons.html
<div data-role="page" id="product">
  <div data-role="header" id="product-header">
    <a data-role="back" href="#products" data-direction="reverse">Back</a>
    <h1>Product</h1>
  </div>

  <div data-role="content" id="product-content">
    <p class="description"></p>
    <span class="price"><strong></strong></span>
  </div>

  <div data-role="footer">
    <h4>&copy; 2012 AwesomeCo</h4>
  </div>
</div>
```

We created a back button in the header <div> that simulates moving backward in the history. The reverse value for the data-direction attribute changes the transition to be left to right. The last step to show a product on the page is to intercept the navigation and load the data. Before, we asked the server to get information about several products. This time, we're going to get information about just one product and build the rest of the product page using that. Let's write some JavaScript to complete our product navigation.

```
jquerymobile/index_icons.html
var productPage = $("#product");

$("#products a").live("tap", function() {
  var productID = $(this).attr("data-product-id");
  $.mobile.showPageLoadingMsg();
  $.getJSON("/products/" + productID + ".json", function(product) {
    $("#product-header h1").text(product.name);
    $("#product-content p.description").text(product.description);
    $("#product-content span.price strong").text("$" + product.price);
  });
  $.mobile.hidePageLoadingMsg();
  $.mobile.changePage($("#product"));
});
```

We start off by binding to the "tap" event, which is a custom event in jQuery Mobile. Since the raw tap events on mobile browsers differ so greatly, the jQuery Mobile tap event removes the inconsistencies and differences in implementation. Next, we store a reference to the product ID so that we can make the call to getJSON(). Inside the Ajax call, we change the text of the product page to use the data we received. Finally, the last line forces jQuery Mobile to animate to the product page.

Now we have a smooth interface that allows us to view products and their information. In Figure 41, *A single product*, on page 177, you can see how a product show page looks.

Further Exploration

On the home page of this application we created a link to a search page that we never created. However, given the method we have already used for creating dynamic pages, it's simple to make a couple additions based on the code we already wrote. We could create a new page for the search and use a form to submit the query.

```
<form id="search-form">
  <input type="search" name="query" id="search-query">
  <input type="submit" name="submit" value="Submit">
</form>
```

We created a form with one input: the search query. From here, we would need to catch the submit event and submit the query with Ajax. With QEDServer's built-in search parameter, we can reuse most of the code from the browse

Figure 41—A single product

products section. However, when making the request with the getJSON() method, we should pass in the value of the search query input.

```
$.getJSON("/products.json?q=" + $('#search-query').val(), function(data) {
  // editing the products page
});
```

Finally, we could just use the changePage() to land on the products page. The jQuery Mobile framework also has a multitude of advanced features for building very powerful applications. We highly recommend reading through the documentation and examples on the jQuery Mobile website.[8]

Also See

- Recipe 10, *Building HTML with Mustache*, on page 67
- Recipe 18, *Accessing Cross-site Data with JSONP*, on page 134
- Recipe 21, *Targeting Mobile Devices*, on page 154
- Recipe 22, *Touch-Responsive Drop-Down Menus*, on page 159

Recipe 25

Using Sprites with CSS

Problem

As mobile data transfer costs rise and total transfer amounts are capped, the cost of loading lots of images on a phone or other mobile device can quickly add up, both in money and in time. We want to minimize the impact of these limitations on our users, while also improving overall load times so that our users have a good mobile experience without eating up their data plan.

Ingredients

- CSS

Solution

In Recipe 21, *Targeting Mobile Devices*, on page 154, we built a mobile interface for the product list we built in Recipe 8, *Accessible Expand and Collapse*, on page 52. We've been asked to add some color and graphics to our site and would like to add some images. However, we want to make sure that we don't take up too much bandwidth with our new images, both so we don't use up our users' limited data and to make sure the pages load quickly. CSS sprites let us cut down the number of files for the user to download by combining multiple icons into one and then using CSS properties to only display the portion of the image that we want. One file needs to be downloaded, but we can use it for multiple situations.

Our graphics department has created a sprite image for us to use on the mobile site, like this:

The sprite contains a + and a - to replace the current text-based way of letting our users know that the list is either open or collapsed. You can get the created graphic by downloading the source code for the example projects from the book's website.

We need to create an images folder inside of the project and place expand_collapse_sprite.png inside of it. We'll be doing all of our work in iPhone.css, which we originally created in Recipe 21, *Targeting Mobile Devices*, on page 154.

In our style.css from Recipe 8, *Accessible Expand and Collapse*, on page 52, we have two CSS rules. These rules dictate what content is shown.

```
css_sprites/style.css
ul.collapsible li.expanded:before {
  content: '-';
}
ul.collapsible li.collapsed:before {
  content: '+';
}
```

We'll override these in iPhone.css, so the browser will use the graphics and not the text. We'll use the sprites by setting the background CSS attribute along with some position adjustments to get the graphics aligned correctly so that only part of the total image is displayed.

```
css_sprites/iPhone.css
ul.collapsible li.expanded:before {
  content: '';
  width:30px;
  height:20px;
  background:url(images/expand_collapse_sprite.png) 0 -5px;
}
ul.collapsible li.collapsed:before {
  content: '';
  width:30px;
  height:25px;
  background:url(images/expand_collapse_sprite.png) 0 -30px;
}
```

The first line in both of our CSS rules set the content to a blank string, overriding whatever text is otherwise there so that we can replace it with our image. Next we specify the height and width of the image since we are showing only part of the image. The background attribute also sets the x and y positions of the sprite, essentially moving the portion of the image, which is visible through the window created by height and width.

Our current graphic has some extra whitespace at the top, so we can start our y position at -5 pixels. The graphic design team got the left edge pretty tight, so that will start that at 0. Our second image is below the first, so all we need to do is slide down to -30 pixels so that the - sign shows through, rather than the +. We can see the fruits of our labor in Figure 42, *Our product list with CSS sprites*, on page 180.

Figure 42—Our product list with CSS sprites

CSS sprites let us streamline the process of switching between multiple images, instead loading everything within a single file and shifting it around to display only the portion we want. With reduced bandwidth and limited data transfer on mobile devices, this can help us give our users a good experience without sucking up resources.

Further Exploration

Now that you have added a CSS sprite into a mobile style sheet, you can take it one step further and implement the same graphic in the desktop version. Since sprites save the number of downloads and help speed up page load time, they will help any version of your site.

The concepts behind CSS sprites can also be used for intricate and impressive animations. Many interactive Google Doodles, the themed replacements of the Google logo to represent important days, use CSS sprites. Searching online for *Google Doodles CSS Sprites*will reveal how to do some advanced tricks using sprites.

Also See

- Recipe 36, *Using Dropbox to Host a Static Site*, on page 268
- Recipe 24, *Creating Interfaces with jQuery Mobile*, on page 169
- Recipe 26, *Rapid, Responsive Design with Grid Systems*, on page 184
- *HTML5 and CSS3: Develop with Tomorrow's Standards Today* [Hog10]

## CHAPTER 5

Workflow Recipes

The tools and processes we use ultimately make or break our productivity. As developers, we're used to looking at better ways to make our clients happy, but we should also look at ways to improve our own workflow. This collection of recipes explores different workflows for working with layouts, content, CSS, and JavaScript, as well as our code.

Recipe 26

Rapid, Responsive Design with Grid Systems

Problem

We're often called on by clients or managers to provide a wireframe or a mock-up of a design (or multiple designs) before we do the actual implementation of a site. This process helps communicate design and layout ideas to our end users, especially when we're asked to design interfaces for mobile phones and tablets as well as desktop computers.

We have lots of options, from paper and pencil to full-blown mock-up tools like OmniGraffle, Visio, or Balsamiq Mockups, but we'd prefer to do these mock-ups in regular HTML and CSS. This way, we could code some interactivity, and we could potentially use some of the code in our actual implementation.

Ingredients

• Skeleton[1]

Solution

Thanks to the arrival of some great HTML and CSS frameworks, we can design layouts much more quickly than we could before, while avoiding some of the more troubling issues with CSS layout, and we can also plan for different screen sizes like mobile phones and tablets from the beginning.

CSS grid frameworks provide a quick and simple way to lay out elements on a page without having to worry about things such as floats and clears. There are a few great frameworks to choose from, but we're going to use Skeleton because it has built-in support for multiple screen sizes.

We've been asked to provide a mock-up for a property listing page. We'll need to show a few pictures of the property, its price, and some details from the property's MLS listing. We need to make sure things are readable on a regular laptop, but also on the iPhone, so the realtors can quickly reference the property information. This mock-up will eventually be turned into a template

---

1. http://getskeleton.com

for an actual web application, so we'll just use some hard-coded text for our examples, and we'll use image placeholders for the property images. Before we start building the mock-up, let's explore what Skeleton is and how it works.

Skeleton's Structure

Skeleton, like other grid-based frameworks, takes a single centered 960-pixel container and divides it into sixteen equal columns, creating a grid. We then use these columns to define the widths of our page regions. A header that stretches across all of these columns would be sixteen columns wide, while a sidebar that's only a fourth of the page would be defined as four columns wide. To illustrate this, take a look at Figure 43, *Defining a two-column layout using Skeleton's grid*, on page 186. Using simple tried-and-true CSS techniques, Skeleton handles the task of floating and aligning elements for us and sets default line heights and font sizes so things flow across columns nicely.

Skeleton provides more than just some CSS to make layout easier. It provides us with a framework for our files. When we download and unpack the Skeleton files, and we get a sample index.html file, a folder for our JavaScript files, a folder for our style sheets, and a folder for images that contains some default icons for our site, including home-screen icons for the iPhone. It also includes a place for us to put our own specific styles and JavaScript code.

On top of all that, Skeleton automatically handles browser resizing and small screens by taking advantage of CSS Media Queries, which we discuss in Recipe 21, *Targeting Mobile Devices*, on page 154.

Now that we know what Skeleton can do for us, let's get started with our mock-up.

Defining Our Layout

Our page will have a header with the property's address, a column with information about the property, and a column with some photographs. When we're done, we'll have a page that looks like Figure 44, *Our finished page*, on page 187.

We'll be using Skeleton version 1.1 for this recipe, which you can find in the book's source code. The Skeleton download gives us a default index.html file that we'll use as our base for our template. Let's open that file and delete everything between the opening and closing <div> with the class container, but we'll keep the container <div> itself, since Skeleton automatically sets that to a width of 960 pixels and centers it on the page.

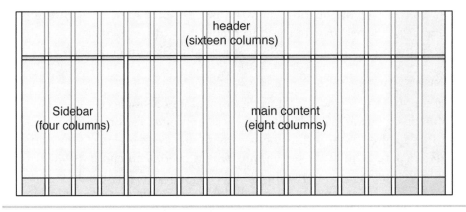

Figure 43—Defining a two-column layout using Skeleton's grid

Let's start by defining the header of the page, which will contain our site's title and the address of the property. We'll use the HTML5 <header> tag for this region.

cssgrids/index.html
```
<header class="sixteen columns">
  <h1>SpotFindr</h1>
  <h3>123 Fake Street, Anytown USA 12345</h3>
</header>
```

We can use all of the HTML5 semantic tags like <section>, <header>, and <footer> in our document; since we've based our page on the default Skeleton template, our <head> section includes the popular HTMLShiv library[2] so that these elements are able to be styled on older browsers.

Next, we define the left column of the page, which holds the price and a brief property description. We'll use a <section> tag to contain this region. We want this one to stretch halfway across the page, so we'll define it as eight columns wide, like this:

cssgrids/index.html
```
<section id="datasheet" class="eight columns">
  <h2 class="price">$109,900</h2>
  <p>
    Simple single-family home on the north side, within walking
    distance to schools and public transportation. New roof in 2005,
    central air in 2006. New windows and doors in 2010. Ready for you to
    move in!
  </p>
</section>
```

---

2. http://code.google.com/p/html5shiv/

SpotFindr

123 Fake Street, Anytown USA 12345

$109,900

Simple single-family home on the north side, within walking distance to schools and public transportation. New roof in 2005, central air in 2006. New windows and doors in 2010. Ready for you to move in!

Year Built: 1964   **Foundation:** Poured

Bedrooms: 4   **Heat:** Gas Forced Air

Baths: 1 Full/1 Half   **Electrical** Circuit Breaker

Square footage: 1,144 (approx)   **Water** City Water

MLS#: 842089   **Sewer** City Sewer

Exterior

Livingroom   Kitchen   Bedroom

Figure 44—Our finished page

Now let's define the right column. We do that by defining another region immediately after the previous <section> tag. Skeleton automatically left-aligns regions until the total column count is sixteen, when it then drops to the next line.

Since we don't have images yet, we'll use some placeholder images that we'll generate using Placehold.it.[3] Using their simple API, we can have images generated for our mock-up on the fly, just by pointing to their site. For example, we can insert an image that's 460 pixels wide by 200 pixels tall with the text "Bedroom" into our page with this request:

```
<img src="http://placehold.it/460x200?text=Bedroom">
```

For our mock-up, we'll use four images, which we'll code up like this:

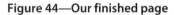
cssgrids/index.html
```
<section class="eight columns">
  <img class="scale-with-grid"
       src="http://placehold.it/460x280&text=Exterior"
       alt="Exterior of house">
  <img src="http://placehold.it/150x100&text=Livingroom"
       alt="Livingroom">
  <img src="http://placehold.it/150x100&text=Kitchen"
       alt="Kitchen">
  <img src="http://placehold.it/150x100&text=Bedroom"
       alt="Bedroom">
</section>
```

---

3. http://placehold.it

When we shrink the browser window or view the page on a smaller device, we want our large image to scale down as well. If we apply the class scale-with-grid to an image, Skeleton will crop the image for us by reducing its width and height to fit the available space.

The only thing we have left to implement is our two columns of data for the house that we want to place below the paragraph in the left column. We'll do that by defining columns within the left column we created earlier.

Columns Within Columns

As it stands right now, our left and right columns have only one row of information. The photos in the right column stack up nicely thanks to the way Skeleton flows its content in the columns, but we can't always rely on this. Sometimes we need to explicitly define a new row within a column.

We do that by inserting an element with the class row inside of our left column, right below the closing <p> tag:

cssgrids/index.html
```
<div class="row">
</div>
```

This "clears the floats," which forces the element to start on a new line. Within this element, we can define new columns. Since we're working within an eight-column region, we will define these new columns to be four columns wide each:

cssgrids/index.html
```
<div class="row">
  <div class="four columns alpha">
    <p><strong>Year Built:</strong> 1964</p>
    <p><strong>Bedrooms:</strong> 4</p>
    <p><strong>Baths:</strong> 1 Full/1 Half</p>
    <p><strong>Square footage:</strong> 1,144 (approx)</p>
    <p><strong>MLS#:</strong> 842089</p>
  </div>
  <div class="four columns omega">
    <p><strong>Foundation:</strong> Poured</p>
    <p><strong>Heat:</strong> Gas Forced Air</p>
    <p><strong>Electrical</strong>Circuit Breaker</p>
    <p><strong>Water</strong> City Water</p>
    <p><strong>Sewer</strong> City Sewer</p>
  </div>
</div>
```

Skeleton adds a small margin around each column so there's a small amount of space. When we define columns within columns, we need to tell Skeleton that we don't want it to add additional margins in these new columns. We do that by adding the alpha class to the first column of the row, which removes the left margin, and we add the omega class to the last column of the row, which removes the right margin.

We now have something that looks pretty nice in a very short amount of time. As we resize the screen, we see our elements restack, as shown in Figure 45, *Our page on an iPhone*, on page 190. Let's finish this mock-up off by adding a shadowed border around the container, but only when the full-width version is displayed.

Styling with Media Queries

The file stylesheets/layout.css contains placeholders and media queries so we can customize how our layout looks. To add a border, we locate the section of that file that starts with "site styles" and add something like this, which makes the page background gray, makes the container background white, and adds a slight drop shadow on the container for browsers that support it.

cssgrids/stylesheets/layout.css
```
/* #Site Styles
================================================ */
body{
  background-color: #ddd;
  margin-top: 20px;
}
.container{
  background-color: #fff;
  -webkit-box-shadow: 5px 5px 5px #bbb;
    -moz-box-shadow: 5px 5px 5px #bbb;
      -o-box-shadow: 5px 5px 5px #bbb;
}
```

The drop shadow looks great in a regular browser, but it takes up valuable real estate when viewed on a mobile phone and prevents the content from stretching as far as it could. We can add a couple lines of code to the style sheet's "Anything smaller than standard 960 section" of the style sheet to make it disappear:

cssgrids/stylesheets/layout.css
```
/* Anything smaller than standard 960 */
@media only screen and (max-width: 959px) {
  body{
    background-color: #fff;
  }

  .container{
    background-color: #fff;
```

Figure 45—Our page on an iPhone

```
    -webkit-box-shadow: none;
      -moz-box-shadow: none;
        -o-box-shadow: none;
  }
}
```

This removes the styles we just added when viewed on a mobile browser or smaller screen. From here, we could make any number of additional customizations for various screen sizes, building off of what Skeleton gives us.

Further Exploration

Skeleton's default template is worth a closer look because it starts us off with a great set of JavaScript and CSS best practices. For example, it loads jQuery from Google's CDN, using a protocol-relative scheme so it supports both HTTP and HTTPS.[5] It uses conditional comments, which older versions of Internet Explorer support, to target these browsers and add version-specific fixes. In fact, we can use those to add in support for media queries for Internet Explorer, by adding something like Respond.js [6] to our page.

---

5. http://paulirish.com/2010/the-protocol-relative-url/
6. https://github.com/scottjehl/Respond

> ### Joe asks:
> # Aren't We Mixing Design and Presentation with Frameworks Like This?
>
> To be honest, yes we are. When we have a <div> with a class of "four columns" and we decide that we need to reorganize things, we will have to touch the markup. So, many purists will look at this as a rather bad idea in theory. While it's not nearly as bad as class="redImportantText", it does couple the content with its presentation.
>
> However, most site redesigns we've seen involve scrapping the existing structure and creating a new layout from scratch, so the reusability of a template and its associated styles is often more theoretical than practical. With systems like this, you're trading strict semantic markup for a productivity gain. As you've seen in this recipe, frameworks like Skeleton are great for creating rapid prototypes of pages, even if you don't roll this markup into the actual site.
>
> If you're still not comfortable with this approach but like the idea of using these systems instead of rolling your own, you can investigate Compass, a framework for style sheets that can abstract grid systems away.[a] Compass uses Sass to build the style sheets, which we discuss in Recipe 28, *Building Modular Style Sheets with Sass*, on page 201.
>
> _____
> a. http://compass-style.org/

Skeleton also includes a very simple tabs implementation, similar to the one we built in Recipe 7, *Swapping Between Content with Tabbed Interfaces*, on page 45, and provides some very pleasant styles for the various HTML form fields.

If you combine Skeleton with an alternative markup language like HAML, you can whip up layouts even faster than HTML.[7] HAML is a Ruby library that lets you write HTML using a nested shorthand notation. In HAML, our page would look like this:

cssgrids/index.haml
```
.container
  %header.sixteen.columns
    %h1 SpotFindr
    %h3 123 Fake Street, Anytown USA 12345
  %section.eight.columns
    %h2.price $109,900
    %p
      Simple single-family home on the north side, within walking...
  %section.eight.columns ...
```

_____
7. http://haml-lang.com/

In HAML, there's no closing tags, because things are scoped by indentation, and the syntax for classes mirrors that of CSS. You then convert HAML to regular HTML so it's usable in the browser. We've used HAML and libraries like Skeleton, along with Sass, which we discuss in Recipe 28, *Building Modular Style Sheets with Sass*, on page 201, to quickly build and deploy production websites.

Also See

- Recipe 36, *Using Dropbox to Host a Static Site*, on page 268
- Recipe 42, *Automate Static Site Deployment with Jammit and Rake*, on page 296
- Recipe 28, *Building Modular Style Sheets with Sass*, on page 201

Recipe 27

Creating a Simple Blog with Jekyll

Problem

We want to create a blog, but our server resources are limited. We don't have access to a database, and we aren't able to run PHP code. This makes solutions such as WordPress and Drupal impossible. We need a way to build a blog that is manageable and gets around these barriers.

Ingredients

- A Ruby interpreter
- The Jekyll library[8]

Solution

To build a blog that doesn't require a database, we're going to use a *static-site generator*. A static-site generator is a tool that helps us build static sites quickly by reusing layout code. Jekyll is a framework designed for blogging. It relies on a rigid, opinionated file structure to form pages and articles. It has a simple and effective layout system, and while it isn't aimed at the average blogger, it's the perfect fit for a proof of concept or for a technical person who wants a fast yet simple blog without the overhead that comes from database-backed solutions.

To learn how to use Jekyll, we're going to create a music blog to share our daily music finds.

Installing Jekyll

To follow along with this recipe, you need to have Ruby and Rubygems installed on your system. If you need assistance with this, see Appendix 1, *Installing Ruby*, on page 305. To install Jekyll, run the following command:

```
gem install jekyll
```

The gem gives us an executable that we can use to build our site.

---

8.   http://jekyllrb.com/

Building the File Structure

Jekyll relies on a specific file and folder structure. It expects two folders for layouts and posts, an index page, and a configuration file. Open a new shell and create these files and folders:

- _layouts/
- _posts/
- index.html
- _config.yml

We can use the configuration file to customize how our site is built, but our site will build correctly if we leave it empty.

Using Layouts

Let's start by creating our index page that lists recent posts. Pages in Jekyll can be nested in a layout, so we'll create a layout that lets us reuse the repetitive HTML for each page. This also enables us to easily change the HTML for the entire blog with one file. In the layouts folder, create a file named base.html. We'll fill this with a standard HTML document.

```
creatingablog/_layouts/base.html
<!DOCTYPE html>
<html lang="en">
  <head>
    <title>My Music Blog</title>
  </head>
  <body>
    <header>
      <h1>My Music Blog</h1>
    </header>
    <section id="posts">
      {{ content }}
    </section>
  </body>
</html>
```

Jekyll uses the Liquid template language[9] to create dynamic pages. Template tags are surrounded by double curly braces. In this case, any other layout file or post file that is rendered with our base.html layout will be inserted in place of the {{content}} area. There are other template tags that we will use later.

Our base layout is created, so we can now move on to creating the rest of the home page. We'll define the content in the index.html file in the root of our

---

9.   http://www.liquidmarkup.org/

directory. The Liquid template language provides an iterator that we can use to create markup for each post. To show the posts, we create an unordered list for the set of posts, like this:

```
creatingablog/index.html
---
layout: base
---

<ul>
  {% for post in site.posts %}
    <li>
      <!-- link to the post -->
    </li>
  {% endfor %}
</ul>
```

The first three lines define a section that contains the YAML front matter, which is a special section where we can set some per-page metadata that Jekyll will look for. YAML[10] is a human-readable format for storing data that works across programming languages, similar to JSON. The front matter is surrounded by three hyphens to mark its beginning and end. We use this to tell Jekyll that our layout for this page is the base.html file. Most of our files will render inside the base.html file that we made before.

```
creatingablog/index.html
<li>
  <a href="{{ post.url }}">{{ post.title }}</a>
</li>
```

Within the context of this iterator, we have a template tag named post that contains the permalink for the post.

Creating Posts

Our home page is able to display posts now, but we haven't written any yet, so we'll do that now. We can write posts in Jekyll in a variety of markup languages including Markdown, Textile, or regular HTML. For now, we'll use Markdown because it is simple and easy to read. While the choice of markup language is flexible, there is a strict rule to abide by when naming our post files. Post files have to begin with a date followed by a title, and we must use hyphens to separate words in our title, like this:

2011-08-12-my-first-post.markdown

---

10. http://yaml.org/

The post files reside in the _posts folder. Create this file now, and use the correct date for today.

Just as the index.html file required a YAML front matter, posts do as well. We use this section to define a layout to use and give our post a human-readable title. While we haven't created a layout specifically for displaying a single post, we will soon. Until then, we will use the base layout. The content of the post comes after the front matter.

```
---
layout: base
title: My First Post
---

Thank you for viewing my music blog! I plan to
write every day about how much I love and enjoy music.
```

Building the Site

To build our site, we run the jekyll command that is packaged with the gem. This generates the static files and puts them in a _site folder. In the root directory of your site, run the following:

```
$ jekyll
```

When we're developing the blog, it's handy to have something serving up your files. Jekyll has this built in by using the --server option.

```
$ jekyll --server
```

This will build the site and start a WEBrick server on port 4000. To view the site, we open a browser and navigate to http://localhost:4000.

Our blog shows the list of posts that we have created and allows us to view each post, as shown in Figure 46, *Our home page*, on page 197.

We can shut down the server that we started by pressing Ctrl+C. Each time we edit the site, we must rebuild the site and restart the server before the changes appear in the browser. Keep in mind that the server is only for development purposes. When we deploy, we use the files that are generated in the _site folder.

Single-Post Layouts

If you follow the link to the post, you'll notice that viewing a post does not give us much information about the post, only its content. Create a file in the layouts folder called post.html. We're going to use it to display the post title.

My Music Blog

- <u>My First Post</u>

Figure 46—Our home page

`creatingablog/_layouts/post.html`

```
---
layout: base
---

<article class="post">

  <h2>{{ post.title }}</h2>
  {{ content }}

</article>
```

Before we're done, we need to tell our post to use the post layout. We simply edit the post we created earlier and change the layout in the front matter. Our new post looks like this:

`creatingablog/_posts/2011-08-12-my-first-post.markdown`

```
---
layout: post
title: My First Post
---

Thank you for viewing my music blog! I plan to write
every day about how much I love and enjoy music.
```

When we rebuild the site and start the server, we can navigate to a post and see its title.

Crafting Layouts

Jekyll is a designer-friendly system. Using CSS and images in your layouts and posts is simple. Any folders and files we create in the root directory are automatically included in the site on generation. To spice up our home page, we're going to write some CSS in an external file. Create a folder named css in the root directory, and create a file inside it named styles.css.

Let's write some simple styles in here to spice up the blog.

> \\//   **Joe asks:**
> ɔ̃̃
> ## Can I Exclude Files or Folders in My Root Directory?
>
> Yes! If you want to keep original assets like Photoshop files in the same folder as your images but you don't want to upload these to the server, you can tell Jekyll to exclude them by modifying the _config.yml file we created at the beginning of the recipe.
>
> To exclude files, we use the exclude option in the configuration file. This option expects a list of files and folders to ignore. Enter the configuration option into the _config.yml file.
>
> ```
> exclude:
> - images/psd/
> - README
> ```
>
> You can learn more about the configuration options for Jekyll at its wiki.[a]
>
> _____
>
> a.   https://github.com/mojombo/jekyll/wiki/Configuration

creatingablog/css/styles.css
```css
body {
  background: #f1f1f1;
  color: #111;
  font-size: 12px;
  font-family: Verdana, Arial, sans-serif;
}

ul {
  list-style: none;
}
```

Lastly, we need to change base.html layout file to load the style sheet.

creatingablog/_layouts/base.html
```html
<link rel="stylesheet" href="/css/styles.css"
      type="text/css" media="screen" charset="utf-8">
```

When we rebuild the site, we can see that the css folder is included. When we pull up the page in our browser, we see our new styles as in Figure 47, *Our finished page*, on page 199.

The same concept applies for including images and JavaScript files. We can create folders named, for example, images and js and reference the files in them.

Figure 47—Our finished page

Static Pages

We can do more than just blogging with Jekyll. We can use the same layout and template system to create static pages too. Pages work nearly the same way that posts do; they have titles, have layouts, and can use template tags.

To create a static page, we're going to reuse the layout we created to render posts. To do that, we first rename the post.html layout to page.html. Then, we edit the HTML so that it uses the page template tag.

creatingablog/_layouts/page.html

```
---
layout: base
---

<section class="post">
  <h3>{{ page.title }}</h3>
  {{ content }}
</section>
```

Jekyll actually treats everything as a page, so we can use the template tag for pages as well as posts, but since we renamed the layout, we broke all of our posts. We have to change the layout of our posts to page instead of post in order to make them display again.

With our layout updated, we can use it to render a static page. In the root directory, create a file named contact.markdown. This file is going to require a YAML front matter that defines the layout as the page and the page title.

creatingablog/contact.markdown

```
---
layout: page
title: Contact
---
```

```
If you would like to get in contact with me,
send an email to
[johnsmith@test.com](mailto:johnsmith@test.com).
```

Jekyll generates static pages based on the filename of the Markdown page. Since we named ours contact.markdown, it generates a file named contact.html. Let's create a link to it on the index page.

```
<a href="/contact.html">Contact Me</a>
```

Now that our blog is ready, we could deploy it to a server by using the contents in the _site folder that is generated when we run the jekyll command.

Further Exploration

If you're currently using WordPress, Drupal, or another blog framework, the Jekyll wiki has information on how to easily transform your posts into a form that is capable of being digested by Jekyll. Also, there are plug-ins available to add syntax highlighting, tag clouds, and more to your blog. For information on the advanced capabilities of Jekyll, refer to the GitHub page for Jekyll.[12]

Also See

- Recipe 36, *Using Dropbox to Host a Static Site*, on page 268
- Recipe 26, *Rapid, Responsive Design with Grid Systems*, on page 184
- Recipe 42, *Automate Static Site Deployment with Jammit and Rake*, on page 296
- Appendix 1, *Installing Ruby*, on page 305

---

12. https://github.com/mojombo/jekyll/wiki

Recipe 28

Building Modular Style Sheets with Sass

Problem

As web developers, we rely heavily on style sheets to create eye-catching interfaces, usable layouts, and readable typography. Style sheets are quite powerful, but they're also very rudimentary. Even novice programmers tend to get frustrated by the things that CSS doesn't provide, like variables and functions to reduce duplication, and so they turn to JavaScript and jQuery to fill in the gaps. While true CSS may not have some of the features we desire, we can use tools that provide these advanced features to *generate* CSS, like Sass.

Ingredients

• Sass[13]

Solution

We can use Sass to build style sheets that are easier to maintain and build upon. Sass takes CSS and extends it, giving CSS features we've longed for, like variables and reusable code. We write our code using Sass's extended CSS syntax and then run this code through a precompiler that spits out regular CSS that web browsers understand. Sass's default syntax supports basic CSS3, so transitioning to Sass involves simply renaming the files from style.css to style.scss.

We've developed some styled buttons in Recipe 1, *Styling Buttons and Links*, on page 2 and some speech bubbles in Recipe 2, *Styling Quotes with CSS*, on page 6. In doing so, we created quite a bit of duplicated code. We'll use Sass and its features to build pieces we can share between the buttons and the speech bubbles, and then we'll stitch the pieces together into one master style sheet we can include in our pages. We won't cover how the CSS code works in this recipe; you should refer to the other recipes for that.

---

13. http://sass-lang.com

Creating a Sass Project

Sass uses a precompiler to convert its files into regular CSS files. There are some graphical tools we can install that will do this conversion, but we'll use the original command-line version written in Ruby. We install this precompiler from the command line like this:

```
$ gem install sass
```

Since only regular CSS files will work in our browser, we'll create two folders: one for our Sass files and one for our CSS files. We'll call those folders sass and stylesheets.

```
$ mkdir sass
$ mkdir stylesheets
```

The sass command-line tool can monitor a directory we specify for changes and convert the Sass files into CSS files. We tell it to watch the sass folder and place the output files in the stylesheets folder like this:

```
$ sass --watch sass:stylesheets
```

This will watch files until we press Ctrl+C or until we restart the computer.

That's all there is to setting up a project. Now let's take a look at one of the simplest, yet extremely powerful, features of Sass: variables.

Using Variables and Imports

Our button has a background color and a border color. When we're working with CSS, we often use the same HTML color codes over and over in our style sheets, which makes changing these colors quite difficult. In programming languages like JavaScript, we solve problems like this by using variables, but regular CSS doesn't have them. Sass does, and they're incredibly easy to use.

Let's create a file in the sass folder called style.scss. We'll add two variables to the top of this new file, one for the background color and one for the border color:

sass/sass/style.scss
```
$button_background_color: #A69520;
$button_border_color: #282727;
```

In Sass, variables start with a dollar sign and get their values assigned the same way we'd assign a value to a CSS property.

To keep our code organized, we'll keep the definition for our CSS button in its own file called _buttons.scss, and we'll place it in the sass folder. Naming it with an underscore lets Sass know that it's not a style sheet of its own, so it won't generate a CSS file from this file directly. We'll put the basic styles for our button in this file, using our two variables for the button's border and background color.

sass/sass/_buttons.scss
```
.button {
  font-weight: bold;
➤ background-color: $button_background_color;
  text-transform: uppercase;
  font-family: verdana;
➤ border: 1px solid $button_border_color;
  font-size: 1.2em;
  line-height: 1.25em;
  padding: 6px 20px;
  cursor: pointer;
  color: #000;
  text-decoration: none;
}

input.button {
  line-height: 1.22em;
}
```

We can then import this partial Sass file into our style.scss file using the @import statement.

sass/sass/style.scss
```
@import "buttons.scss";
```

When we process our files, the Sass compiler will see the @import statement, pull in the contents of our other file, and create one CSS file. This is a great way to keep sections of style sheets organized during the development process, but we can take organization a step further by reducing duplication.

Using Mixins to Share Code

Both our buttons and our speech bubbles have gradient backgrounds and rounded corners. In addition, our button has a different gradient background definition when the user hovers over the button. Defining these gradients and rounded corners requires a lot of CSS because we have to support different definitions for the various browsers. On top of that, our buttons also have a drop shadow we'll need to define, and we may want to share that code with other elements on the page so we have consistent shadows.

We can define these rules as *mixins* that we can share across style definitions. Let's create a new file called _mixins.scss to hold the mixins we'll define and then add the import statement to style.scss.

sass/sass/style.scss
```
@import "mixins";
```

In _mixins.scss, let's first define a mixin for the rounded corners. A mixin looks a lot like a function declaration in JavaScript, with parentheses for the parameters and curly braces for the content.

sass/sass/_mixins.scss
```
@mixin rounded($radius){
        border-radius: $radius;
    -moz-border-radius: $radius;
  -webkit-border-radius: $radius;
}
```

With the mixin declared, we can add it to our .button definition in _buttons.scss by using the @include statement.

sass/sass/_buttons.scss
```
@include rounded(12px);
```

It fits in like any other CSS rule.

Next, let's create a mixin for our gradients, which will be a little more complex.

sass/sass/_mixins.scss
```
@mixin gradient($color1, $color2, $alpha1: 100%, $alpha2: 100%){
  background:
    -webkit-gradient(linear, 0 0,
                     $alpha1, $alpha2,
                     from($color1), to($color2));
  background: -moz-linear-gradient($color1, $color2);
  background: -o-linear-gradient($color1, $color2);
  background: linear-gradient(top center, $color1, $color2);
}
```

Since WebKit-based browsers like Google Chrome, Safari, and those on many mobile devices support alpha transparency for the gradients, we'll make our mixin take those as parameters too. Our button styles don't make use of the alpha transparency, but our speech bubbles do, so we assign these default values of 100 percent. Now we can include this mixin into our _buttons.scss file.

sass/sass/_buttons.scss
```
@include gradient(#FFF089, #A69520 );
```

We also need to use the gradient code when we hover over the button. Let's look at how Sass handles pseudoclasses.

Reducing Duplication with Nesting

With regular CSS, we end up duplicating selectors. To define styles for a hyperlink, we often end up writing code like this to handle the regular state and the hover state:

```
a{
  color: #300;
}
a:hover{
  color: #900;
}
```

With Sass, we can nest the pseudoclass definition *within* the parent rule:

```
a{
  color: #300;
  &:hover{
    color: #900;
  }
}
```

This nesting doesn't save us a lot of keystrokes in this case, but it does help us keep things more organized.

In _buttons.scss, we'll use this nesting technique to include our gradients mixin for the hover pseudoclass.

```
sass/sass/_buttons.scss
&:active, &:focus {
  @include gradient(#A69520, #FFF089 );
  color: #000;
}
```

When developing a more complex style sheet, we often use this nesting feature to dramatically reduce repeating selectors, turning this:

```
#sidebar a{
  color: #300;
}
#sidebar a:hover{
  color: #900;
}
```

into this:

```
#sidebar a{
  color: #300;
  &:hover{
    color: #900;
  }
}
```

This way, we use nesting for the scope of the selectors, instead of repeating the selection hierarchy over and over.

With these mixins created, we can create the file _speech_bubble.scss and define the bubbles like this:

```
sass/sass/_speech_bubble.scss
Line 1  blockquote {
          width: 225px;
          padding: 15px 30px;
          margin: 0;
     5    position: relative;
          background: #faa;
          @include gradient(#c40606, #ffaaaa, 20%, 100%);
          @include rounded(20px);
          p {
    10        font-size: 1.8em;
              margin: 5px;
              z-index: 10;
              position: relative;
          }
    15    + cite {
              font-size: 1.1em;
              display: block;
              margin: 1em 0 0 4em;
          }
    20    &:after {
              content: "";
              position: absolute;
              z-index: 1;
              bottom: -50px;
    25        left: 40px;
              border-width: 0 15px 50px 0px;
              border-style: solid;
              border-color: transparent #faa;
              display: block;
    30        width: 0;
          }
        }
```

We call our mixins starting on line 7, and on line 15, we use Sass's nesting support to keep things organized. Now we can tell style.scss to import this new file as well:

```
sass/sass/style.scss
@import "speech_bubble.scss";
```

Before we wrap up, let's take a look at one last item in Sass' bag of tricks: iteration.

Generating CSS with Iterators

If we glance back at the pure CSS implementation of the buttons, we see that we need to write one last bit of code to finish up our buttons—the drop-shadow code.

Like the rounded-corners code, we have to declare the shadow multiple times, once for each type of web browser. Rather than code that by hand, we can use a loop. In _mixins.scss, we'll add this code:

```
sass/sass/_mixins.scss
@mixin shadow($x, $y, $offset, $color){
  @each $prefix in "", -moz-, -webkit-, -o-, -khtml- {
    #{$prefix}box-shadow: $x $y $offset $color;
  }
}
```

This lets us iterate over the browser prefixes and use them to generate the CSS properties. The first entry in the list of prefixes is an empty string, because box-shadow should be included in the list, as it's the version of the property that's in the CSS specification.

We then add that to our _buttons.scss file to apply the shadow.

```
sass/sass/_buttons.scss
@include shadow(1px, 3px, 5px, #555);
```

As we've been working, the Sass command has been stitching all of our individual style sheets together, producing a single style.css file we can include into our page. Our Sass files can stay in our source code repository, nicely organized.

Further Exploration

With the powerful features Sass brings to the table, it's hard to imagine doing style sheets any other way. We've managed only a small amount of CSS in this recipe, but imagine how much more maintainable the style sheets for a large content management system would be. You could define your own library of mixins that you could share across the various functional pieces of the site, and you could use variables to hold the values for measurements, colors, and font choices so you could quickly alter them when needed.

Sass is just the beginning. With Compass, a CSS framework built on Sass, you can take advantage of many prebuilt mixins and plug-ins for things like grid frameworks and CSS3.[14]

---

14. http://compass-style.org/

A Tale of Two Syntaxes

Sass actually has two syntaxes—the SCSS syntax that we used in this recipe and another syntax commonly referred to as "Indented Sass" or "Sass Classic." Instead of curly braces, it uses indentation and is aimed at developers who favor conciseness over similarity to regular CSS. It also eliminates semicolons from the definitions. A Sass style sheet that defines different link colors for sidebar and main regions of a page would look like this, using this alternative syntax:

```
#sidebar
  a
    color: #f00
  &:hover
    color: #000
#main
  a
    color: #000
```

You only need to use the .sass extension instead of .scss extension. The end result and workflows don't change. Both of these syntaxes are interoperable and will be supported well into the future, so the choice is yours.

Also See

- Recipe 1, *Styling Buttons and Links*, on page 2
- Recipe 2, *Styling Quotes with CSS*, on page 6
- Recipe 29, *Cleaner JavaScript with CoffeeScript*, on page 209
- Recipe 42, *Automate Static Site Deployment with Jammit and Rake*, on page 296
- *Pragmatic Guide to Sass* [CC11]

Recipe 29

Cleaner JavaScript with CoffeeScript

Problem

JavaScript is the programming language of the Web, but it's often misunderstood, which leads to poorly written and terribly performing code. Its rules and syntax can lead to developer confusion and frustration, which slow down productivity. Since JavaScript is everywhere, we can't simply remove it or replace it with a language with a more comfortable syntax, but we can use other languages to *generate* good, standard, and well-performing JavaScript.

Ingredients

- CoffeeScript[15]
- Guard[16] and the CoffeeScript add-on[17]
- QEDServer

Solution

CoffeeScript lets us write JavaScript in a more concise format, similar to languages like Ruby or Python. We then run our code through an interpreter that emits regular JavaScript that we can use on our pages. While this interpretation adds a step to our development process, the productivity gains are often worth the trade-off.

For example, we won't accidentally forget a semicolon or miss a closing curly brace, and we won't forget to declare variables in the proper scope. CoffeeScript takes care of those issues and more, so we can focus on the problem we're solving.

We'll test-drive CoffeeScript by using it with jQuery to fetch the products from our store's API. We'll use our test server, just like we did in Recipe 14, *Organizing Code with Backbone.js*, on page 93.

---

15. http://coffeescript.org/
16. https://github.com/guard/guard
17. https://github.com/netzpirat/guard-coffeescript

CoffeeScript is a language of its own, which means we need to learn a new syntax for declaring things like variables and functions. The CoffeeScript website and Trevor Burnham's book, *CoffeeScript: Accelerated JavaScript Development* [Bur11] explain a lot of these fundamentals in excellent detail, but let's take a look at a couple of basic CoffeeScript concepts we'll need to understand to move forward.

CoffeeScript Basics

CoffeeScript's syntax is designed to be similar to JavaScript but with much less noise. For example, instead of declaring a function like this in JavaScript:

```javascript
var hello = function(){
  alert("Hello World");
}
```

We can express it with CoffeeScript as follows:

```coffeescript
hello = -> alert "Hello World"
```

We don't need to use the var keyword to declare our variables. CoffeeScript will figure out which variables we've declared and add the var statement in the appropriate place for us.

Second, we use the -> symbol instead of the function keyword to define functions in CoffeeScript. Function arguments come before the -> symbol, and the function body comes immediately after, with no curly braces. If the function body goes for more than one line, we indent it, like this:

```coffeescript
hello = (name) ->
  alert "Hello " + name
```

While there are many more powerful expressive features of CoffeeScript, those two make it possible to turn something like this:

```javascript
$(function() {
  var url;
  url = "/products.json";
  $.ajax(url, {
    dataType: "json",
    success: function(data, status, XHR) {
      alert("It worked!");
    }
  });
});
```

into this:

```
$ ->
  url = "/products.json"
  $.ajax url,
    dataType: "json"
    success: (data, status, XHR) ->
      alert "It worked!"
```

The CoffeeScript version of the code is a little easier on the eyes, and it takes less time to write. If we made syntax errors, we'll find out as soon as we try to convert our CoffeeScript to JavaScript, which means we won't be spending time hunting these things down in the web browser.

Installing CoffeeScript

There are numerous ways to get CoffeeScript running, but the absolute simplest way to test it is through the browser. This way, we don't have to install anything on our machines to try a quick demo. We download the CoffeeScript interpreter[18] and include it on our web page like this:

coffeescript/browser/index.html
```
<script
  src="http://ajax.googleapis.com/ajax/libs/jquery/1.7/jquery.min.js">
</script>
<script src="coffee-script.js"></script>
```

Then we can place our CoffeeScript code in a <script> block, like this:

coffeescript/browser/index.html
```
<script type="text/coffeescript">
$ ->
  url = "/products.json"
  $.ajax url,
    dataType: "json"
    success: (data, status, XHR) ->
      alert "It worked!"
</script>
```

Since the web browser doesn't know how to handle <script> elements with text/coffeexcript, it will simply ignore them, but when we include the CoffeeScript interpreter on the page, it finds these <script> elements and evaluates their contents. It then writes the resulting JavaScript to the page, where the browser executes it. CoffeeScript's interpreter is actually *written* in Coffee-Script, which is then compiled down to JavaScript.

This in-browser approach is great for experimenting, but it's not something you'll ever want to roll out in production because the CoffeeScript interpreter

---

18. http://jashkenas.github.com/coffee-script/extras/coffee-script.js

is a very large file, and interpreting the CoffeeScript on the client machine is going to be much slower. We want to convert our CoffeeScript files ahead of time and serve only the resulting JavaScript files from our website. For that, we'll need to install a CoffeeScript interpreter, and we'll need a good workflow to go along with that.

People usually install the CoffeeScript interpreter with Node.JS and NPM, the Node Package Manager,[19] but we can also use it with Ruby. Since we've used Ruby for other recipes, we'll go that route. Assuming you've installed Ruby following the instructions in Appendix 1, *Installing Ruby*, on page 305, you can type this on the command line:

```
$ gem install coffee-script guard guard-coffeescript
```

This installs the CoffeeScript interpreter and Guard, which we'll use to automatically convert CoffeeScript files to JavaScript files whenever we make changes to them. The guard-coffeescript gem does the automatic conversion for us.

Let's set up our project and get a demo going.

Working with CoffeeScript

We'll use QEDServer and its product management API as our development server. We'll place all of our files in the public folder in our workspace so our development server will serve them properly, and our Ajax requests will work without issue.

Since we're going to turn CoffeeScript files into JavaScript files, let's create folders for each of those types of files.

```
$ mkdir coffeescripts
$ mkdir javascripts
```

Now, let's create a very simple web page that loads jQuery, the Mustache library we learned about inRecipe 10, *Building HTML with Mustache*, on page 67, and app.js, which will contain the code that fetches our data and displays it on the page:

coffeescript/guard/index.html
```
<!DOCTYPE html>
<html lang="en">
  <head>
    <script
      src="http://ajax.googleapis.com/ajax/libs/jquery/1.7/jquery.min.js">
    </script>
    <script src="javascripts/mustache.js"></script>
```

---

19. http://npmjs.org/

```
    <script src="javascripts/app.js"></script>
  </head>
  <body>
  </body>
</html>
```

We'll need to place mustache.js in the javascripts folder, but app.js will be generated from CoffeeScript when we're done.

Now we'll add a simple Mustache template to the page, which we'll use to display each recipe.

coffeescript/guard/index.html
```
<script id="product_template" type="text/html">
  <div class="product">
    {{#products}}
    <h3>{{name}}</h3>
    <p>{{description}}</p>
    {{/products}}
  </div>
</script>
```

Next, we'll create the file coffeescripts/app.coffee.

coffeescript/guard/coffeescripts/app.coffee
```
$ ->
  $.ajax "/products.json",
    type: "GET"
    dataType: "json"
    success: (data, status, XHR) ->
      html = Mustache.to_html $("#product_template").html(), {products: data}
      $('body').append html

    error: (XHR, status, errorThrown) ->
      $('body').append "AJAX Error: #{status}"
```

Instead of the unfriendly jQuery shortcut $(function(){}), we simply use $ -> to define the code that runs when the document is ready. We define a variable for our URL, and we call jQuery's AJAX() method, rendering the Mustache template if we get a response and displaying the failure message when we don't. The logic and flow are identical to a pure JavaScript implementation, but it's several lines fewer. Of course, this code won't work yet because our page is requesting a JavaScript file that we still need to generate. We'll do that with Guard.

Using Guard to Convert CoffeeScript

Guard is a command-line tool we can configure to watch files for changes and then perform tasks in response to those changes. The guard-coffeescript plug-in gives Guard the ability to convert our CoffeeScript files.

We need to tell Guard to watch files within the coffeescript folder for changes and convert them to JavaScript files, placing those in the javascripts folder. We do that by creating a file called Guardfile in the root of our project, which tells Guard how to handle our CoffeeScript files. We can create this file by hand or by running the following:

```
$ guard init coffeescript
```

Then we open the newly generated Guardfile and change the input and output folders so they point to our folders:

coffeescript/guard/Guardfile
```
# A sample Guardfile
# More info at https://github.com/guard/guard#readme
guard 'coffeescript', :input => 'coffeescripts', :output => "javascripts"
```

Now we can start up Guard from our shell, and it will start watching our coffeescripts folder for changes:

```
$ guard
Guard is now watching at '/home/webdev/coffeescript/public/'
```

When we save the coffeescripts/app.coffee file, Guard will notice and do the conversion from CoffeeScript to JavaScript:

```
Compile coffeescripts/app.coffee
Successfully generated javascripts/app.js
```

When we view the page at http://localhost:8080/index.html, everything works! If we inspect the generated app.js file, we'll see that all of the required curly braces, parentheses, and semicolons are where they should be. We now have a workflow we can use to write better JavaScript, so we can continue making changes to our application. When we're done, we can deploy the javascripts folder and leave the coffeescripts folder in our source code repository.

Further Exploration

More and more JavaScript projects are moving to CoffeeScript as a development platform to develop their projects because of its ease of use and because it provides some of the niceties of languages like Ruby, including list comprehensions and string interpolations. For example, instead of concatenating strings like this in JavaScript:

```
var fullName = firstName + " " + lastName;
```

we can use #{} within double-quoted strings like this:

```
fullname = "#{firstName} #{lastName}"
```

the expressions within the #{} markup are evaluated and converted to strings.

And when we're working with arrays or lists of items, we often find ourselves writing code like this:

```
var colors = ["red", "green", "blue"];
for (i = 0, length = colors.length; i < length; i++) {
  var color = colors[i];
  alert(color);
}
```

```
alert color for color in ["red", "green", "blue"]
```

We developers like shortcuts, and we can use JavaScript libraries to achieve the same thing, but then we make our end users download additional code just so we can write less of it ourselves. CoffeeScript's output is regular, standard JavaScript that works anywhere JavaScript works, without any additional libraries.

To get more comfortable with CoffeeScript, try to implement some of the recipes in this book in CoffeeScript.

In addition to CoffeeScript, Guard also has support for Sass, which we talk about in Recipe 28, *Building Modular Style Sheets with Sass*, on page 201 via the guard-sass gem. Using Guard, Sass, and CoffeeScript together gives you an incredibly powerful workflow for managing your sites. And if you really want to integrate CoffeeScript into your web development workflow, you could use a tool like MiddleMan, which makes building static sites with Sass and CoffeeScript a breeze.[20] Combining that with an automated deployment strategy like the one we talk about in Recipe 42, *Automate Static Site Deployment with Jammit and Rake*, on page 296 can create an efficient and enjoyable development experience.

Also See

- *CoffeeScript: Accelerated JavaScript Development* [Bur11]
- Recipe 28, *Building Modular Style Sheets with Sass*, on page 201
- Recipe 14, *Organizing Code with Backbone.js*, on page 93
- Recipe 42, *Automate Static Site Deployment with Jammit and Rake*, on page 296

---

20. http://middlemanapp.com/

Recipe 30

Managing Files Using Git

Problem

As web developers, we often find ourselves in situations where we're asked to juggle multiple versions of our code. Sometimes we need to experiment with the latest and greatest plug-in. Then there are the times where we're in the zone, cranking away on a new feature, but then get sidetracked because we need to fix a critical bug. We all use some form of version control, even if it is just keeping multiple copies of a file. But that multiple-file situation breaks down pretty fast because it's all on our machine and isn't easy to manage. We need something that's fast, robust, and modern—something that we can use to manage our code but also something we can use to collaborate with others.

Ingredients

- Git[21]

Solution

Today we have many options for version control. Git is very popular among developers, because it's local and fast, faster than making local copies. Git also allows us to work on multiple versions in parallel. We can save changes often, giving us many restore points. All of these features make it the choice VCS for many of today's open source projects.

During our morning meeting, our boss turned to us and said, "I need you to take those two mocks you presented last week and develop actual versions of the site using those templates. Oh, and while you're working on that, we also need a few bugs fixed in the existing site."

Now we have three versions of our site to maintain. Let's use Git to keep our files organized and in sync.

---

21. http://git-scm.com/

Setting Up Git

Let's get started by installing Git. Head over to Git's website[22] and download the appropriate packages for your operating system. If you're running Windows, you should use MsysGit,[23] and you'll want to choose the option to use Git Bash, since you'll need to use that instead of the normal command prompt to follow along with this recipe.

Git tracks the person who made the change based on their configured Git username. This makes it easy to see who made what changes and when. Let's configure Git by specifying our name and email address. Open a new shell and type the following:

```
$ git config --global user.name "Firstname Lastname"
$ git config --global user.email "your_email@youremail.com"
```

Now that we have Git installed and configured, let's get comfortable with the basics.

Git Basics

Let's start by turning our project into a Git repository. Let's create a folder for this web project called git_site and initialize it as a Git repository. From the command line (or from Git Bash if you're on Windows), type the following:

```
$ mkdir git_site
$ cd git_site
$ git init
```

After we initialize the directory, we will get a confirmation message:

```
Initialized empty Git repository in /Users/webdev/Sites/git_site/.git/
```

This creates a hidden folder called .git in the root of our directory. All of the history and other details about our repository will all go in this folder. Git will track changes to our folder and store "snapshots" of our code, but first we have to tell Git what files we'd like to track.

Let's copy our website files into our new git_site folder. You can find these files in the git folder of the book's source code.

With the files in place, let's add them all to the repository so we can get back to where we started if something goes wrong. To add all the files, simply issue the following command:

```
$ git add .
```

---

22. http://git-scm.com/
23. http://code.google.com/p/msysgit/

The add command doesn't show anything; we need to use the a git status. We can use a Git status command at any time to see the current status of our Git repository.

```
# On branch master
#
# Initial commit
#
# Changes to be committed:
#   (use "Git rm --cached <file>..." to unstage)
#
#       new file:   index.html
#       new file:   javascripts/application.js
#       new file:   styles/site.css
#
```

This is called "staging our files." This way, we can see what is ready to be committed and can have one more chance to change our minds before we commit the files to the repository. Staging files just means that Git is ready to look for changes. Everything looks good, so let's actually commit these files.

$ **git commit -a -m "initial commit of files"**

The two flags we passed in were -a and -m. The -a tells Git that we want to add all the changes to the index before committing, and the -m specifies a commit message. Unlike other version control systems, Git requires that every commit must have a commit message. This helps greatly when tracking commits, so don't take commit messages lightly! After our commit finishes, we'll get confirmation of what it did as shown in the following code snippet:

```
                        [master (root-commit) 94c75a2] Initial Commit
1 files changed, 17 insertions(+), 0 deletions(-)
create mode 100644 index.html
create mode 100644 javascripts/application.js
create mode 100644 styles/site.css
```

We can verify that the files were committed with git status When we run that, we see that everything is up-to-date:

```
# On branch master
nothing to commit (working directory clean)
```

We now have a "snapshot" of our code, which means we can start making and tracking changes.

Working with Branches

Branching allows us work on multiple features of our website. We can effectively develop a new feature while maintaining our current deployed code. Unlike other VCSs, branching is an easy and very commonly used feature of Git.

Our boss wanted us to start work on implementing two site layouts, which we'll call *layout_a* and *layout_b*. Let's create a branch for *layout_a*.

```
$ git checkout -b layout_a
Switched to a new branch 'layout_a'
```

Now when we run git status we see that our current branch is *layout_a*. Let's go into the index.html file and change the text in the <h1> tag to say "Layout A" and save the file. Now when we do Git status, we see the following:

```
# On branch layout_a
# Changed but not updated:
#   (use "Git add <file>..." to update what will be committed)
#   (use "Git checkout -- <file>..." to discard changes in working directory)
#
#       modified:   index.html
#
no changes added to commit (use "Git add" and/or "Git commit -a")
```

Let's commit the changes to the *layout_a* branch.

```
$ git commit -a -m "changed heading to Layout A"
```

While we were working on our branch, our boss sent us an email that says "On the home page, it says that we offer one day shipping. We no longer offer that shipping promotion. We need to update it to two-day shipping and we have to do it right now before anyone else holds us to that option!" Let's switch back to our *master* branch and get that change made.

```
$ git checkout master
```

Now when we open the index.html we won't see the text we changed in the *layout_a* branch. The changes we made are in another branch, and instead of us moving files around, we simply let Git alter the file's contents when we change branches. Now we can make the changes to the home page that our boss wanted us to, and then we can commit back to the *master* branch.

```
$ git commit -a -m "fixed shipping promotion from one day to two-day"
  [master d00d2de] fixed shipping promotion from one day to two-day
  1 files changed, 1 insertions(+), 1 deletions(-)
```

We made this change on the *master* branch, but if we change back to our other branches, we won't see the change, and it would be a Really Bad Thing if we lost the work we just did by accident, so let's get these changes into our *layout_a* branch so we can get back to working on that layout.

```
$ git checkout layout_a
$ git merge master
```

This takes anything that wasn't changed in *layout_a* but was changed in *master* and applies it to the *layout_a* branch.

Next let's create a branch for our *layout_b* option. We want this to start off based on our current production site, not our *layout_a* version, so we need to switch back to the *master* branch and then create a branch for *layout_b*.

```
$ git checkout master
$ git checkout -b layout_b
```

This time we'll change the text inside of the <h1> tag to say "Layout B." Let's save and commit this change.

```
$ git commit -a -m "Changed heading to Layout B"
```

This version of our layout requires us to add a products.html file and a about_us.html file. Let's create those files and then stage those files for check-in.

```
$ touch products.html
$ touch about_us.html
$ git add .
```

Now if we do a git status, we'll see that we have two new files that have been staged.

```
# On branch layout_b
# Changes to be committed:
#   (use "Git reset HEAD <file>..." to unstage)
#
#       new file:   about_us.html
#       new file:   products.html
#
```

Let's commit those files.

```
$ git commit -a -m "added products and about_us, no content"
```

Now, let's add an <h1> to the products.html with the text of "Current Products" to comply with our design.

While we were doing that, we just got another email from our boss that says "We need to change the shipping time on the home page back to one day. We

Joe asks:

Why Are We Committing Changes So Often?

Think of commits as snapshots, or restore points, for your project. The more commits you make, the more powerful and flexible Git becomes. If we keep our commits small and focused on a particular feature, we can use Git's "cherry-pick," which lets us take a commit from one branch and apply it to other branches. And if the idea of lots of small commits seems messy to you, you can always squash commits together using rebase when you've completed a feature.

struck a deal with a major shipping company. Get these changes made ASAP!!!" We need to make these changes and get them pushed out right away. However, we are not ready to commit the changes we just made.

Git's stash command is meant for situations like this. We can use stash to store our changes so we can switch branches. Stashes are a great way to store something you are working on without actually having to commit them.

```
$ git stash
```

Now if we do a Git status, we will see that there are no changes that need to be committed. Let's switch over to our *master* branch:

```
$ git checkout master
```

Now we can make our changes to the shipping information index.html and commit the changes.

```
$ git commit -a -m"updated shipping times"
```

Let's switch back over to our *layout_b* branch with Git checkout layout_b and explore what we can do with stashes. Let's see what stashes are available by using the Git stash list command:

```
$ git stash list
stash@{0}: WIP on layout_b: f8747f4 added products and about_us, no content
```

When we open up our products.html, we see that it's empty. Let's get the changes we made to that file back. We do that with this command:

```
$ git stash pop
```

Now when we look at our products.html file, we'll have our <h1> tag that we added before we got sidetracked.

After several more tweaks to both layouts (and several other "important" distractions), our boss decided that the *layout_b* option was the best and wants to roll that out into production. Let's merge this work into our *master* branch.

```
$ git checkout master
$ git merge layout_b
$ git commit -a -m "merged in layout_b"
```

In traditional version control systems, it's common to leave branches in a repository indefinitely. Git differs from this in that both branches and tags refer to a commit. With Git, when we delete a branch, Git does not remove any of the commits; it only removes the reference. Since we have merged our changes back into *master*, we can delete our branches that we used for development. First let's look at the branches we currently have by using the git branch command. It shows us that we are on *master* and lists *layout_a* and *layout_b*. Let's delete those branches, like this:

```
$ git branch -d layout_a
$ git branch -d layout_b
```

Git also will tell us whether the branch has not been merged into the current branch. We can override this by using -D, which will force delete the branch.

Working with Remote Repositories

So far we have worked only with a local repository. While it is great to keep our local code under version control, having a remote repository allows us to collaborate with others and keep our code in two places.

Let's set up a remote Git server on our development VM we created in Recipe 37, *Setting Up a Virtual Machine*, on page 272. We can save ourselves the extra step of having to type our password whenever we log in or transfer files by creating SSH keys. Creating an SSH key and placing it on the server will allow us to authenticate quickly and without a password every time we want to push to our remote repository.

SSH keys consist of two components: a private key that we keep to ourselves and a public key we give to another server. When we log in to that server, it checks to see whether our key is authorized, and then our local system proves we are who we say we are by matching the public key with the private key. With Git, this handshaking process is all done transparently during the login process.

Before we continue, you should check to see whether you have any SSH keys on your system. Try to change directories into ~/.ssh. If you get a message saying the directory doesn't exist, then you'll need to generate keys. If you see files like id_rsa and id_rsa.pub, then you already have keys, and you can skip the next step.

Let's generate a new SSH key with the ssh-keygen command. We'll pass our email address, which will be placed into the key as a comment.

```
$ ssh-keygen -t rsa -C "webdev@awesomeco.com"
```

The comment will help us or other server administrators quickly identify who owns the key when it is uploaded to a server.

The ssh-keygen program will ask you for a place to store the SSH key; you can simply hit the Enter key to save it in the default location. It will also ask you to enter a passphrase. This adds an additional layer of security to the key, but we'll just leave it blank for now. Simply press the Enter key again.

Now that we have our keys generated, let's add them to our VM. We can pipe our local public key into the file authorized_keys on the server. This lets the VM know that our machine can have access.

```
$ cat ~/.ssh/id_rsa.pub | ssh webdev@192.168.1.100 \
"mkdir ~/.ssh; cat >> ~/.ssh/authorized_keys"
```

After executing this command, our server will ask for our password to make sure this is a legitimate request. After the command finishes, we can test our key by trying to SSH into the VM:

```
$ ssh webdev@192.168.1.100
```

and this time it will not ask us for our password.

Now that we're logged in to our VM, we use Ubuntu's package manager to install Git on the server:

```
$ sudo apt-get install git-core
```

And now we can create a "bare" repository on the VM, which is nothing more than a directory, usually with a .git extension, since this makes it easier for us to identify these. Then, inside the directory, we use the git command to initialize the folder, using the --bare switch.

```
$ mkdir website.git
$ cd website.git
$ git init --bare
```

With the repository created on the remote machine, we can log out of the VM by typing exit.

Back on our local machine, let's add the location of our remote repository and push up our *master* branch.

```
$ git remote add origin ssh://webdev@192.168.1.100/~/website.git
$ git push origin master
```

Let's say we wanted to work on a new feature with another developer. We can create a branch for this new feature called *new_feature* and then work on our design implementation. Once our design work is done, we can push the branch to the remote repository.

```
$ git checkout -b new_feature
$ git push origin new_feature
```

Now that we've pushed our branch, let's see what branches are out on the remote repository.

```
$ git branch -r
```

We'll end up with a list of branches. We won't see *layout_a* and *layout_b* because we deleted them locally, and we never pushed them out.

```
origin/HEAD -> origin/master
origin/new_feature
origin/master
```

To get our developer access to our Git repository, we can have him clone the full project. After he clones the whole project, we can have him check out the *new_feature* branch. Lastly, he can make sure he is up to-date on the project by pulling the remote branch from the server into his local branch.

```
$ git clone ssh://webdev@192.168.1.100/~/website.git
$ git checkout -b new_feature
$ git pull origin new_feature
```

With the branch on the developer machine also, the cycle begins again. Git gives us the power to work side by side on the same code and merge the changes with ease, like we did locally earlier in the chapter.

Further Exploration

Now that you have explored the basics of Git, you might start seeing other uses for it. In this recipe, we worked only with text files, but Git supports any type of file. You could use Git to version control your Photoshop documents, so you can easily maintain multiple versions as you build out designs. You can explore how to pull out previous versions of files, so you can recover that change your boss didn't like last week but wants to look at one more time.

You can also use Git to collaborate on open source projects with others. For example, you can go out to GitHub[24] and find an open source project like

---

24. http://www.github.com

jQuery (or one of the other libraries you've learned about in this book) and clone it, which pulls it down to your computer as a Git repository. You can then use techniques such as branching to develop new features for that project, which you could then submit these new features back to the original maintainers to help the community grow.

Also See

- Recipe 36, *Using Dropbox to Host a Static Site*, on page 268
- Recipe 37, *Setting Up a Virtual Machine*, on page 272
- *Pragmatic Version Control Using Git* [Swi08]

## CHAPTER 6

Testing Recipes

We need to ship, but we have to ship code that *works*. We often ensure our apps do what we want them to do by testing them in the browser manually. Sometimes we'll get other people to test things for us. In these recipes, we'll explore how to debug our code as we build it and also how to create repeatable acceptance tests that we can run whenever we make changes to our code so we can see whether things still work the way they did before.

Recipe 31

Debugging JavaScript

Problem

Some changes were recently made to our site, and some the JavaScript has stopped working as expected and nobody knows what happened or how to fix it. We need to figure out what's broken and what needs to be done to get everything working as it should.

Ingredients

- A modern browser
- Firebug Lite[1]

Solution

Finding out what is happening inside JavaScript code can be a time-consuming, tedious process without the right tools. Fortunately, there are multiple options available to us to aid in inspecting the code. Many browsers now include a console that allows us to run JavaScript from a command line, interact with the elements of the page, and see how things work without having to save the page and reload it every time we make a change. Even older browsers that don't include a console can use Firebug Lite, a JavaScript bookmarklet that creates a console in the browser for you and works in all major browsers.

Firebug Lite provides all that we need for this chapter, so we won't get in to the differences between the native tools available in each browser. Everything that we'll do with Firebug Lite should be available in the native tools as well as extensions, including the full Firebug extension for Firefox. We'll use Firebug so that you can use your browser of choice in these tests, but feel free to use the tools provided with the browser as well. The names of the tools and the labels on buttons may vary slightly, but the concept will remain the same.

---

1. http://getfirebug.com/firebuglite

> \|/ **Joe asks:**
> ஃ̆ **What If I Want to Use a Built-in Tool or Browser Extension?**
>
> Firebug Lite lets us do everything covered in this chapter, but more advanced tools are available for digging deeper into the code and improving performance. Here's how to get at some of them.
>
> - Chrome: View > Developer > JavaScript Console
> - Safari: Safari > Preferences > Advanced > Show Develop menu in menu bar and *then* Develop > Show Web Inspector
> - Firefox: Install Firebug[a]
> - Firefox: Tools > Web Console will load a JavaScript console without Firebug
> - IE: Install IE Developer Toolbar[b]
>
> _____
>
> a.   http://getfirebug.com
> b.   http://www.microsoft.com/download/en/details.aspx?id=18359

The Basics of Firebug

Once Firebug Lite has been added to our bookmark bar, we just need to click it to open the Firebug console on the bottom of the browser window. This console will enable us to run JavaScript and inspect page elements in the browser so we can see what happens when our code is run.

Let's get an idea of how the console works by creating an alert box on the page, just to make sure everything is working properly. In the bottom of window after the >>> type alert('Pretty neat!'); and hit Enter. You'll see an alert box with the message in it like Figure 48, *Executing JavaScript in Firebug*, on page 230.

Firebug also gives us the ability to inspect the rendered HTML, the CSS, and the even the DOM, as shown in Figure 49, *Inspecting elements in Firebug*, on page 231. We can click the inspect button on the top left of the Firebug console and then move the cursor to any element in the page. The left pane shows the current element's location in the HTML, and the right pane shows its CSS. When we click an element, we can begin to inspect and manipulate the element inline, make changes to CSS, or switch to the DOM tab to check the attributes of the element.

Firebug can do much more, but this basic overview covers everything we'll need to start debugging our Javascript. Visit http://getfirebug.com to learn more about what Firebug can do.

```
>>> alert('Pretty neat!');
```

Figure 48—Executing JavaScript in Firebug

Debugging with Firebug

Now that we've looked in to Firebug's basics, it's time to fix that broken site we talked about at the beginning of this recipe. Someone has made some changes to the code from Recipe 5, *Creating and Styling Inline Help Dialogs*, on page 24, and now the links aren't being converted. Unfortunately, we didn't use Git,[4] and nobody has a copy of the previous version of the code, so we have to figure out what went wrong. To get our version running, we need to download the files from Recipe 5, *Creating and Styling Inline Help Dialogs*, on page 24 and replace the contents of helper-text.js with helper-text-broken.js.

```
javascriptdebugging/helper-text-broken.js
function display_help_for(element) {
  url = $(element).attr("href"); //The URL to load via AJAX
  help_text_element =
    "#_"+$(element).attr("id")+"_"+
    $(element).attr("data-style");
  //If the content is already loaded, don't get it again
  if ($(help_text_element).html() == "") {
    $.get(url, { },
      function(data){
        $(help_text_element).html(data);
```

---

4. Learn about source control in Recipe 30, *Managing Files Using Git*, on page 216.

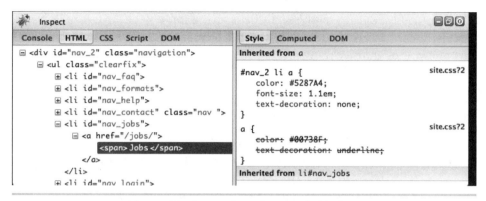

Figure 49—Inspecting elements in Firebug

```
      if ($(element).attr("data-style") == "dialog") {
        activate_dialog_for(element,$(element).attr("data-modal"));
      }
      toggle_display_of(help_text_element);
    });
  }
  else { toggle_display_of(help_text_element); }
}
```

When we load the page with the broken JavaScript, we see right away that the link text is not being replaced. Recall that we were setting that link in the append_help_to() function, replacing the HTML of the link element with our icon. Something is breaking in this function, perhaps preventing the code from executing that line. Let's check by calling it ourselves. Since the function is expecting an element to be passed, we'll use the Inspect option to grab the ID of the link on the page, and then we'll switch back to the console and call append_help_to($('#help_link_1'));.

Nothing happened. To confirm that we're in the right place and that the code is executing, let's log information back to the console. We can do this by calling console.log() in helper-text-broken.js, which will print whatever is passed to it in the console.

javascriptdebugging/helper-text-broken.js
```
helperDiv.setAttribute("title", title);

console.log(element);
console.log(helperDiv);
console.log(icon);

$(element).after(helperDiv);
$(element).html(icon)
```

The value passed in console.log() can be a string, an object, or a function call. In this case, we want to take a look at the element that we're interacting with and the values that we're inserting into the page to see whether any of them are the culprit.

Once we've updated our code, we'll need to refresh the page and then open Firebug and run append_help_to($('#help_link_1')); again, as shown in Figure 50, *Inspecting elements in Firebug*, on page 233.

We were expecting to see three things returned by our calls to console.log(): the element we're working with, the <div> that we insert for the helper text, and the value for our icon replacement. Instead, we see only the first two, and the icon replacement value is being printed as undefined, which indicates that our icon value is not being set properly.

javascriptdebugging/helper-text-broken.js
```
Line 1 function set_icon_to(help_icon) {
   2   is_image = /jpg|jpeg|png|gif$/
   3   if (help_icon = undefined)
   4     { icon = "[?]"; }
   5   else if (is_image.test(help_icon))
   6     { icon = "<img src='"+help_icon+"'>"; }
   7   else
   8     { icon = help_icon; }
   9 }
```

When we look at the set_icon_to() function, we see what has gone wrong. On line 3, we're setting help_icon to undefined with a single = rather than a double == for comparing help_icon to see whether it already is undefined. Let's fix that and reload the page to see what happens.

```
if (help_icon == undefined)
```

Everything looks good now! help_icon is being set properly, and we're good to go. Thanks to Firebug, we were able to easily ensure that our functions were being called, check the properties of different variables and elements, and figure out what was happening in our code.

Further Exploration

When we called console.log(), we passed in an element at one point. Run it again and try clicking the entry in the console. We get the same effect as when we inspect and click an element in the page. This can be very helpful when we're writing new JavaScript, because it helps ensure that we're working with the element we expected. Additionally, we can use the CSS and DOM tabs in the

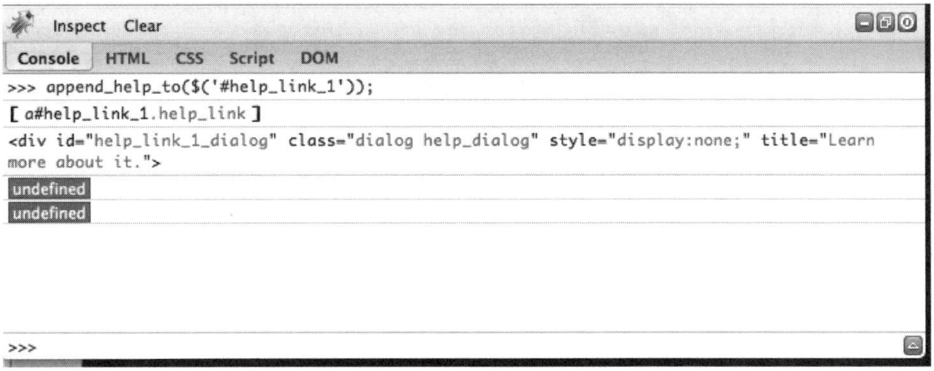

Figure 50—Inspecting elements in Firebug

right tab to confirm that any attributes that were changed by JavaScript were set as expected.

All of the JavaScript we ran in the console was single-line calls. What if we wanted to write a function using Firebug? On the far-right side of the console's text entry is an icon with a triangle on it. Clicking that gives us a split-pane interface so we can write JavaScript functions with line breaks and then click Run and see what happens. This is great for testing new function ideas out before messing with existing code on the page.

Writing tests for our JavaScript would've helped us quickly find this problem. A thorough test suite, as discussed in Recipe 35, *Testing JavaScript with Jasmine*, on page 255, helps us quickly track down the effects of changing code. Take a look at the chapter and try writing tests for Recipe 5, *Creating and Styling Inline Help Dialogs*, on page 24, or any of the other JavaScript chapters in the book.

Also See

- Recipe 35, *Testing JavaScript with Jasmine*, on page 255
- Recipe 5, *Creating and Styling Inline Help Dialogs*, on page 24

Recipe 32

Tracking User Activity with Heatmaps

Problem

When running a promotion or redesigning a site, it's helpful to know what works and what doesn't so we know where to spend our time. We need to quickly identify the most used regions of our page.

Ingredients

- A server running PHP
- ClickHeat[5]

Solution

We can track where our users click the page and display the results in a graphical overlay called a *heatmap*, giving us an at-a-glance idea of the most-used parts of our page. While there are several commercial products that can create heatmaps based on user activity, we'll use the open source ClickHeat script because setting it up on modern web hosts is almost as easy as using a commercial solution.

Let's use ClickHeat to solve an internal dispute. One of our clients is launching a new product, and the two partners are at odds on whether the "Sign Up" or "Learn More" button is actually useful. These buttons are placed right next to each other on the interface. We can easily add some tracking to this page to see which one is getting clicked more.

Setting Up ClickHeat

ClickHeat needs PHP to work, but we can use it against any website we want. We just need to download ClickHeat from the project's web page and place ClickHeat's scripts in a PHP-enabled folder on our server. For this recipe, we'll use a virtual machine running on our own network at http://192.168.1.100. Check out Recipe 37, *Setting Up a Virtual Machine*, on page 272 to learn how to build your own virtual machine for testing.

---

5. http://www.labsmedia.com/clickheat/index.html

When we unzip the ClickHeat archive, we'll find a clickheat folder. We'll upload this folder into /var/www, the folder on our virtual machine that contains our existing web pages. Since our virtual machine has SSH enabled, we can copy the files up with a single command by using scp:

```
scp -R clickheat webdev@192.168.1.100:/var/www/clickheat
```

Or we can transfer them over to the server's /var/www folder with an SFTP client like FileZilla.

Once we've copied the code out to the server, we need to modify the permissions on a few folders within the clickheat folder structure so that we can write the logs and modify permissions. We'll log into our server and use the chmod command to make the config, tmp, and logs folders writeable:

```
$ ssh webdev@192.168.1.100
$ cd /var/www/clickheat
$ chmod -R 777 config logs cache
$ exit
```

With the files in place, we can complete the configuration by browsing to http://192.168.1.100/clickheat/index.php. ClickHeat will verify that it can write to the configuration folder, and we'll be able to follow the link to configure the rest of the settings.

We can leave the values alone for this case, but we'll enter values for the administrator username and password. Once we click the Check Configuration button and we see no errors, we're done configuring ClickHeat. Now let's attach it to our web page so we can capture some data.

Tracking Clicks and Viewing Results

To begin tracking clicks, we simply need to add a few lines of JavaScript to our home page, right above the closing <body> tag:

heatmaps/index.html
```
<script type="text/javascript"
  src="http://192.168.1.100/clickheat/js/clickheat.js"></script>
<script type="text/javascript">
  clickHeatSite = 'AwesomeCo';
  clickHeatGroup = 'buttons';
  clickHeatServer = 'http://192.168.1.100/clickheat/click.php';
  initClickHeat();
</script>
```

We're defining a "site" and a "group" for this heatmap. This lets us track multiple sites.

Figure 51—Our heatmap

When we redeploy our page to our server, clicks from our users will be recorded to ClickHeat's logs. After a few hours, we can visit http://192.168.1.100/clickheat/index.php to see the results of our test, which look similar to Figure 51, *Our heatmap*, on page 236.

It looks like more people are clicking the Sign Up! button!

Further Exploration

ClickHeat is relatively low-maintenance once it's running, but there are a lot of options we can adjust, such as the number of times we'll record a click from the same user. We can also configure ClickHeat to record its results to the Apache logs and then parse them out with a script, which is a great approach for servers where PHP might be too slow to invoke on each request. Finally, ClickHeat can be set up on its own server, so it can collect data from more than one site or domain. Check out the documentation at the ClickHeat website for more options or just explore its interface.

If you'd like something with a little more power, you might want to investigate hosted commercial solutions like CrazyEgg,[6] which has similar functionality.

Finally, when you're looking at heatmaps of your own sites, you might get a little unexpected guidance from your users. If you notice a bunch of click activity on part of your page that doesn't have a link, consider making that region active. Heatmaps can oftentimes show you things you never saw before.

Also See

- Recipe 37, *Setting Up a Virtual Machine*, on page 272

---

6.   http://www.crazyegg.com/

Recipe 33

Browser Testing with Selenium

Problem

Testing is a hard and tedious process. As websites become more complex, it becomes more important to have tests that are repeatable and consistent. Without automated testing, our only chance at having a consistent working website was to have a top-notch QA person that worked long hours and had very long checklists. That process could be painfully slow. We need to speed up the testing process and create tests we can run on-demand so that we can verify things work the way we want today, as well as several months from now when we start adding new features.

Ingredients

- Firefox[7]
- Selenium IDE[8]
- QEDServer (for our test server); see *QEDServer*, on page xiv

Solution

We can use automated tools to test our web projects in addition to manual testing. The Selenium IDE plug-in for Firefox lets us build tests in a graphical environment by recording our actions as we use a website. As we move through a site, we can create *assertions*, or little tests that ensure that certain things exist on the pages. We can then play them back any time we want, creating a set of automated, repeatable tests.

Our development team has built a product management website, and our boss wants some safeguards in place to make sure this will always work. The development team has added some unit testing to their business logic underneath, but we're tasked with building some automated tests for the user interface. Automated testing will give both the development team and us peace of mind if we make changes to the UI down the road.

---

7. http://getfirefox.com
8. http://seleniumhq.org/download/

Setting Up Our Test Environment

First, we need to install the Firefox web browser. Go to the Firefox website and follow the instructions for your operating system.

Once we have Firefox working, we need to get the Selenium IDE installed. Open Firefox, visit the Selenium website,[9] and download the latest version.[10]

With the tools installed, let's write our first test.

Creating Our First Test

We'll create our test by recording our movements with the Selenium IDE against our test server, which we'll run on our own machine using QEDServer. Start QEDServer and then launch Firefox. Go to http://localhost:8080 to bring up the test server, where you'll see an interface like the one in Figure 52, *Our home page screen*, on page 239.

Since this is a product management application, we'll start off with a test to make sure we always have the "Manage products" link on the home page and that the link goes where we expect it to go.

Open up the Selenium IDE by selecting it from the Tools menu in Firefox. To start recording, we need to make sure the Record button is active. Then, in the browser, we click the "Manage products" link. As we click the link, we'll see some items begin to show up in Selenium IDE, just like in Figure 53, *Our first test with the Selenium IDE*, on page 240. At the top, the Base URL is now set to http://localhost:8080, and then we see one of the most useful commands in the Selenium IDE: the clickAndWait() method. When we use web applications, we spend a lot of time clicking on links or buttons and waiting for pages to load. That is exactly what this command does. Every time we click a link, the Selenium IDE adds this method to our test along with some text that identifies the link. When we play the test back, it uses this method and the associated link text to drive the browser.

The Selenium IDE shows us the three parts of a Selenium test action. The first is Command, which is the action that Selenium is performing. The second is Target, which is the item that Selenium is performing the action on. The third is Value, which we'll use to set a value for fields that take inputs, such as when we're filling out a text box or selecting a radio button.

---

9. http://seleniumhq.org/download/
10. If you have Firefox 4, you may need to install the Add-On Compatibility Reporter Extension version 0.8.2.

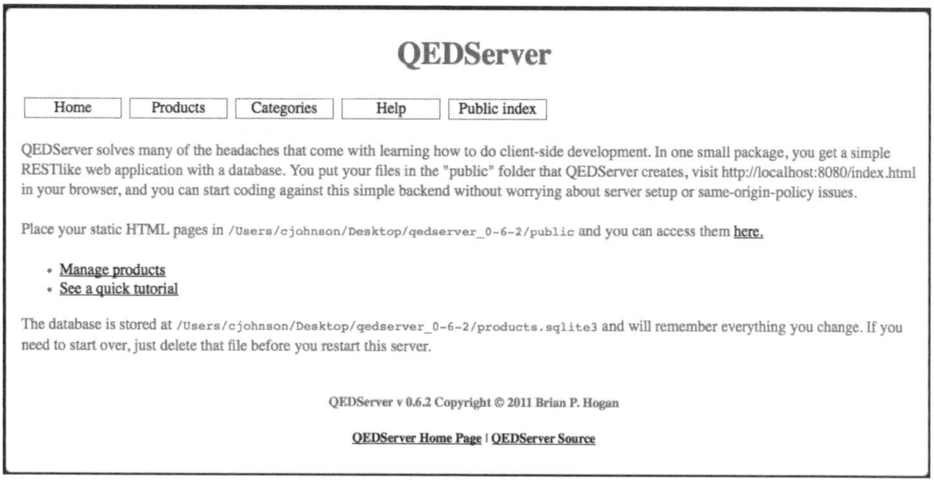

Figure 52—Our home page screen

A powerful part of Selenium is its locator functions. We can use these to find an element on the page not only by its id but also via the DOM, an XPath query, a CSS selector, or even plain text. When we clicked "Manage products," the target we used is link= Manage products. The link= is the selector that allows us to choose a block of text to perform an action on. One thing we should keep in mind is that locators default to looking for an ID first followed by that string of text. Identifying elements for testing with IDs is a great way to speed up your tests and improve accuracy, but it can make tests harder to read.

Now that we have an understanding of locators, let's look at what the commands do. Commands are the actions that Selenium performs when we run a test. Selenium can do anything a human would do, with one small exception —it can't upload a file without some significant modifications. The ability to manipulate a browser the way a human would allows us to simulate human interaction, giving our tests the ability to flex our code realistically.

Let's test that once we click "Manage products" we are taken to a page where "Products" is present. First we need to click the "Manage products" link. Next we want to make sure the word "Products" is on the screen. To add a test for that, locate Products on the web page and right-click it. Choose the command verifyTextPresent from the context menu. We could also do this by using the Selenium IDE and clicking in the whitespace just below the clickAndWait() command and using the form fields to choose our command, target, and value, but the Selenium IDE adds some test helpers to the context menu, which makes the process much faster.

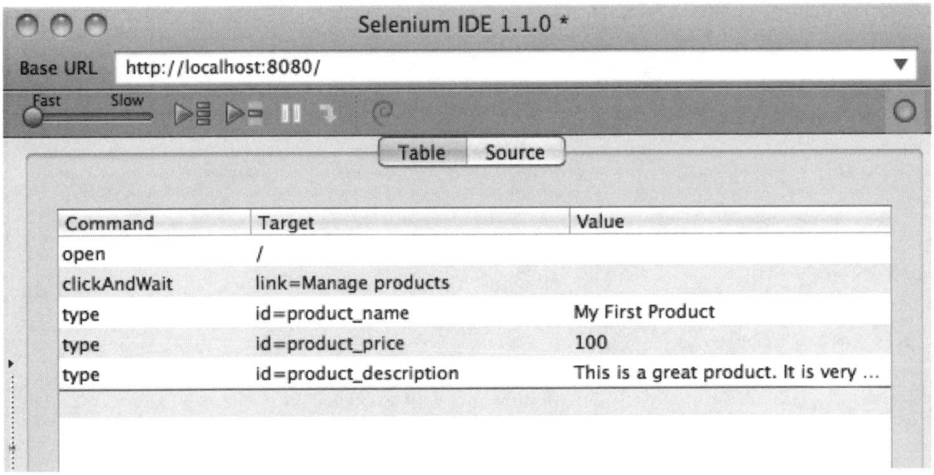

Figure 53—Our first test with the Selenium IDE

We can save this test by choosing Save Test Case from the Selenium IDE's File menu. We can then run the test by clicking the play button below the Base URL window. As the test runs, the browser moves through our pages, and the background color for each step changes to green as it passes. If a step fails, it will turn red and will also show some bold red text in the log window below that with descriptions of what went wrong. This visual cue lets us know something went wrong so we can address it.

Creating an Advanced Test

We want to make sure that our product management application functions, and we can create a new product and delete a product. We also want to make sure we can view the details of a product. This is a multistep process; let's use Selenium to automate it.

Let's go back to the home page at http://localhost:8080 and start up the Selenium IDE. Click the "Manage products" link and wait for the page to load. Then select the "New Product" text, right-click it, and select "verifyTextPresent New Product." Next, leave the form blank and click the Add Product button. Our application requires that we fill in at least some of the product details, so we now have a form that did not submit, along with an error message on the screen.

Let's make this part of our test. Right-click the "The product was not saved" error message, and use the verifyTextPresent command to add an assertion that verifies that the error message show up on the Products page.

Now that we've shown that our error message works, we can now fill out all of the information in the form and submit it. The Selenium IDE adds a row to our test for each field we fill out. It also shows the value we typed in.

When we submit the form this time, it takes us back to the products page where we'll see the message "Created." We can use the verifyTextPresent() command again to make sure this text is displayed.

Now we have a feature-rich example that we can save and run later. If anyone changes the site, we'll know what's broken, simply by replaying the test.

Further Exploration

Now that we have test coverage, we can take this to the next level by automating our entire test suite. We currently have to run each test individually by loading it into the Selenium IDE, and this breaks down when we have a lot of tests. You'll want to investigate Selenium Remote Control and Selenium Grid,[11] which let you build automated test suites that run against multiple browsers.

And while Selenium IDE is primarily a testing tool, you could use it as an automation tool as well. For example, if you have a process that has a less-than-friendly user interface, such as a time-tracking system or a repetitive and clunky management console, you might try using Selenium IDE to save you some keystrokes and mouse clicks.

Also See

- Recipe 34, *Cucumber-Driven Selenium Testing*, on page 242
- Recipe 35, *Testing JavaScript with Jasmine*, on page 255

---

11. http://selenium-grid.seleniumhq.org/

Recipe 34

Cucumber-Driven Selenium Testing

Problem

Browser testing can be a tedious and time-consuming activity. In Recipe 33, *Browser Testing with Selenium*, on page 237, we learned how to build tests using Selenium IDE. Unfortunately, that limits our tests to Firefox only, which is only one of the browsers used to visit our site. We want to make sure that we can test in all of the browsers that might be used. Manually testing sites in multiple browsers would require having access to installations of every browser we want to test. What we need is a way to automate testing across multiple browsers without having to keep our own versions installed.

Ingredients

- Cucumber Testing Harness[12]
- QED Server[13]
- Sauce Labs Account[14]
- Sauce Connect[15]
- Bundler[16]

Solution

Our testing server has an administrative interface to manage products. We've tested it locally in Firefox and Safari but need to expand our tests to include several other browsers. Using a combination of tools, including Cucumber and Selenium, we can set up an automated multibrowser testing environment.

Tools

As we found out in Recipe 33, *Browser Testing with Selenium*, on page 237, Selenium is a great tool that simulates a user's experience on a website. In that recipe, we used the Selenium IDE to record our actions as we went

---

12. http://pragprog.com/book/wbdev/web-development-recipes
13. http://webdevelopmentrecipes.com/files/qedserver.zip
14. http://www.saucelabs.com
15. https://saucelabs.com/downloads/Sauce-Connect-latest.zip
16. http://gembundler.com/

through the site. Now we'll use Cucumber to extend Selenium by programming our tests.

In Recipe 35, *Testing JavaScript with Jasmine,* on page 255, we'll also look at behavior-driven development (BDD) and talk about its outside-in approach to test writing. Cucumber gives us a chance to take BDD to a higher level and include our business stakeholders. Cucumber tests are written in plain text, making them effective for communicating features and goals between business and technological stakeholders.

```
selenium2/cucumber_test/features/manage_products.feature
Line 1  Feature: Manage products with the QED Server
     2    Scenario: When I view the product details of a new product it should take me
     3            to the page where the product information is displayed
     4      Given I am on the Products management page
     5      And I created a product called "iPad 3" with a price of "500"
     6        dollars and a description of "My iPad 3 test product"
     7      When I view the details of "iPad 3"
     8      Then I should see "iPad 3"
     9      And I should see a price of "500"
    10      And I should see a description of "My iPad 3 test product"
```

As you can see, Cucumber uses regular language, which makes it easy to understand what the test covers.

As noted earlier, the Selenium IDE allows us to test only against Firefox. To test in all browsers, we have a couple of options: we can install every browser on our machine and manually test everything, or we can use a cloud-based Selenium testing service, like the one offered by Sauce Labs. To avoid the hassle of installing multiple browsers (during just the writing of this book both Firefox 5 and 6 have been released!), we'll use Sauce Labs to run our tests. Sauce Labs records our test runs, so we can play them back and watch both the passing and failing tests. These videos are also great for our stakeholders because they can see the application functioning without having to manually test it. At the time of writing, Sauce Labs provides every user with 200 testing minutes a month for free.

The tool that brings everything together is the Cucumber Testing Harness (CTH), which is a bare-bones framework developed to get people writing tests easily and quickly. Often the barrier to entry in testing is very high, which is the case with Cucumber and Selenium. Using tools like the CTH and Sauce Labs make that barrier lower and easier to overcome. Sauce Labs takes care of managing runaway Selenium processes and making sure remote controls are available for Cucumber to control. It also tests and makes available many versions of each browser, which helps us test the experience for users on older computers too. Not having to maintain all of these installs lets us focus on the testing. Additionally, because Sauce Labs is a cloud service, there is less strain on our local machine while running tests. The CTH helps by organizing code, managing dependencies, and providing hooks for working with Sauce Labs. We just have to modify a few configuration files, and then we can start running our tests.

Setting Up Our Environment

To use the CTH, we're going to need Ruby on our system. If you don't have Ruby set up yet, check out Appendix 1, *Installing Ruby*, on page 305 to get everything ready to go before proceeding with the rest of this chapter.

Since we're going to be using Sauce Labs OnDemand to run our tests, let's sign up for a free Sauce Labs account.[17]

The majority of our work is going to be done in the CTH. Download the CTH from the book's site,[18] and then extract cucumber_test.zip into a directory where our tests will live and run. After the CTH is extracted, let's open the shell and navigate to the directory it was saved on your computer.

Inside of the CTH, we have a Gemfile that holds a list of all the necessary Ruby gems we need to install for the CTH to work properly. To take advantage of the Gemfile, we'll first need a gem called bundler, which will read the Gemfile and install the rest of the gems for us. Let's install bundler and then run it in the shell.

```
$ gem install bundler
$ bundle install
```

Now that the gems installed, we can move on to the next part of our setup, adding our Sauce Labs API key to the CTH.

Log in to Sauce Labs and go to the My Account page to get your API key. At the time of writing, the View My API Key link shows the account's API key (see Figure 54, *Finding our Sauce Labs API key*, on page 245). Take this key and place it in the config/ondemand.yml file.

selenium2/cucumber_test/config/ondemand.yml
```
#---
username: my_sauce_user_name
access_key: my_super_secret_key
```

---

17. https://saucelabs.com/signup
18. http://pragprog.com/book/wbdev/web-development-recipes

Figure 54—Finding our Sauce Labs API key

The ondemand.yml will be used by the CTH when we run our tests against Sauce Labs. We'll replace the username with our Sauce Labs username.

To make things easier to keep track of, we can refer to a hostname in our tests. Since we're using our local testing server, let's use a hostname of "qedserver.local." We need to tell our computer that requests to that hostname where to go, so we'll add it to the hosts file. On OS X and Linux, open /etc/hosts or on Windows open C:\Windows\system32\drivers\etc\hosts, and add the following:

```
127.0.0.1 qedserver.local
```

Adding this line to our hosts file tells our computer to take requests for "qedserver.local" and direct them to 127.0.0.1, which is our local machine. Let's start up our testing server and test our hostfile by pointing our browser to http://qedserver.local:8080.

Next we need a way for Sauce Labs to talk to our test server. Luckily for us, it has created Sauce Connect,[21] which is a direct connection between the Sauce Labs servers and our machine. Once Sauce Connect is downloaded, we'll need to unzip it and navigate to that directory in a new shell and execute the Java jar with the following command, replacing "USERNAME" and "API_KEY" with our username and API key.

```
$ java -jar Sauce-Connect.jar USERNAME API_KEY
```

Now when we run tests on Sauce Labs servers, it'll be able to access our local machine without us having to know our public IP address or open ports on our router.

With the connection to Sauce Labs open, let's finish configuring our CTH. Inside of the configfolder is a cucumber.yml file. We're setting up a few default

---

21. https://saucelabs.com/downloads/Sauce-Connect-latest.zip

> \|/ **Joe asks:**
> ꙮ # What If We Want to Do Everything Locally?
>
> We could use the CTH on our local machine as well, but if we want to test more than
> just Firefox, some additional installs like Ant[a] and Selenium Grid[b] are required. Using
> a local install of Selenium Grid brings our testing barrier way up, because it can be
> a difficult tool to manage, but if an external solution isn't an option for you, it's defi-
> nitely possible to set everything up on your own computer or server.
>
> ———————
> a. http://ant.apache.org
> b. http://selenium-grid.seleniumhq.org/download.html

options that are common for all browsers and then adding specifics for each
of the browsers we want to test against.

selenium2/cucumber_test/config/cucumber.yml
```
<% defaults = "HOST_TO_TEST=http://qedserver.local
               APP_PORT=8080
               HUB=sauce" %>
```

Here we are defining a defaults variable that contains a string with several values.
HOST_TO_TEST is the URL of the application we are testing, which in this case is
our local QED Server. Since our test server runs on port 8080, we set that
in the APP_PORT declaration. The HUB declaration tells our test suite that we
want to use the *sauce* hub, which is handled by Sauce Labs.

Our main goal in setting this up is to have the ability to run multibrowser
tests. Next we can define profile flags that will easily let us switch between
browsers we want to test against. We want to support users of Internet
Explorer 7, 8, and 9 along with the latest versions of Safari, Firefox, and
Chrome. It is always good to use a naming convention, and with this many
browsers, it will really make it easier to quickly identify our profiles. We'll
start each profile name with sauce, since this test is going to run at Sauce
Labs, followed by a shorthand for the browser and operating system we're
testing on. For the IE7 profile, let's use sauce_ie7_03, where ie7 indicates Internet
Explorer 7, and 03 is short for Windows Server 2003.

selenium2/cucumber_test/config/cucumber.yml
```
sauce_ie7_03: BROWSER=iehta VERSION='7.' <%= defaults %>
sauce_ie8_03: BROWSER=iehta VERSION='8.' <%= defaults %>
sauce_ie9_08: BROWSER=ietha VERSION='9.' OS='Windows 2008'<%= defaults %>
sauce_f_03: BROWSER=firefox VERSION='3.' <%= defaults %>
sauce_s_03: BROWSER=safariproxy  VERSION='5.'   <%= defaults %>
sauce_c_03: BROWSER=googlechrome VERSION=' '    <%= defaults %>
```

Now we have a full set of browsers to be tested. We have kept most of our tests running on Windows Server 2003; the only exception is Internet Explorer 9, which is available only on Server 2008.[22] As we find other browser and server configurations that we need to test, we can add them to this list.

Writing Our First Test

For our first test, let's start with something simple: making sure we have the links "Manage products" and "See a quick tutorial" on our home page.

Cucumber tests are organized by features, in which the test focuses on a feature of our application. In a feature we describe the behavior of the application and group those behaviors into scenarios. Scenarios are written in a given, when, then pattern. This pattern clearly defines what the test is testing.

Given statements set the context of the test, saying "Don't worry about the flow before this; I am here and in this state." When statements describe an action that needs to take place. Then statements are the assertion of the test; they verify the result of the then statement is the desired result of the scenario.

Since our first feature is about the test server's home page, we'll put it in the qedserver_home_page.feature file. Let's start with a feature statement followed by a scenario for each of our two test cases.

```
selenium2/cucumber_test/features/qedserver_home_page.feature
Feature: Testing the QED Server home page to make sure we have the
  manage products link and the See a quick tutorial link

  Scenario: Verify the manage products link is on the home page
    Given I am on the QED Server home page
    Then I should see the "Manage products" link

  Scenario: Verify the See a quick tutorial link is on the home page
    Given I am on the QED Server home page
    Then I should see the "See a quick tutorial" link
```

This feature describes what we expect from the home page. It contains two scenarios, one for each of the links whose presence we want to test. Our scenarios in this case have only given and then statements. Later, in *Writing a More Complex Test*, on page 250, we'll cover some scenarios that perform actions.

With our feature written, let's run the test. This is where the profiles we created earlier will come into play. We're using the command $ cucumber -p sauce_f_03, which tells cucumber to use the sauce_f_03 or Firefox on Sauce Labs profile.

---

22. https://saucelabs.com/docs/sauce-ondemand/browsers

When we run the Cucumber features, we'll see a response in our shell like the following:

```
$ cucumber -p sauce_f

Using the sauce_f profile...
Feature: Testing the test server home page to make sure we have the
manage products link and the See a quick tutorial link

Scenario: Verify the manage products link is on the home page
# features/qedserver_home_page.feature:3
  Given I am on the QED Server home page
# features/qedserver_home_page.feature:4
  Then I should see the "manage products" link
# features/qedserver_home_page.feature:5

Scenario: Verify the See a quick tutorial link is on the home page
# features/qedserver_home_page.feature:7
  Given I am on the QED Server home page
# features/qedserver_home_page.feature:8
  Then I should see the "See a quick tutorial" link
# features/qedserver_home_page.feature:9

2 scenarios (2 undefined)
4 steps (4 undefined)
0m26.580s

You can implement step definitions for undefined steps with these snippets:

Given /^I am on the QED Server home page$/ do
  pending # express the regexp above with the code you wish you had
end

Then /^I should see the "([^"]*)" link$/ do |arg1|
  pending # express the regexp above with the code you wish you had
end
```

The Cucumber output shows us many things about our test. It tells us which profile was run and then displays the feature statement. Next we see the scenarios with the line number for each of the statements in the tests. After the scenarios, the output tells us about what happened in our test run. In this case, we had two scenarios, but two of them were undefined, and four steps, all four of which were also undefined. The last part of the output includes some stubbed code so we can get started implementing the steps required by the feature.

Next we'll implement the steps needed to make our features pass. Let's create a file called /features/step_definitions/qedserver_home_page_steps.rb to hold our step definitions, which consist of Ruby code that the features execute to drive Selenium to perform actions within the browser.

```
Given /^I am on the QED Server home page$/ do
  pending # express the regexp above with the code you wish you had
end

Then /^I should see the "([^"]*)" link$/ do |arg1|
  pending # express the regexp above with the code you wish you had
end
```

Now we have a step file defined, but it doesn't actually tell Selenium how to test anything. Let's update the pending lines to actually test the content of the page. The first step calls a given statement that requires our test to start from the home page. Then we'll use a Selenium locator for the next step to determine whether the link is there.

selenium2/cucumber_test/features/step_definitions/qedserver_home_page_steps.rb
```
Line 1 Given /^I am on the QED Server home page$/ do
   2    @selenium.open("/")
   3  end
   4  Then /^I should see the "([^"]*)" link$/ do |link_text|
   5    @selenium.element?("link=#{link_text}").should be_true
   6  end
```

On lines 2 and 5, we started off with the @selenium object, which is made available by the CTH to pass commands to Selenium. On line 2, we used the open() method and passed in a string of "/". Because we set our HOST_TO_TEST in the CTH's cucumber.yml file, Selenium knows that the base URL it should use is http://qedserver.local:8080.

On line 5, we use the element?() method with a locator string. Without going too deeply into the underlying Ruby, we are building the locator string dynamically with string interpolation, which lets us use a variable called link_text rather than a hard-coded value. The link_text is pulled out of the then statement with a regular expression.

Now that we have some tests completed, let's run our tests again and watch them pass.

```
$ cucumber -p sauce_f
....
2 scenarios (2 passed)
4 steps (4 passed)
0m36.439s
```

Now that we have test coverage on our home page, let's head over to Sauce Labs and watch the test runs and look at the information they provide about each test. By clicking the My Jobs[23] link, we see a list of all the tests we ran.

---

23. https://saucelabs.com/jobs

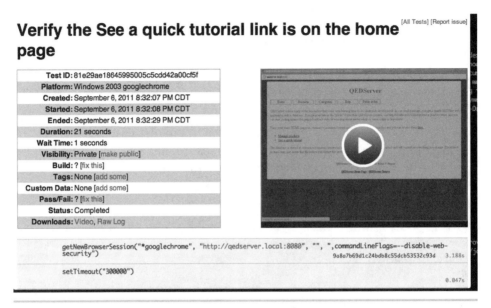

Figure 55—Post-test run information

Clicking the name of a test, we get to see some information similar to that shown in Figure 55, *Post-test run information*, on page 250 about the test run along with the video of our test.

Writing a More Complex Test

Simple tests are great, but we need to make sure that our product management interface works correctly too. Let's create a feature to test that, beginning with creating another feature file, manage_products.feature. Our feature statement will be "Manage products with the QED Server." We can test our entire workflow with a scenario describing the ability to create a new product and view its details.

```
selenium2/cucumber_test/features/manage_products.feature
Line 1  Feature: Manage products with the QED Server
    2    Scenario: When I view the product details of a new product it should take me
    3           to the page where the product information is displayed
    4      Given I am on the Products management page
    5      And I created a product called "iPad 3" with a price of "500"
    6        dollars and a description of "My iPad 3 test product"
    7      When I view the details of "iPad 3"
    8      Then I should see "iPad 3"
    9      And I should see a price of "500"
   10      And I should see a description of "My iPad 3 test product"
```

We are using the same basic structure that we used in our first test. We start off with the feature statement followed by a scenario and then the test lines. On line 5, we are adding an additional statement to our vocabulary, and, which we can use to chain additional statement together. We also are using and statements on lines 9 and 10. We can determine when to use an and by reading the statements out loud; if there is a natural pause or and sounds good while reading it, then it's a good time to use one. On line 7, we're describing an action by using a when statement.

Continuing down our test writing path, let's run our new feature to generate the needed step definitions. We want to target a specific feature; this is accomplished by adding the file we want to run to the end of the Cucumber command. To spice things up, let's run this feature using Google Chrome this time.

```
$ cucumber -p sauce_c_03 features/manage_products.feature
...
1 scenario (1 undefined)
6 steps (1 skipped, 5 undefined)
0m9.701s

You can implement step definitions for undefined steps with these snippets:

Given /^I am on the Products management page$/ do
  pending # express the regexp above with the code you wish you had
end

Given /^I created a product called "([^"]*)" with a price of "([^"]*)"
dollars and a description of "([^"]*)"$/ do |arg1, arg2, arg3|
  pending # express the regexp above with the code you wish you had
end

When /^I view the details of "([^"]*)"$/ do |arg1|
  pending # express the regexp above with the code you wish you had
end

Then /^I should see a price of "([^"]*)"$/ do |arg1|
  pending # express the regexp above with the code you wish you had
end

Then /^I should see a description of "([^"]*)"$/ do |arg1|
  pending # express the regexp above with the code you wish you had
end
```

We used the sauce_c_03 profile and then specified the file we wanted to run. Since we haven't set anything up for this test yet, it didn't pass. Let's create a new step file manage_products_steps.rb alongside qedserver_home_page_steps.rb and paste in the step stubs that Cucumber generated for us so that we can get everything passing.

Let's work our way down the list of step definitions we need to implement. Our first definition is similar to our last set of step definitions where we need to open a specific page.

```
selenium2/cucumber_test/features/step_definitions/manage_products_steps.rb
Given /^I am on the Products management page$/ do
  @selenium.open("/products")
end
```

In this step, we run the same open() method but told Selenium we wanted to go load "/products" instead of "/" this time.

The next step definition will fill out the form and submit the form to add the product to the database. We're accomplishing this by telling Selenium to place each of the values from our given statement into its correct box on the page and then clicking the Add Product button.

```
selenium2/cucumber_test/features/step_definitions/manage_products_steps.rb
Line 1 Given /^I created a product called "([^"]*)" with a price of "([^"]*)"
   2 dollars and a description of "([^"]*)"$/ do |name, price, description|
   3   @selenium.type("product_name", name)
   4   @selenium.type("product_price", price)
   5   @selenium.type("product_description", description)
   6   @selenium.click("css=input[value='Add Product']")
   7 end
```

By changing the variable names at the end of the given statement, we can keep track of what values are being passed in. Name, price, and description are easier to recognize than arg1, arg2, and arg3. On line 3, we used the method type(), which tells Selenium to place the contents of the name into the textbox with an ID of product_name. On lines 4 and 5, we did the same thing by setting the value and textbox ID.

To tell Selenium to click the Add Product button, we use the click() method, which requires us to pass in a locator to identify the button. Here we use a CSS selector to find the button to click. A CSS selector lets us target elements the same way we would in CSS and then evaluates an expression like value='Add Product' and determines whether this is the element we want. The locator we used will find a button on the page with a value of Add Product.

With a product created, we need to make sure it shows up in the list and confirm that there is a details link we can click to show us the details page.

```
selenium2/cucumber_test/features/step_definitions/manage_products_steps.rb
When /^I view the details of "([^"]*)"$/ do |product_name|
  @selenium.is_element_present("css=td:nth(0):contains(#{product_name})")
  @selenium.click("css=td:nth(1) > a:contains(Details)")
end
```

Like last time, we changed the variable name from arg1 to product_name, making it easier to recognize the content of the variable. To determine whether the product name is present, we use the is_element_present() method, which takes a locator, similar to what we used to locate the Add Product button earlier. The CSS locator we're using looks for a <td> that contains the value of the product_name variable. To click the details link for that product, we used a CSS locator to get the correct <a> for the link, which is contained in the second child <td> in the row.

Our final two step definitions of our feature perform similar tasks: checking for text to be present on the page. The CTH provides a couple step definitions for us, one of which will help us with our feature. The step definition Then I should see "some text" uses the text?() method to find the passed-in block of text on the page. Let's use this included step definition to simplify our test implementation by calling the step from inside of our step.

```
selenium2/cucumber_test/features/step_definitions/manage_products_steps.rb
Then /^I should see a price of "([^"]*)"$/ do |price|
  Then "I should see \"#{price}\""
end

Then /^I should see a description of "([^"]*)"$/ do |description|
  Then "I should see \"#{description}\""
end
```

In both of the tests, we use the same syntax and pass in our variable to the string. Because Cucumber uses regular expression matching, we needed to escape the quotes inside of string with a \. Let's run our tests with Google Chrome again and watch them pass.

```
$ cucumber -p sauce_c_03
....
3 scenarios (3 passed)
10 steps (10 passed)
0m43.184s
```

With our tests running and passing on Google Chrome, we can try other browser combinations such as Internet Explorer 7 by running $ cucumber -p sauce_ie7_03 or Safari by running $ cucumber -p sauce_s_03. Seeing our tests pass against other browsers gives us confidence that our application is performing in each environment. We can also look at the screenshots to make sure our styles are rendering correctly for each environment.

Further Exploration

Our example tests some of the functionality of our test server. We can add more tests to cover other parts of the application, such as deleting a product. We can also take the Cucumber Testing Harness and modify it for use on a separate site.

We can also explore some of the other features from Sauce Labs such as Sauce Scout. Sauce Scout will allow us to look at our website through our tunnel in any of the supported browsers at Sauce Labs. Scout actually lets us drive the browser and click around when we need to troubleshoot something.

Rather than using Sauce Labs, you could use the selenium-rc gem[24] to run the tests locally against browsers you have installed on your own computer. As mentioned, be aware that this can be a very system-intensive way to run your tests.

Also See

- Recipe 33, *Browser Testing with Selenium*, on page 237
- Recipe 35, *Testing JavaScript with Jasmine*, on page 255
- *The Cucumber Book: Behaviour-Driven Development for Testers and Developers* [WH11]

---

24. http://selenium.rubyforge.org/getting-started.html

Recipe 35

Testing JavaScript with Jasmine

Problem

The flexibility and dynamic nature of JavaScript can make it difficult to accurately test well because it is a moving target. You could do things like using the Selenium IDE (Recipe 33, *Browser Testing with Selenium*, on page 237), but that still requires manual JavaScript debugging (Recipe 31, *Debugging JavaScript*, on page 228) and doesn't give us direct information into what function is broken. What we really need it is a full testing framework for JavaScript.

Ingredients

- jQuery
- Jasmine[25]
- Jasmine-jQuery[26]
- Firefox[27]

Solution

Jasmine is a JavaScript testing framework created by Pivotal Labs to allow behavior-driven development (BDD) in JavaScript. Jasmine's syntax is very similar to that of Ruby's RSpec testing framework[28] (you can find out more about RSpec and BDD in *The RSpec Book* [CADH09]). BDD is an outside-in approach to testing that focuses on behaviors rather than structure.

For our first fully tested JavaScript application, let's build a to-do application using jQuery. We'll still use the test-driven development (TDD) approach by writing the test and then implementing the code to make it pass—the only difference being we'll describe behaviors and not specific elements of code.

To get started, let's create a folder for our application and then download and extract into that folder the Jasmine testing libraries from GitHub. We also

---

25. http://pivotal.github.com/jasmine/downloads/jasmine-standalone-1.0.2.zip
26. https://github.com/downloads/velesin/jasmine-jquery/jasmine-jquery-1.2.0.js
27. http://www.mozilla.com/en-US/firefox/new/
28. http://rspec.info/

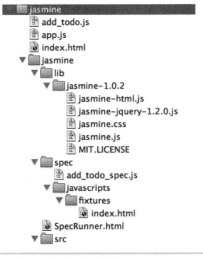

Figure 56—Our folder structure

want to get the Jasmine-jQuery plug-in and put that in the jasmine/lib/jasmine-1.0.2 folder. The Jasmine-jQuery plug-in gives us some additional functionality that we'll use later when we work with fixtures.

Inside of the Jasmine folder we find three folders and a SpecRunner.html file. We can remove the two .js files inside the spec and src folders. These are sample files that come with the Jasmine libraries so we don't need them.

Now we can build out our tests and application. We'll start with the basics and add items as we need them. Let's add add_todo_spec.js inside the spec folder. Our directory structure should look like Figure 56, *Our folder structure*, on page 256. To get oriented, let's take a look at the mock-up of the application (Figure 57, *Our to-do list mock-up*, on page 257).

Writing Our First Test

Let's start off by creating a describe() block, which is a way to group related tests. As described in our mock-up (Figure 57, *Our to-do list mock-up*, on page 257), the primary function of our application is adding an item to the to-do list. Here you may notice the similarities to Ruby's RSpec framework. We have a describe() function that takes a message and another function. Inside of the describe() block we'll add our examples that describe specific behaviors.

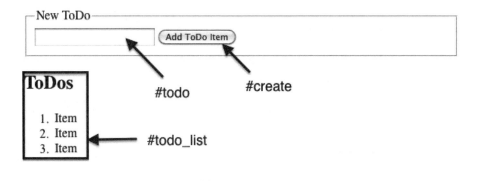

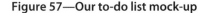

Figure 57—Our to-do list mock-up

```
jasmine/jasmine/spec/add_todo_spec.js
Line 1 describe('I add a ToDo', function () {
2    it('should call the addToDo function when create is clicked', function () {
3    });
4    it('should trigger a click event when create is clicked.', function() {
5    });
6 });
```

Our first example on line 2 describes the behavior of what to do when we click the create button. With this test we are saying that when the button is clicked, the to-do application should call a function to add the to-do. Our second example is describing what event is fired when the create is clicked. In this situation, we are going to want to make sure the click() event is called.

Before we can use Jasmine, we need to tell it where our test, application, and third-party libraries are. To configure Jasmine, we'll modify SpecRunner.html, removing references to the spec files we deleted earlier and adding the location of add_todo_spec.js

```
jasmine/jasmine/SpecRunner.html
<!--The jQuery additional commands, for fixtures and such -->
<script type="text/javascript"
  src="lib/jasmine-1.0.2/jasmine-jquery-1.2.0.js">
</script>

<!-- include source files here... -->
<script type="text/javascript"
  src="http://ajax.googleapis.com/ajax/libs/jquery/1.7/jquery.min.js"
  charset="utf-8">
</script>
<script src="../add_todo.js" type="text/javascript" charset="utf-8"></script>

<!-- include spec files here... -->
<script type="text/javascript" src="spec/add_todo_spec.js"></script>
```

To run our specs, open SpecRunner.html in Firefox. Everything is green, and it looks like all the tests have passed! Well, not quite. If we look back at the tests we wrote, they don't actually do anything. We want to actually test things, so now we'll write some tests that will fail and then implement the actual code and watch them go green.

Let's work on our first test. We want to make sure that the addToDo() function gets called when we click the Create button.

jasmine/jasmine/spec/add_todo_spec.js
```
$('#create').click();
expect(ToDo.addToDo).toHaveBeenCalledWith(mocks.todo);
```

We'll want to test that the click event actually triggers the addToDo() function. To call the click event, we're going to need some HTML to actually execute the JavaScript against. One benefit of the Jasmine-jQuery plug-in is its fixture support, which lets us create pieces of HTML code that we can rely on to be consistent and make our tests repeatable. Since our application is going to be a form with one text box and a Create button followed by a list, we can mock out the application in a fixture file. Jasmine looks for fixtures in the jasmine/spec/javascripts/fixtures/ directory of our application. Let's create an index.html file in that location to represent our to-do application.

jasmine/jasmine/spec/javascripts/fixtures/index.html
```html
<fieldset>
  <legend>New ToDo</legend>
  <form>
    <input type="text" id="todo"/>
    <button id="create">Add ToDo Item</button>
  </form>
</fieldset>
<h2>ToDos</h2>
<ol id="todo_list">
</ol>
```

Now that we created a fixture, we need to tell our tests to use it. We'll use Jasmine's beforeEach() function to do some setup before each one of our tests. We'll want the beforeEach() function just inside of the describe() function and use the loadFixtures() function to load our fixture.

jasmine/jasmine/spec/add_todo_spec.js
```
beforeEach(function () {
  loadFixtures("index.html");
});
```

By having the beforeEach() function inside of the describe() function, Jasmine will execute the code for all of the tests that are also inside the describe() function.

> ### Joe asks:
> ## Why Use Firefox?
>
> Firefox is a stable browser with third-party support that has been in many developers' toolbox for many years. One add-on in particular, Firebug,[a] is the Swiss Army knife of web development. It has tools for inspecting and modifying markup, JavaScript, and CSS. Firebug will even analyze load time for each element on a page and show you their load order. It has extensive JavaScript debugging capabilities and is covered more in Recipe 31, *Debugging JavaScript*, on page 228.
>
> ---
>
> a.   http://getfirebug.com/

The beforeEach() function is the perfect place to put any code you need executed for each of the tests below it.

We are going to want to test our application's functionality of adding a to-do item. We just created a fixture; let's get some mock data to work with. Mocks are a tool that simulate real data and are consistent for every test run. Let's start by creating a blank mocks object that we can attach different values to. Right above the beforeEach() we need to add the following:

`jasmine/jasmine/spec/add_todo_spec.js`
```
var mocks = {};
```

Creating a global variable in the top of our test gives us an object that we can add functions and values to. Since our Jasmine test interacts with our application code, using a mock object will keep the test objects separated.

Inside of the beforeEach(), we'll add a todo variable to the mocks object. We can use jQuery to set the value of the to-do text box with the mocked todo. We know that the text box needs to have an id of todo from our wireframe.

`jasmine/jasmine/spec/add_todo_spec.js`
```
mocks.todo = "something fun";
$('#todo').val(mocks.todo);
```

Here we're giving our todo a value of "something fun" and then filling the textbox with that value.

Since we're using a TDD approach, we write our test first and then the code to make them pass. Since we haven't written any actual code yet, the test will fail when we run it, and we'll get an output similar to Figure 58, *Failing first test*, on page 260.

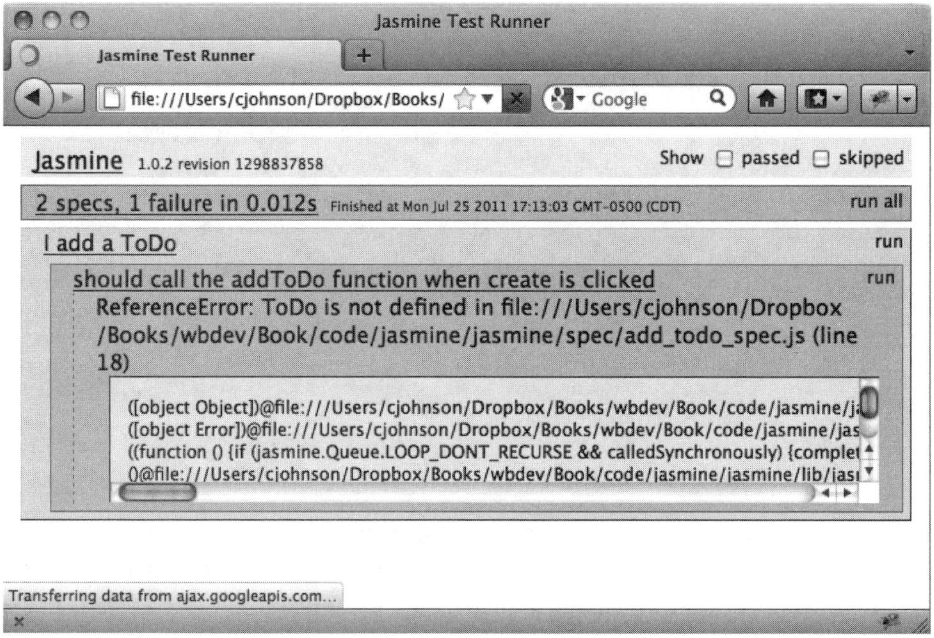

Figure 58—Failing first test

Going Green

We need a place to keep our application code. Let's create a file named add_todo.js in the root of the application. We'll use a JavaScript object called ToDo to organize our functions and make them more testable. Inside of our ToDo object, we'll add three functions:

```
jasmine/add_todo.js
var ToDo = {
  setup: function(){
  },
  setupCreateClickEvent: function(){
  },
  addToDo: function(todo){
  }
};
```

With our add_todo.js file in place, we need to add all of the functionality to make the application work. We'll start with a setup() function, which we'll invoke in both our application and our tests. Its job is to call the setupCreateClickEvent() function, which binds a click() event to the create button. When a user clicks the create button, the browser will fire a click() event, which triggers the addToDo() function.

```
jasmine/add_todo.js
var ToDo = {
  setup: function(){
    ToDo.setupCreateClickEvent();
  },
  setupCreateClickEvent: function(){
    $('#create').click(function(event){
      event.preventDefault();
      ToDo.addToDo($('#todo').val());
      $('#todo').val("");
    });
  },
  addToDo: function(todo){
    $('#todo_list').append("<li>" + todo + "</li>");
  }
};
```

In the setupCreateClickEvent() function, we call preventDefault() on the event that is passed into the click() function, which prevents the button from actually submitting the form. We then call the addToDo() function, passing in the value from our todo text field. Then we'll set the value of todo to a blank string so it's ready for the next to-do. In our addToDo() we are adding the to-do to our list using jQuery's append() function.

Let's jump to our spec and add the ToDo.setup() call to the beforeEach() block.

```
jasmine/jasmine/spec/add_todo_spec.js
ToDo.setup();
```

Now before every test our ToDo.setup() function will be called, and the create click() event will be bound to the create button in our fixture.

Our main focus of the first test is that the ToDo.addToDo() gets called. To assert that the function was called, we'll need to use a "Jasmine spy."[30] A spy is a multiuse test double, which can be used as a stub, fake, or mock. A stub is a predefined response to something, usually a method that returns a specific value. The stub doesn't care what parameters are passed into it and always returns the predefined response. A fake is an object that still has working parts but takes shortcuts—it pretends to be a method that exists but only does a shorthand version of the original. A mock is similar to a fake but does more: it actually inspects what is going on, like who is calling it and how many times it was called and with what parameters. Attaching a spy to a function enables assertions for that function like checking to see whether the function was called, the number of times it was called, and even the arguments from each call. For our expect(ToDo.addToDo).toHaveBeenCalledWith(mocks.todo); to

---

30. http://pivotal.github.com/jasmine/jsdoc/symbols/jasmine.Spy.html

perform an assertion, and not actually call the function, we need to add a spyOn() to the top of the test. In this case, the spy is going to hijack our addToDo() function when it gets called. Then it's going to check that the assertion toHave-BeenCalledWith(mocks.todo) is true, in other words, that the function was called with whatever value is in mocks.todo.

```
jasmine/jasmine/spec/add_todo_spec.js
spyOn(ToDo, 'addToDo');
```

We're spying on the ToDo object's addToDo() function. Our assertion is that we are expecting the function to be called with the value in mocks.todo. This test is giving us a clear picture of the code we are going to need to implement to make this pass.

Now that we know what spies do, let's work on our second test and make sure a click event is triggered when Create is clicked. Our test needs to spy on the click() event, then click the Create button, and assert that the click() has been called. Let's add this code inside of our second test.

```
jasmine/jasmine/spec/add_todo_spec.js
spyOnEvent($('#create'), 'click');
$('#create').click();
expect('click').toHaveBeenTriggeredOn($('#create'));
```

We don't want to actually execute the click() function, but we want to make sure that it was called. By using spyOnEvent(), we are using Jasmine again to hijack the click() event, so our assertion can be evaluated.

Since we have our tests and related code completed, let's go watch the tests pass. Open SpecRunner.html in Firefox. We'll see the specs passing in Figure 59, *Passing Jasmine specs*, on page 263.

With working tests, let's finish up the last part and build the index.html page and have a functioning to-do list.

Finishing Touches

To finish up, we'll create a JavaScript file to hold our DomReady() function. Creating a separate file for this little bit of JavaScript makes sure we can set the state of our tests and not have them influenced by outside sources. At the root of the project, let's create app.js.

```
jasmine/app.js
$(function() {
  ToDo.setup();
});
```

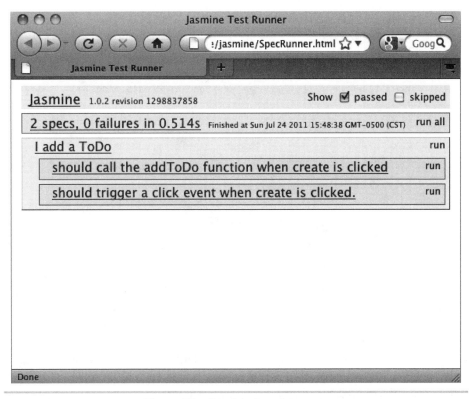

Figure 59—Passing Jasmine specs

Here we are just calling our ToDo.setup() function. This gives us the most flexibility, because we are keeping the majority of the code in add_todo.js.

Lastly, let's create the index.html based on our fixture. We'll need to include both the app.js and the add_todo.js files. Let's start off our index.html with a simple header.

```
jasmine/index.html
<!DOCTYPE html>
  <head>
    <title>My Great ToDo List</title>
    <script type="text/javascript"
      src="http://ajax.googleapis.com/ajax/libs/jquery/1.7/jquery.min.js">
    </script>
    <script type="text/javascript" src="app.js"></script>
    <script type="text/javascript" src="add_todo.js"></script>
  </head>
```

For the body of the page, we'll want to grab the code from our fixture. This way, our tests are executing against the same code as our application is.

```
jasmine/index.html
  <body>
    <fieldset>
      <legend>New ToDo</legend>
      <form action="#" method="post" accept-charset="utf-8">
        <input type="text" id="todo"/> <button id="create">Add ToDo Item</button>
      </form>
    </fieldset>

    <h2>ToDos</h2>
    <ol id="todo_list">
    </ol>

  </body>
</html>
```

Now when we open index.html in the Firefox, we'll see Figure 60, *Our working application*, on page 265.

We have now gone through a cycle of the TDD process and brought our tests to green, and we have a working application to show for it.

Further Exploration

To expand on our Jasmine exploration, go and add some tests to other recipes in this book. Try your hand at adding tests to the Recipe 9, *Interacting with Web Pages Using Keyboard Shortcuts*, on page 59 or Recipe 11, *Displaying Information with Endless Pagination*, on page 73. You could continue this recipe by adding tests and functionality to restrict adding blank to-dos. You can also use Jasmine with CoffeeScript (see Recipe 29, *Cleaner JavaScript with CoffeeScript*, on page 209), which gives you testable JavaScript with the syntax safety of a compiler.

Also See

- Recipe 33, *Browser Testing with Selenium*, on page 237
- Recipe 34, *Cucumber-Driven Selenium Testing*, on page 242
- Recipe 29, *Cleaner JavaScript with CoffeeScript*, on page 209
- Recipe 31, *Debugging JavaScript*, on page 228

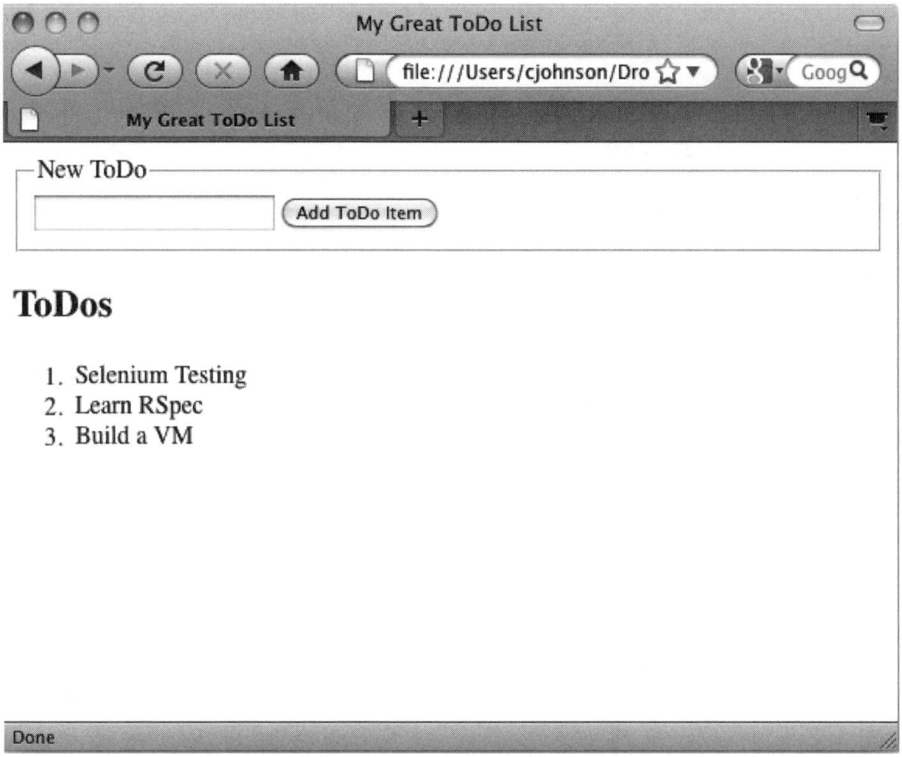

Figure 60—Our working application

## CHAPTER 7

Hosting and Deployment Recipes

We want to get our work out there for others to see, but that's only the beginning. Once our sites are live, we have to make sure they're secure. In this collection of recipes, you'll learn how to deploy your work and how to work with the Apache web server to redirect requests, secure content, and host secure sites.

Recipe 36

Using Dropbox to Host a Static Site

Problem

We need to collaborate on a website with another person who is working remotely. The remote person does not have VPN access to our server farm, and our firewall allows deployment only from within our network. It would also be nice to have a publicly accessible URL so we can share our work with others.

Ingredients

- Dropbox[1]

Solution

We can use Dropbox to collaborate on static HTML files and share them with external users. With Dropbox we don't need to worry about firewalls, FTP servers, or emailing files. Because Dropbox is cross-platform, we don't have to waste time with different applications for each OS, making Dropbox a productivity win.

Our company and our partner company, AwesomeCableCo, are sponsoring "Youth Technology Days." AwesomeCableCo has its own designer, Rob. We need a way to work with Rob on this site and show our bosses the progress we are making.

Let's walk through the installation process so we can document it and send it off to Rob. Let's head to Dropbox's website and get the installer.

After the installer finishes, we can go to the Dropbox folder on our local computer. Dropbox automatically creates a Public folder, as shown in Figure 61, *The folders Dropbox creates*, on page 269, which we can use to distribute files with anyone in the world. Let's make a "youth_tech_days" folder inside of that public folder.

---

1. http://www.dropbox.com

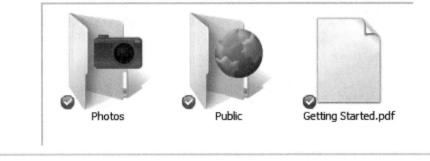

Figure 61—The folders Dropbox creates

Now that we have a workspace, we need to invite Rob to collaborate on files in this folder with us. When we right-click the folder we created, we'll see a context menu that gives us the option to share this folder, like the one in Figure 62, *Sharing context menu*, on page 270.

When we choose Share This Folder, we get taken to the Dropbox website to finish the sharing process, as shown in Figure 63, *Dropbox online sharing form*, on page 270. We simply fill out the information to share this folder with Rob.

Now we can move the files for the website into the youth_tech_day folder, which you can find in the book's source code in the dropbox folder. Now we will have a directory that looks like Figure 64, *Youth Technology Days website files*, on page 271.

Whenever we drop files into this folder, they'll show up on Rob's computer as well. When Rob updates the files, our copy will be updated to stay in sync. As we work on the files, we'll want to communicate with Rob about what we're doing so that we don't overwrite his work. Dropbox has checks in place to handle conflicts if we edit a file at the same time as Rob, saving multiple copies of the file and appending a message to the filename indicating the conflict. This works fine for our simple situation, but if we are doing heavy active collaboration, we would should be using Git, as mentioned in Recipe 30, *Managing Files Using Git*, on page 216.

Now we just need to show our bosses what we've done. Since we put the files in the public folder, they are available on the Web to anyone who knows the URL. To find the address of our index file, we simply need to right-click it and choose "Copy public link," which will put the URL on our clipboard. We can test this URL by opening it from a browser. We will have a URL similar to http://dl.dropbox.com/u/33441336/youth_tech_days/index.html.

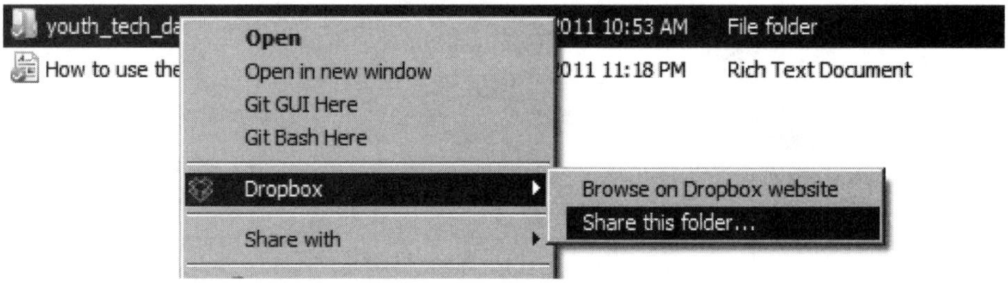

Figure 62—Sharing context menu

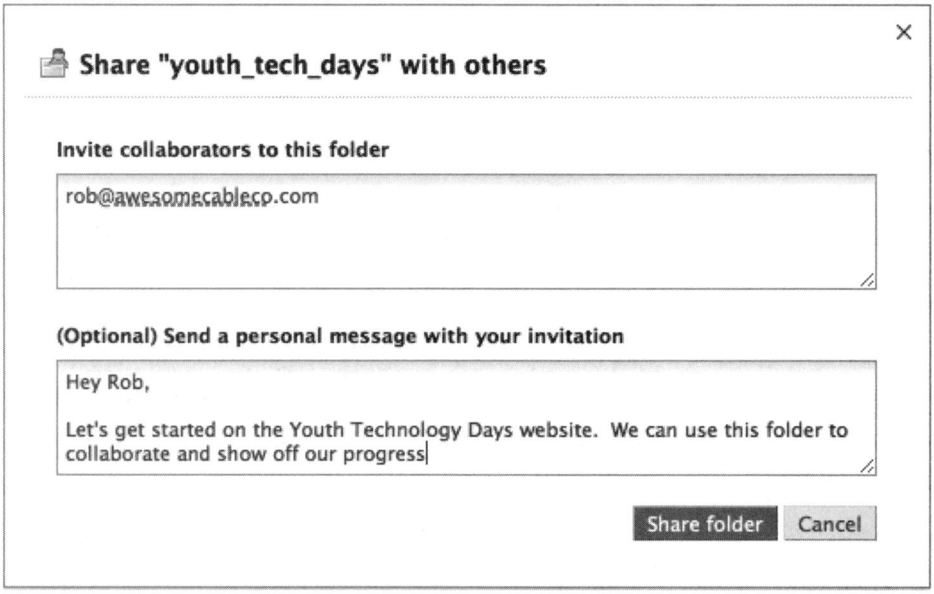

✉ Share "youth_tech_days" with others   ✕

Invite collaborators to this folder

rob@awesomecableco.com

(Optional) Send a personal message with your invitation

Hey Rob,

Let's get started on the Youth Technology Days website. We can use this folder to collaborate and show off our progress|

[Share folder] [Cancel]

Figure 63—Dropbox online sharing form

This is a great, simple way to collaborate with people outside our company and easily show progress without the need for an FTP server, web server, or VPN connection. We can add other contributors to our project and share the URL with anyone who is interested in the progress we are making.

Further Exploration

We can further explore by sharing nonpublic folders with co-workers and friends. We can also use this tool to back up files and share them among several of our own computers. We can also use the public folders to send Mom an Internet Explorer patch she just can't seem to find or provide our

Figure 64—Youth Technology Days website files

clients with a place to send us photos or other assets they'd like us to post on their sites. Other uses include the following:

- Hosting files you want to share on a blog post
- Sharing a folder with each of your clients for easy collaboration
- Forwarding a vanity domain to a public site
- Creating a blog with Jekyll and hosting it from Dropbox

If your registrar or DNS provider supports redirection, you could set up a URL that's easier for people to remember when they want to check out your pages on Dropbox.

Also See

- Recipe 30, *Managing Files Using Git*, on page 216
- Recipe 27, *Creating a Simple Blog with Jekyll*, on page 193

Recipe 37

Setting Up a Virtual Machine

Problem

We need to set up a local server that looks like our production server so that we have a place to test PHP scripts and configurations in an environment in which we can safely experiment.

Ingredients

- VirtualBox[2]
- Ubuntu 10.04 Server image[3]

Solution

We can use virtualization and open source tools to create a server playground that runs right on our laptop or workstation. We'll use the free VirtualBox software and the Ubuntu Server Linux distribution to build this environment, and we'll then set up the Apache web server with PHP so we can use this environment to test some PHP web projects.

Creating Our Virtual Machine

We need to grab two pieces of software: the Ubuntu server operating system, and VirtualBox, an open source virtualization program. VirtualBox lets us create virtual workstations or servers that run on top of our operating system, giving us a sandbox that we can play in without modifying our actual operating system.

First, we need to visit the Ubuntu download page[4] and grab the 32-bit *server* version of Ubuntu 10.04 LTS instead of the most recent release. LTS stands for "Long-term Support," which means we can get updates for a much longer period without having to do a complete OS upgrade. The LTS releases don't always have the most up-to-date features, but they're perfect for servers.

---

2. http://www.virtualbox.org/

3. http://www.ubuntu.com/download/ubuntu/download

4. http://www.ubuntu.com/download/server/download

While that's downloading, we can go to the VirtualBox web page[5] and download the latest edition of VirtualBox. You'll want to get the one for your platform. Once it's downloaded, install it using the defaults and then launch the VirtualBox program.

Once VirtualBox is running, we need to click the New button to bring up the Virtual Machine Wizard. We need to give our virtual machine a name, such as My Web Server. Then we'll choose Linux for the operating system and Ubuntu for the version. We also need to decide how much memory and disk space to give to the virtual machine, and we can use the defaults, which are pretty sensible. We'll end up with a virtual machine that has 512MB of memory and an 8GB hard disk.

With our virtual machine created, we can click the Settings button to configure additional options. We need to change our network type from NAT to Bridged, as shown in Figure 65, *Setting the network type to bridged*, on page 274, so that we can access our servers from our host machine.

Now we can click the Start button to fire up the new virtual machine. VirtualBox detects that we are running it for the first time and will walk us through the steps to get the Ubuntu operating system running. We'll need to choose media for our operating system, and we can use a CD, but we can also use the ISO image we downloaded. Once we select our installation media, the virtual server starts and the installation of Ubuntu is underway.

For our purposes, we can accept all of the default settings in the Ubuntu installation process. You'll be asked for a hostname, and you can enter whatever you like, but the default will work just fine. You'll also be asked about disk partitioning, and you should accept the defaults and answer yes whenever you're prompted to write changes to disk. Since this is a virtual machine, you're not going to erase data on your computer's actual hard drive.

Toward the end of the process, we'll be asked to create a user account. This is the user we'll use to log in to our server and do our web server configuration, so let's call it "webdev." We can use that value for both the full name and the username. We'll also need a password, which you can create on your own. Just don't forget it!

When asked whether you'd like to install any predefined software, simply choose Continue. We'll install things ourselves at the end of the process.

---

5.   http://www.virtualbox.org/

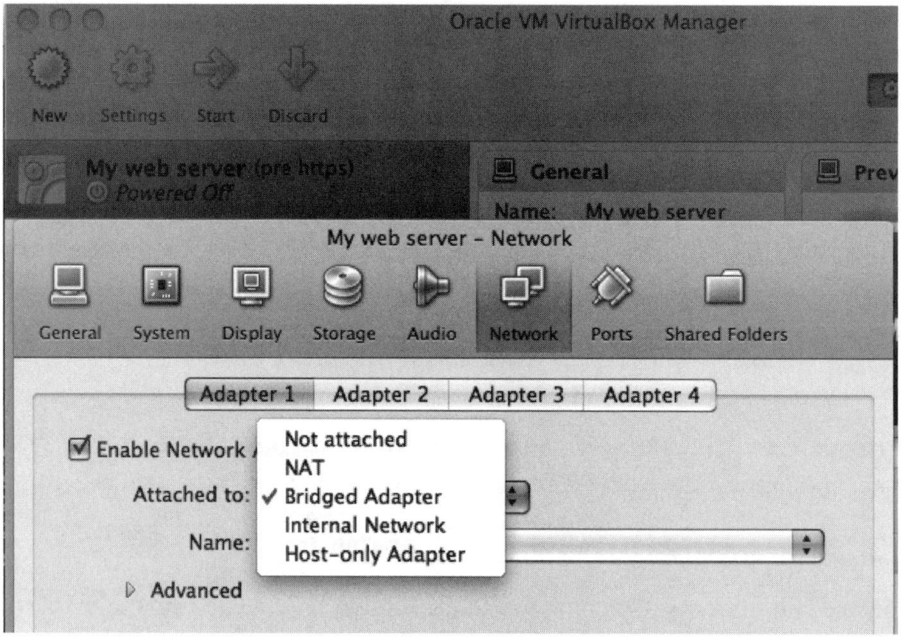

Figure 65—Setting the network type to bridged

When the installation finally ends, the virtual machine will restart, and we'll be prompted to log in with the username and password we created. Let's do that and get our web server running.

Configuring Apache and PHP

Thanks to Ubuntu's package manager, we can quickly get the Apache web server running with PHP by logging into our server and typing the following:

```
$ sudo apt-get install apache2 libapache2-mod-php5
$ sudo service apache2 restart
```

The first command installs the Apache web server and the PHP5 programming language and sets up Apache to serve PHP pages. The second reloads Apache's configuration files to ensure the new PHP settings are enabled. Now let's set up our VPS so we can copy files into our web server's directory.

Getting Files to Our Virtual Server

To really work with our virtual server, we need to set up services so we can copy our files there.

Apache is serving all of the web files out of the /var/www folder, and the only user who can put files into that folder is the root user. Let's change that by taking ownership of that folder and all its contents with this command:

```
$ sudo chown -R webdev:webdev /var/www
```

Now, let's set up OpenSSH so we can use an SFTP client to copy files, just like we would if we were using a hosting company.

```
$ sudo apt-get install openssh-server
```

And now we can log in using any SFTP client. We just use the IP address of our virtual machine, which we can find by typing the following:

```
$ ifconfig eth0
```

Our IP address is the one that looks like this:

```
inet addr: 192.168.1.100
```

We can now use an SFTP client to connect to that address with the username and password we set when we built the virtual machine. From a Windows machine, we could use FileZilla, and from a Mac we can use Cyberduck or even the command line, using the scp command to transfer a file. For example, if we had a simple HTML file in our home directory, we could transfer it to our server like this:

```
scp index.html webdev@192.168.1.100:/var/www/index.html
```

We specify the source filename, followed by the destination path, which is the username we want to connect with, followed by the @ sign and the IP address of the server and a colon, and then by the full path where we'll place the file.

With our virtual machine in place, we can now start using it as a testing playground. When it comes time to deploy our code to our production environment, we'll have had enough practice.

Further Exploration

Virtual machines give us a playground where we can test, experiment, and break things, but we can do more than that. VirtualBox's "snapshot" feature lets us create restore points that we can revert to if we goof something up. This is perfect for those times when we're interested in playing with a new piece of technology. In addition, we can create "appliances," or specific virtual machines with preloaded packages. We could create a PHP appliance, which has PHP, MySQL, and Apache already configured, and then share that virtual machine with others so they can get started quickly.

Virtual machines are extremely useful for deploying actual applications. For example, we can snapshots in production to restore our machine after a failed upgrade or a security exploit, and we can clone virtual machines to scale things out. Closed source products like VMware provide enterprise-level solutions for hosting multiple virtual machines on a single physical server.[6] VMware even provides some tools for taking a physical machine and converting it to a virtual one.[7]

Also See

- Recipe 39, *Securing Apache with SSL and HTTPS*, on page 283

---

6. http://www.vmware.com/virtualization/
7. http://www.vmware.com/products/converter/

Recipe 38

Changing Web Server Configuration Files with Vim

Problem

When we have to make changes to our server's configuration files, it's often much quicker to edit the file directly on the server than it is to download the file, make the change on our development workstation, and then upload the file back to the server.

Ingredients

- Our virtual machine, created in Recipe 37, *Setting Up a Virtual Machine*, on page 272[8]

- The Vim text editor

Solution

Many production servers use Linux and don't give us access to a graphical interface, but we can use Vim, a command-line text editor to make the changes we need quickly. Vim is a powerful text editor designed with efficiency in mind. It's a great choice for working with files on a server because it's almost always available, is lightweight, and is extremely configurable.

We've recently deployed a site to our client's production server, but we've forgotten to configure the web server to display a proper 404 "Page Not Found" error page. The default "Page Not Found" message is a little more technical than our client would like, so we'll modify the message by configuring Apache to serve up a custom 404 page.

For this recipe, we'll use the VM we built in Recipe 37, *Setting Up a Virtual Machine*, on page 272. Before we customize our error page, let's get acquainted with editing files in Vim.

---

8. You can grab a premade VM from http://www.webdevelopmentrecipes.com/.

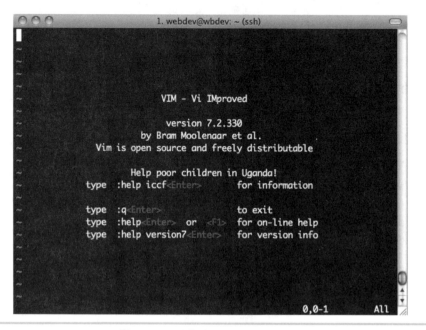

Figure 66—Vim's opening screen

Editing Files with Vim

Let's start by logging in through the virtual machine's console. Once logged in, we can start Vim by typing the following:

```
$ vim
```

at the server's prompt. When we open Vim without specifying a file, we'll see a screen like the one in Figure 66, *Vim's opening screen*, on page 278, which gives us a little introduction to the editor itself.

We'll use the keyboard for absolutely *everything* in Vim, from moving our cursor around the screen to saving and opening files. We do this through Vim's various *modes*.

Vim has four main modes: normal, insert, command, and visual.

- Normal mode is for navigating around a file and switching to other modes.

- Insert mode is for entering text or making changes to the file.

- Command mode is where we execute specific commands such as saving and opening files.

- Visual mode is for selecting text so we can manipulate it.

When we first open Vim, we start in Normal mode. We can go into Insert mode by pressing i. When we do that, we'll see -- INSERT -- at the bottom of the screen.

In Insert mode, type *Welcome to Vim*, press the ENTER key, and then type *Let's have some fun!* We should now have a file that looks like this:

```
Welcome to Vim
Let's have some fun!
```

Since we're done adding text, we want to go back to normal mode, which we do by pressing the ESC key. In normal mode we can navigate around our file character by character using either the arrow keys or the h, j, k, and l keys. These navigation keys keep your fingers on the keyboard's home row and, with practice, will let you move around files very quickly. The h key moves the cursor left, while the l key moves right. The k key moves up one line, and j moves down. If you need help remembering which key moves up and which key moves down, just imagine that the j key looks like an arrow pointing downward, so pressing that key moves the cursor down one line.

From normal mode, we can save and close this file. We press : to switch to Vim's Command mode. To save a file, we use :w, or "write." We can pass a filename to this command, so to save this file as test.txt, we use the following command:

```
:w test.txt
```

Any time we are editing an existing file, we can just use :w to save the file we are working on, so we don't always have to pass the filename.

Finally, we can quit Vim with the :q command.

There's a lot more to Vim than these simple commands, but we now know enough to modify our configuration to show a friendlier error page to our client's users.

Creating and Serving Custom Error Page

There are a few ways to customize the error pages Apache displays to our end users. We could modify the main Apache configuration file, we could change the configuration file for our web site, or we could use a special file called .htaccess. Using an .htaccess file lets us configure the Apache web server on a per-directory basis, giving us more flexibility. In some hosting environments, this is often the only way for us to configure things like error pages, since we may not have permission to edit the other configuration files. Let's configure Apache to use .htaccess files.

First, we need to enable Apache's mod_rewrite extension to Apache, which we discuss in more detail in Recipe 41, *Rewriting URLs to Preserve Links*, on page 291. We do this by typing this command at the server's prompt:

```
$ sudo a2enmod rewrite
```

Next, we need to tell Apache to allow overriding of configuration properties for this site. If we don't do this, Apache will ignore anything we put in our .htaccess file. Let's use Vim to modify the configuration file for the default website:

```
$ sudo vim /etc/apache2/sites-enabled/000-default
```

Instead of the arrow keys, let's use Vim's navigation keys (h, j, k, and l) to move down and change the AllowOverride value for our web directory /var/www. Navigate to the end of AllowOverride None and press i to go into insert mode. Then, delete None and replace it with All. Our file should now look like this:

```
<Directory /var/www>
    Options Indexes FollowSymLinks MultiViews
    AllowOverride All
    Order allow,deny
    allow from all
</Directory>
```

Before we can save the file, we have to press the Esc key to leave insert mode. Then we can save the file with :w. We can then quit Vim with :q.

Next we'll need to create a file to use as our 404 page. Let's navigate to the root of our sample website and use Vim to create a new 404 page called 404.html.

```
$ cd /var/www
$ vim 404.html
```

We'll be presented with a blank file, so we can press i to enter insert mode and then type in some basic markup for this page.

```
<h1>We're sorry</h1>
<p>
  The page you are looking for can't be found.
  It may have been moved to a new location.
</p>
<p>
  You might be able to find what you're looking for
  <a href="/">here</a>.
</p>
```

Once again, we'll press the Esc key to leave insert mode. We can then type :wq to save and close Vim with a single command.

Now that our 404 page is created, we need to tell the web server to display it. We'll create the .htaccess file in the same directory that contains our other web files, in /var/www.

```
$ vim .htaccess
```

Then, we add a *directive*, or *configuration rule*, to define the location of our 404 page. Press i to enter insert mode, and enter this rule:

```
ErrorDocument 404 /404.html
```

The location of the file is actually relative to the site's URL, not the location of the file on the server's disk.

We then press Esc to leave Insert mode and then type :wq again to save the file. We can test it by trying to load a page that doesn't exist on our site with a browser, and we'll see our 404 page. With our friendlier 404 page online, we've bought ourselves some time to fix the actual application and make a real 404 page.

Further Exploration

Saying that Vim is just a text editor is like saying that bacon is just meat. Bacon is more than meat—it is super tasty. By using the right mixture of plug-ins, we can turn Vim into a full-fledged super-tasty IDE. There is a Vim installation for every major OS,[9] so you can download and install it on your development machine. Then you can find some plug-ins that relate to your daily activities.[10]

Once you have found some plug-ins that interest you, you might consider using Pathogen[11] to manage those plug-ins. Normally, you install Vim plug-ins into specific folders, but Pathogen makes managing plug-ins easier by letting you keep the plug-ins in a central location so you can update them easily. You simply download plug-ins into a .vim/bundles folder, and Pathogen tells Vim to look in that folder and all of its subfolders for your plug-ins. Since some of the most popular Vim plug-ins are available on GitHub, many developers simply use Git to clone those plug-ins directly into their .vim/bundles folder. This way they can use git pull to update the plug-ins.

To learn more about using Vim for different tasks, check out VimCasts.[12] They post screencasts that go into detail about using Vim and various plug-ins.

---

9. http://www.vim.org/download.php
10. http://www.vim.org/scripts/script_search_results.php
11. http://www.vim.org/scripts/script.php?script_id=2332
12. http://vimcasts.org/

Also See

- Recipe 37, *Setting Up a Virtual Machine*, on page 272
- Recipe 39, *Securing Apache with SSL and HTTPS*, on page 283
- Recipe 41, *Rewriting URLs to Preserve Links*, on page 291

Recipe 39

Securing Apache with SSL and HTTPS

Problem

When our applications and websites deal with people's information, we owe it to them to safeguard it. We want to make sure our servers and databases safely store that information, but we also need to protect that data during its trips from their computer to our servers and back. We need to configure our web server so it connects to web browsers using SSL.

Ingredients

- A virtual machine running Ubuntu for testing
- The Apache web server with SSL support

Solution

To set up a secure web server, we need to set up SSL certificates. Production websites use signed SSL certificates that are verified by a third-party authority. This verification gives customers a sense of security.

Signed SSL certificates cost money, and we don't want to pay for certificates for our development environments. For testing purposes, we can create "self-signed" certificates, which are ones we verify ourselves.

We'll use the virtual machine we created in Recipe 37, *Setting Up a Virtual Machine*, on page 272 so we can get some practice.[13] That way, when we have to set up our production machine, we'll know exactly what to do. We'll do all of the commands in this recipe from our virtual machine's console, *not* on your local machine.

Creating a Self-Signed Certificate for Development

The process for getting an SSL certificate is the same whether we're getting a verified one or a self-signed one. We start by creating a certificate request. This request usually gets sent to a certificate authority along with a payment, and they then send back a verified SSL certificate we can install on our

---

13. To save time, you can grab a premade VM from http://www.webdevelopmentrecipes.com/.

server. In our case, we'll be acting as both the certificate requester and the certificate authority.

To create the request, we fire up our virtual machine, log into the console, and type the following:

```
$ openssl req -new -out awesomeco.csr
```

This creates both a certificate request and a private signing key that requires a passphrase.

We'll need to provide a passphrase for this new key, and we'll be asked for our company name and other details. You'll want to fill these out with real data, especially if you plan to use this to request a key from a certificate authority!

The key we created requires that we enter a passphrase every time we use it. If we request a certificate with this key, we'll have to enter that passphrase every time we restart our web server. This is secure but pretty inconvenient. It's also not very manageable in a production environment. Let's create a key we can use that doesn't require a password.

```
$ sudo openssl rsa -in privkey.pem -out awesomeco.key
```

Now that we have our request, we can sign it ourselves by passing both our request and our key.

```
$ openssl x509 -req -days 364 -in awesomeco.csr \
-signkey awesomeco.key -out awesomeco.crt
```

The certificate we created will be good for one year.

Finally, we need to copy our certificate and our keyfile to the appropriate locations.

```
$sudo cp awesomeco.key /etc/ssl/private
$ sudo cp awesomeco.crt /etc/ssl/certs
```

Now let's modify the default Apache website to use SSL.

Configuring Apache for SSL Support

We need to enable the Apache module for SSL support on our server. To do that, we can either manually edit the list of installed modules or type the following:

```
$ sudo a2enmod ssl
```

This will do the modification for us.

Now we need to tell Apache to serve web pages using SSL.

Let's create a separate configuration file for our SSL site. Create the file /etc/apache2/sites-available/ssl_example and add the following configuration to the file:

```
<VirtualHost *:443>
ServerAdmin webmaster@localhost
DocumentRoot /var/www
<Directory /var/www/>
  Options FollowSymLinks
  AllowOverride None
</Directory>
SSLEngine on
SSLOptions +StrictRequire
SSLCertificateFile /etc/ssl/certs/server.crt
SSLCertificateKeyFile /etc/ssl/private/server.key
</VirtualHost>
```

We're creating a new virtual host on port 443, listening on all addresses. The document root specifies where our web pages are, and the directory section sets up some basic permissions.

The last few lines set up the actual SSL connections, turning on SSL support, ensuring it's strictly enforced, and ensuring that it knows where our self-signed certificate and key are located.

With this new configuration file saved, we need to enable it and tell Apache to reload its configuration.

```
$ sudo a2ensite ssl_example
$ sudo /etc/init.d/apache2 restart
```

Now we can visit our website's URL over SSL. We'll get some warnings from the browser, though, because a certificate we created by ourselves isn't considered safe for the average user. And that makes sense. If anyone could create a certificate that was automatically trusted by every browser, it really would not be that secure. We need to get a third party involved to get a trusted certificate. That's where a certificate provider comes in.

Working with a Certificate Provider

We don't want our users thinking we're trying to steal their credit card information or do other evil things with their data, so we need to get a trusted certificate. To do that, we generate a certificate request and a key in the same fashion we did for our self-signed certificate. We then send the certificate request to the certificate authority along with our payment, and they'll send back a certificate we can install along with other instructions.

Some certificate authorities do more than just take your money in exchange for a certificate that removes the error message. Some will actually verify that your entity is a legitimate business. When your users review the details of the certificate in their browser, they can see this information, which adds an additional layer of trust. It also adds extra costs for you, but depending on your industry, it may be worth it.

There are many certificate authorities out there. Thawte[14] and VeriSign[15] are well-known and trusted certificate authorities, but you'll need to research some on your own to find ones that meet your needs. If you're working with a hosting provider, you can often work with them to get a signed certificate for your site.

Further Exploration

There are actually several types of SSL certificates we can use. We can get certificates that cover a single server, or we can get a "wildcard" certificate that we could apply to all servers within our domain. Wildcard certificates are much more expensive than single-server certificates.

Finally, *Server Name Indication* (SNI) certificates are a much cheaper option, but they work only with the most modern browsers and operating systems. SNI certificates are great for internal organizations where you have control over the browsers your clients use, but you'll want to rely on more traditional host or IP-based certificates for the general public.

Also See

- Recipe 37, *Setting Up a Virtual Machine*, on page 272

---

14. http://www.thawte.com
15. https://www.verisign.com/

Recipe 40

Securing Your Content

Problem

When we're managing files on servers, it's often handy to have an easy way to lock certain files or folders. When we just want a select group of people to be able to access the files, we need a way to create very simple authentication.

Ingredients

- Development server with Apache

Solution

When we put files on our web server, they're available for anyone to see. Since we don't want the entire world to have access to any important documents we are storing, we can create some basic authentication to secure files. Apache allows us to create configuration files that specify which directories and files shouldn't be served without authentication. We'll take a look at how we build these configuration files to secure our server.

Using Basic HTTP Authentication

When Apache is serving up files, it's always looking for the file .htaccess. This special file tells Apache the configuration for a specific folder on your server. With the .htaccess file, we can enable password protection of files, block users based on certain criteria, set redirects and error documents, and much more.

Let's start by creating a file to ask for authentication. If you haven't already, be sure to read through Recipe 37, *Setting Up a Virtual Machine*, on page 272 so that you have a development server to test with. After we log into our development server, let's also make sure Apache is running.

```
$ sudo service apache2 restart
```

Now that Apache is running, we can start to build the authentication. For basic HTTP authentication, we need to create a file to hold the usernames and passwords allowed to log in. We can use the htpasswd command to generate a username with an encrypted password. Let's create the user now, and let's keep the file in our home directory.

\\//   **Joe asks:**
ᵕᵕ   # Where Should I Keep My .htpasswd Files on a Live Server?

With most shared hosts, you're limited to only working in your home directory. This means that the document root for Apache is set up to point most often to something like /home/webdev/mywebsite.com/public_html. Since you will often be hosting multiple websites, it's nice to have each website in its own folder. For security reasons, you should place each site's .htpasswd file in that site's folder. For example, to generate the file for mywebsite.com, we'd run something like this:

```
$ htpasswd -c ~/mywebsite.com/.htpasswd webdev
```

This allows us to keep the users for different websites separate from each other.

```
$ htpasswd -c ~/.htpasswd webdev
New password:
Re-type new password:
Adding password for user webdev
```

When we call htpasswd, we pass a location for the file and our username, and it prompts us for a password to encrypt. We used the -c flag to create a new file if one does not exist. If we want, we can use the cat command to check what's in that file so far.

```
$ cat .htpasswd
webdev:mT8fQuzEhguRg
```

Now that our user is created, we can start locking down directories. Let's navigate to the document root and create an .htpasswd file.

```
$ cd /var/www
$ touch .htaccess
```

Let's open up our new file with our text editor and add some directives to lock down the root directory.

```
AuthUserFile /home/webdev/.htpasswd
AuthType Basic
AuthName Our secure section
Require valid-user
```

Since we created this file in the top level of the document root, we've locked down every document on our server. Let's use our browser and navigate to http://192.168.1.100/. You should see an authentication modal dialog like the one in Figure 67, *HTTP basic authentication dialog*, on page 289.

Figure 67—HTTP basic authentication dialog

Thanks to Apache's HTTP authentication, we have an easy method for securing the content on our servers.

Denying Off-Site Image Requests

We're paying a pretty penny for our hosting plan, so bandwidth and server load are always a concern. Also, we don't want anyone to be able to use our images without the correct rights and permissions. Thankfully, we can write a rule in .htaccess that will block off-site linking of images.

First, we need to enable Apache's mod_rewrite since we'll want to use it to deliver a broken image to the request. If you want to learn more about mod_rewrite, refer to Recipe 41, *Rewriting URLs to Preserve Links*, on page 291.

```
$ sudo a2enmod rewrite
```

We're going to add a rule that rewrites the URLs for incoming requests to instead deliver an image that doesn't exist. Let's open up our .htaccess file and add these lines:

```
RewriteEngine on
RewriteCond %{HTTP_REFERER} !^http://(www\.)?mywebsite.com/.*$ [NC]
RewriteRule \.(jpg|png|gif)$ - [F]
```

The first line tells Apache to use mod_rewrite. Next, we added a condition that applies our rewrite rule only if the referring website is different from our own URL. Last, we create a rewrite rule to look for any requests that end in an image extension. We use the [F] flag to tell Apache that these URLs are forbidden.

With that, any image request to our server returns a broken image in place of the image that was being used.

Further Exploration

When it comes to locking down a server, there are many methods we can use to keep information and content hidden. Aside from password protection and rewrite rules, we can also block users by IP address or even by the website they are coming from. With Apache's configuration files, we can secure our content in many ways. To see more advanced applications of the rewrite engine, read through Recipe 41, *Rewriting URLs to Preserve Links*, on page 291. Also, you can refer to Apache's own .htaccess tutorial.[16]

Also See

- Recipe 38, *Changing Web Server Configuration Files with Vim*, on page 277
- Recipe 41, *Rewriting URLs to Preserve Links*, on page 291
- Recipe 37, *Setting Up a Virtual Machine*, on page 272
- Recipe 42, *Automate Static Site Deployment with Jammit and Rake*, on page 296

---

16. http://httpd.apache.org/docs/current/howto/htaccess.html

Recipe 41

Rewriting URLs to Preserve Links

Problem

We want to redesign our site around a new CMS, and our URLs are going to change as a result. We have a lot of incoming links to pages and don't want to lose out on that traffic. Trying to figure out who links to us and ask them to change the links would take a lot of work and isn't a very reasonable plan, nor is leaving the old pages around with a link to the new ones. We need a way to redirect users from the old URLs to the new ones with as little overhead as possible.

Ingredients

- The Apache server
- mod_rewrite

Solution

The Apache server and mod_rewrite give us the ability to tell the server to load a specified file when another is requested. This will enable us to dictate what to load when a user visits our site. We can even use regular expressions so that we don't have to write an entry for every page in the site. Additionally, we can set headers so that search engines know to direct users to the new locations.

In this recipe, we'll assume that we're working with a virtual machine with Apache on it, as covered in Recipe 37, *Setting Up a Virtual Machine*, on page 272. If you're using a server hosted by another company, you may have to contact a server admin to set up mod_rewrite.

The first thing we need to check is whether mod_rewrite has been installed. The easiest way to do this is by making a page called phpinfo.php that contains one line of code:

```
<?php phpinfo(); ?>
```

We place this file on our server with the rest of our web pages and then load it in the browser. We'll see all sorts of information about our environment,

> \\// **Joe asks:**
> ٤‿ᵕ‿ **Why Can't We See the .htaccess File?**
>
> Just because you don't see the file in your file browser doesn't mean it's not there. Files that begin with a . may not show up because they're typically system or configuration files and are hidden. Enabling the display or hidden files in the file browser will allow you to see them. You can see a list of all files by running ls -la in Terminal on OS X or Linux or by running dir /a on Windows.

but we're looking for "mod_rewrite" in the "apache2handler" section under "Loaded Modules," just like in Figure 68, *Using phpinfo() to see loaded modules*, on page 293. (If you're checking on a production server, you should remove this file once you've finished checking, because it exposes details of your server configuration that would be best kept private.) If it's there, we're good to go. If not, we'll SSH to the server and install it by running sudo a2enmod rewrite in terminal. Next open /etc/apache2/sites-available/default and change the line AllowOverRide None in the <Directory /var/www/> section of the file to AllowOverRide All. Finally restart Apache with

```
sudo /etc/init.d/apache2 restart
```

and mod_rewrite will be ready to use.

mod_rewrite uses an .htaccess file to know how to handle requests for files and redirect them to the appropriate location.

```
RewriteEngine on
RewriteRule ^pages/page-2.html$ pages/2
```

Our initial .htaccess file only handles the display of a single page, but it's enough to ensure that everything is set up correctly. The first line simply activates the RewriteEngine, allowing us to use mod_rewrite. The second line creates a RewriteRule, which consists of three parts. First we declare that we're creating a RewriteRule, and then we use a regular expression to identify URLs that match the incoming request by the user. Finally, we tell Apache what it should load instead. The rule takes any request for pages/page-2.html and renders the content from pages/2 instead. As far as the user can tell, they're still on pages/page-2.html. This allows us to override a page like Figure 69, *An old page without mod_rewrite*, on page 293 with Figure 70, *A new page*, on page 294 so that the user sees Figure 71, *A new page displaying at the old URL with mod_rewrite*, on page 294 when they visit our site.

This is great, but do we really want to make a rule for every page? We can use regular expressions to avoid having to create a URL for every page. Let's

Configuration

apache2handler

Apache Version	Apache/2.2.14 (Ubuntu)
Apache API Version	20051115
Server Administrator	[no address given]
Hostname:Port	drinkatpuzzles.com:0
User/Group	www-data(33)/33
Max Requests	Per Child: 0 - Keep Alive: on - Max Per Connection: 100
Timeouts	Connection: 300 - Keep-Alive: 15
Virtual Server	Yes
Server Root	/etc/apache2
Loaded Modules	core mod_log_config mod_logio prefork http_core mod_so mod_alias mod_auth_basic mod_authn_file mod_authz_default mod_authz_groupfile mod_authz_host mod_authz_user mod_autoindex mod_cgi mod_deflate mod_dir mod_env mod_mime mod_negotiation mod_php5 mod_reqtimeout mod_rewrite mod_setenvif mod_status

Figure 68—Using **phpinfo()** to see loaded modules

Figure 69—An old page without **mod_rewrite**

assume that we're deploying a new version of a site. The old URLs were at pages/page-2.html, while the new CMS uses pages/2.

```
RewriteRule pages/page-(\d+) pages/$1 [L]
```

This rule tells the server to find the first set of numbers in the URL after matching the string pages/page- and use the match for the path to the page it should actually load. pages/page-3.html will load pages/3, and pages/678.html will try to load the actual pages/678.html file, since it doesn't match the regular expression. The final option we're passing—[L]—tells Apache that it should not apply any more RewriteRules if this one had a successful match.

Now that our new content is loading through the old URLs, we've realized that having the same content available at two URLs—pages/page-2.html and

Figure 70—A new page

Figure 71—A new page displaying at the old URL with mod_rewrite

pages/2—is not ideal because it's not clear what page should be linked to and it's making updating pages more difficult. Instead, we'd like to redirect the browser to the new URL entirely and make sure that any search engine robots also know to update their records.

To do this, we open .htaccess again and add the option R=301 to our RewriteRule to make Apache respond with a 301 Redirect header when the original URL is requested, which means that the resource at the given URL has been moved permanently. In addition, the new URL, which .htaccess has determined, is passed along so that browsers and search engine robots can continue along to the new location and still access the information.

```
RewriteRule pages/page-(\d+) pages/$1 [R=301,L]
```

With some regular expressions and a few RewriteRules, we can move to a new website without being restricted by its previous content structure or fear of breaking existing inbound links.

Further Exploration

How could we use mod_rewrite and .htaccess to redirect requests to a new domain name? We can specify a full URL in RewriteRule, so what would it look like to redirect users from a.com to b.com? What if a section of our site was moved from a directory to a subdomain?

Also, what if we changed server-side languages from PHP to Ruby on Rails? What would it take to preserve all of our URLs from /display.php?term=foo&id=123 while loading content from /term/foo or /term/123? Executing this well could mask the fact that we ever changed our backend.

Also See

- Recipe 38, *Changing Web Server Configuration Files with Vim*, on page 277
- Recipe 37, *Setting Up a Virtual Machine*, on page 272
- Recipe 39, *Securing Apache with SSL and HTTPS*, on page 283

Recipe 42

Automate Static Site Deployment with Jammit and Rake

Problem

Web developers working with static sites typically use tools like FTP to transfer web pages and associated assets into production. This practice works on a small scale, but as things get more complicated, manual processes break down. A file might accidentally get left out or even copied to the wrong location. In addition, concepts such as asset packaging, where multiple JavaScript files are combined into a single, compressed file, are becoming quite common and can be easily added to an automated deployment process. We need to develop a simple process that's easy to maintain yet flexible enough to extend.

Ingredients

- Our virtual machine, created in Recipe 37, *Setting Up a Virtual Machine,* on page 272[17]
- Jammit[18]
- Guard[19]
- Rake[20]

Solution

As developers, we spend a lot of time automating the processes for our customers and clients, so it makes sense for us to invest some time in automating our own processes. Nearly every command shell has its own scripting language that we could use to automate website deployment, but we can leverage some powerful Ruby-based tools that work whether we're deploying from Windows, OS X, or Linux.

At AwesomeCo, we're getting ready to expand our newly acquired "daily deals" to some new markets, and we've been asked to develop a simple microsite to collect email addresses from people so we can let them know when the service

---

17. You can grab a premade VM from http://www.webdevelopmentrecipes.com/.
18. http://documentcloud.github.com/jammit/
19. https://github.com/guard/guard
20. https://github.com/jimweirich/rake

is available in their area. When we're done, it will look like Figure 72, *Our landing page*, on page 298.

We'll build a quick prototype of the site using a tool called Jammit to combine and compress our JavaScript and style sheet files. Then we'll write a script that anyone can use to quickly push updated versions of the site to the servers using a tool called Rake. Let's start by taking a quick look at how we can develop our project with asset management in mind.

Improving Performance with Asset Packaging

A web page containing two JavaScript includes, a style sheet link, and a single image takes a total of five requests to the server. The browser first pulls down the page and then makes additional requests to the server to grab the other assets. Some browsers are limited to only two simultaneous requests to the same server at a time. Instead of including multiple JavaScript files on a page, we can combine them into a single file. We can reduce the loading time even further by *minifying* that file, which means we remove comments and whitespace. This makes the file size smaller so there's less data to transfer to the client. We then include this single, minified file in our web page.

To avoid losing our clean indentation, our comments. and our well-organized files, we do the minification automatically as we develop but only push the minified versions of our files to production. This is similar to how we work with CoffeeScript in Recipe 29, *Cleaner JavaScript with CoffeeScript*, on page 209. To do this, we'll use Jammit to manage this process for us.

Jammit takes a simple approach to minifying CSS and JavaScript files. We build a configuration file that specifies the output files and the input files, and Jammit takes care of the rest. Let's set up our project and quickly build our landing page.

We install Jammit from the command line using the `gem` command that comes with Ruby. If you don't have Ruby set up on your machine yet, take a quick look at Appendix 1, *Installing Ruby*, on page 305 before going forward. We'll also install Guard with the Jammit plug-in so that we can tell Jammit to rebuild our style sheets and JavaScript files whenever we change the master files.

```
$ gem install jammit guard guard-jammit
```

Now that we have our tools installed, let's get to work on our page.

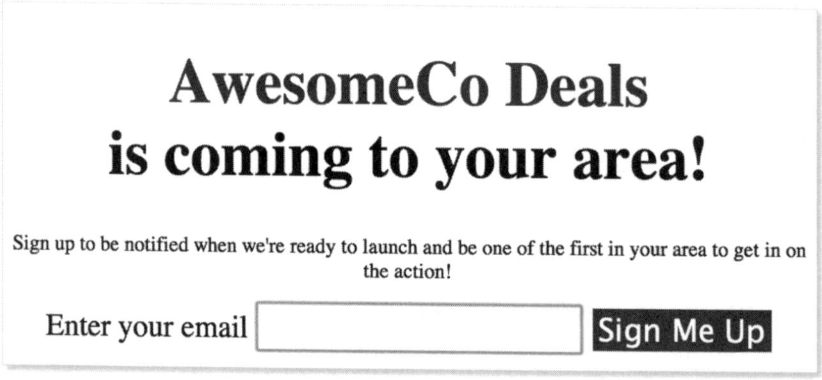

AwesomeCo Deals
is coming to your area!

Sign up to be notified when we're ready to launch and be one of the first in your area to get in on the action!

Enter your email [   ] **Sign Me Up**

Figure 72—Our landing page

Building Our Landing Page

In our project folder, we'll create a folder for our JavaScripts, a folder for style sheets, and a public folder that will contain all of the files we'll be pushing to production.

```
$ mkdir public
$ mkdir javascripts
$ mkdir stylesheets
```

Instead of loading jQuery from Google's API, we'll package it with our other assets. This means we'll need to download jQuery and place it in our javascripts folder.

Our form will have a piece of JavaScript that will send the user's email address to our servers using Ajax, so let's create a file called javascripts/form.js to hold that code.

Now let's create a simple skeleton for our landing page, which we'll place in public/index.html:

```
static/deploy/public/index.html
<!DOCTYPE html>
<html>
  <head>
    <title>AwesomeCo Deals</title>
➤    <link rel="stylesheet" href="assets/app.css" type="text/css">
➤    <script type="text/javascript" src="assets/app.js"></script>
  </head>
  <body>
  </body>
</html>
```

Notice the <head> section of our page: we're including the CSS and JavaScript files and from a folder called assets rather than our javascripts and stylesheets folders. This is because Jammit will construct this folder and these files for us, by stitching the files in the javascripts and stylesheets folders. All we have to do is tell Jammit how we'd like that to work.

Jammit looks for a file called config/assets.yml, so we'll create one in our project. In the file, we specify the output files and the corresponding inputs.

static/deploy/config/assets.yml
```
stylesheets:
  app:
    - stylesheets/style.css

javascripts:
  app:
    - javascripts/jquery-1.7.min.js
    - javascripts/form.js
```

Next, we'll configure Guard to watch files in the stylesheets and javascripts folders for changes by creating a Guardfile like this:

static/deploy/Guardfile
```
guard 'jammit' do
  watch(/^stylesheets\/(.*)\.css/)
  watch(/^javascripts\/(.*)\.js/)
end
```

With our files in place, let's fire up Guard and have it start building the assets for us.

```
$ guard
```

Now, let's add the markup for our form to index.html.

static/deploy/public/index.html
```
<!DOCTYPE html>
<html>
  <head>
    <title>AwesomeCo Deals</title>
➤   <link rel="stylesheet" href="assets/app.css" type="text/css">
➤   <script type="text/javascript" src="assets/app.js"></script>
  </head>
  <body>
  </body>
</html>
```

When the user fills in their email address and submits the form, we'll capture the form submission and send the result with Ajax. We'll hide the form and display a confirmation message. For this demo, we'll leave the actual Ajax piece out. In javascripts/form.js, we'll add this code:

```
static/deploy/javascripts/form.js
(function() {
  $(function() {
    return $("form").submit(function(event) {
      var element;
      event.preventDefault();
      element = $("<p>You've been added to the list!</p>");
      element.insertAfter($(this));
      return $(this).hide();
    });
  });
}).call(this);
```

When we save the file, Guard triggers Jammit, which updates the public/assets/app.js file, which now contains both jQuery and our form handling code in a single, minified file.

All that's left to do is add some simple CSS to stylesheets/style.css. First we center the page and set some font sizes:

```
static/deploy/stylesheets/style.css
#container {
  width: 960px;
  margin: 0px auto;
  text-align: center;
  box-shadow: 5px 5px 5px #ddd;
  border: 1px solid #ddd;
}

#container h1 {
  font-size: 72px;
}

#container h1 span.name {
  color: #900;
  display: block;
}

#container p {
  font-size: 24px;
}
```

and then we change the borders and text sizes on the form fields.

```
static/deploy/stylesheets/style.css
#container form {
  margin-bottom: 20px;
}
```

```
#container input, #container label {
  height: 50px;
  font-size: 36px;
}
#container input {
  border: 1px solid #ddd;
}

#container input[type=submit] {
  background-color: #900;
  color: #fff;
}
```

When we open index.html in our browser, we'll see everything working together. But now, let's extend this a step further by turning this development workflow into a deployment workflow.

Automating Deployment with Rake

Rake is a command-line tool written in Ruby that makes creating automated tasks a breeze. We'll use Rake to package up our assets and push all of our files to our server. We'll use the virtual machine we created in Recipe 37, *Setting Up a Virtual Machine*, on page 272 as our server for this recipe.

We install Rake the same way we installed Jammit, via our shell:

```
$ gem install rake
```

We define tasks in a file called Rakefile, and these tasks can use any Ruby library, or even call out to other command-line programs. A simple task looks like this:

```
desc "remove all .tmp files from this folder"
task :cleanup do
  FileUtils.rm_rf "*.tmp"
end
```

This defines a single task called cleanup, which deletes all files with the .tmp from the current directory. It uses Ruby's FileUtils library to handle deletes in a cross-platform way, so this task would work on any operating system that can run Ruby. We'd run this from the shell like this:

```
$ rake cleanup
```

The desc line before the task definition lets us document what the task does. We can then see all of the available tasks in a Rakefile with the following:

```
$ rake -T
```

> ### Joe asks:
> ## What About Deploying to Windows Servers?
>
> You can install OpenSSH[a] on your Windows servers and use the same scripts we're building in this recipe. If that's not an option, you could mount the server's disks as network drives on your client machine and simply copy the files over instead of using SCP. We've used both of these approaches successfully and highly recommend automating your deployment regardless of your target platform.
>
> ---
>
> a.   http://sshwindows.sourceforge.net/

Tasks without a desc line directly above will not show up when we list the available tasks, so it's a good practice to add those for every task you define.

Let's create a Rakefile in our project that has two tasks. The first task will use a simple Ruby script to load our Guardfile and execute all of the tasks:

static/deploy/Rakefile
```
task :build do
  require 'guard'
  Guard.setup
  Guard::Dsl.evaluate_guardfile
  Guard::guards.each{|guard| guard.run_all}
end
```

Next, we'll define the task to copy the public folder to the /var/www folder on the virtual machine. We'll use Ruby's Net::SCP library to transfer the files, which works on Windows, OS X, and Linux. We'll assume our server is located at 192.168.1.100 and that the username and password are both "webdev."[22]

static/deploy/Rakefile
```
desc "Deploy the web site to the dev server"
task :deploy => :build do
  require 'net/scp'
  server = "192.168.1.100"
  login = "webdev"

  Net::SCP.start(server, login, {:password => "webdev"} ) do |scp|
    scp.upload! "public", "/var/www", :recursive => true
  end
end
```

---

22. Remember that you can use the ifconfig command on your server's console to locate its IP address.

How to Avoid Storing Passwords in Scripts with SSH Keys

In Recipe 30, *Managing Files Using Git*, on page 216, we discussed how to create SSH keys. By uploading your public key to your servers, you can remove the :password => part of the deployment script. Ruby's SCP library will automatically use your SSH keys if you don't specify a password. This is a much more secure way of scripting deployments.

The definition of this task looks a tiny bit different. We can use the => (or *hashrocket*, as Rubyists call it) to specify that this task depends on a previous one. When we run this task, it will automatically run our build task first.

Now, when we execute the following:

```
$ rake deploy
```

our code will be pushed to our server, and we can pull it up in the browser at http://192.168.1.100/index.html. When it comes time to push our code to the production server, we only need to change the login details in the script.

Further Exploration

Once you have a good deployment workflow in place, you can start working more things in. Our workflow already uses Guard, which means you could incorporate CoffeeScript and Sass into this process quite easily. To do that, you would install the CoffeeScript and Sass libraries and their respective Guard plug-ins:

```
$ gem install coffee-script guard-coffeescript
$ gem install sass guard-sass
```

You would then write the style sheet with Sass, placing it in sass/style.scss. Similarly, you would develop the form handler code in CoffeeScript in coffee-scripts/form.coffee. You would then modify the Guardfile to place the generated CSS and JavaScript files into a temporary directory, watching those files for changes:

static/sassandcoffee/Guardfile
```
➤ guard 'sass', :input => 'sass', :output => 'tmp'
➤ guard 'coffeescript', :input => 'coffeescripts', :output => 'tmp'

  guard 'jammit' do
➤   watch(/^tmp\/(.*)\.css/)
➤   watch(/^tmp\/(.*)\.js/)
    watch(/^stylesheets\/(.*)\.css/)
    watch(/^javascripts\/(.*)\.js/)
  end
```

Finally, you would modify Jammit's configuration file to pull the generated style sheet and JavaScript files together.

static/sassandcoffee/config/assets.yml

```
stylesheets:
  app:
    - tmp/style.css

javascripts:
  app:
    - javascripts/jquery-1.7.min.js
    - tmp/form.js
```

This approach lets you mix regular JavaScript and CSS with CoffeeScript and Sass, which means you can use jQuery, Backbone, Knockout, Skeleton, Jekyll, or any of the other techniques in this book in your automated build chain. Since the resulting files all end up in the public folder, our deployment tasks in the Rakefile don't have to change at all.

To take deployment to the next level, you could investigate Capistrano,[23] a Ruby-based tool that lets you write recipes to deploy sites from version control systems like Git. While Capistrano was originally designed to deploy Ruby on Rails applications, it works great for deploying static sites, PHP applications, or even software packages.

Also See

- Recipe 28, *Building Modular Style Sheets with Sass*, on page 201
- Recipe 29, *Cleaner JavaScript with CoffeeScript*, on page 209
- Recipe 27, *Creating a Simple Blog with Jekyll*, on page 193
- Recipe 30, *Managing Files Using Git*, on page 216

---

23. https://github.com/capistrano/capistrano/wiki/

Installing Ruby

Several of the recipes in this book use the Ruby programming language or its interpreter. Ruby is a powerful cross-platform interpreted language that's most well known for the Ruby on Rails web development framework. Many Ruby developers work on the Web, and they've used Ruby to create some amazing tools like Cucumber[1] and SassOS X[2] to speed up the web development process. To use these tools, we'll need the Ruby interpreter and its package management system, RubyGems, installed. In this appendix, we cover how to do just that on Windows, OS X, and Ubuntu.

A1.1 Windows

Windows installation is a two-part process. First, download the Ruby Installer for Windows.[3] Grab the one for Ruby 1.9.2. The installation will give you the option to add Ruby executables to your PATH, which you should do. This way you'll be able to use Ruby and other libraries you install from your command prompt no matter what folder you're currently in.

Once that's done, download the development kit, which you can find on the same download page. While we won't be writing our own Ruby programs in these recipes, some of the components we want to install need to be compiled, because they're actually written in the C programming language. The development kit contains these compilers.

The development kit is a self-extracting archive, which you should extract to c:\ruby\devkit. Then, open a command prompt and run the following commands:

---

1. http://cukes.info/
2. http://sass-lang.com
3. http://rubyinstaller.org/downloads/

```
c:\> cd \devkit
c:\> ruby dk.rb init
c:\> ruby dk.rb install
```

To test your setup, install the Cucumber gem by opening your command prompt and typing the following:

```
$ gem install cucumber
```

That's all there is to it. Now you can use libraries like Cucumber and SASS in your development projects.

A1.2 Mac OS X and Linux with RVM

OS X and many Linux distributions have prebuilt Ruby interpreters available; OS X even has it installed by default. We'll use RVM, or Ruby Version Manager, to install and manage our Ruby installations.[4] While RVM works exactly the same on every platform it supports, each platform has its own unique setup process. We'll cover setting up RVM for OS X and Ubuntu.

Setting Up RVM on OS X

To use RVM on OS X, you need to install Xcode.[5] We won't be using Xcode in this book, but it's the easiest way to get the C compilers we need. You can find Xcode on your OS X installation DVD or through the Mac App Store. You'll also need to install Git for OS X, which we discuss in Recipe 30, *Managing Files Using Git*, on page 216, because we'll need that to fetch RVM.[6]

Next, execute this command from your Terminal to install RVM.

```
$ bash < <(curl -s https://rvm.beginrescueend.com/install/rvm)
```

This fetches RVM and installs it to your home directory.

Next, run the following command so that RVM and its files are available every time you start a new Terminal session:

```
$ echo '[[ -s "$HOME/.rvm/scripts/rvm" ]] && \
source   "$HOME/.rvm/scripts/rvm"' >> ~/.bashrc
```

Finally, close and restart your Terminal session to ensure that RVM is now available and then continue to *Installing Ruby with RVM*, on page 307.

---

4.   http://rvm.beginrescueend.com
5.   http://developer.apple.com/xcode/
6.   http://code.google.com/p/git-osx-installer/

Setting Up RVM on Ubuntu

RVM has several dependencies for Ubuntu. This command will work nicely, because it installs the compilers, prerequisites, and Git, which we discuss in Recipe 30, *Managing Files Using Git*, on page 216:

```
$ sudo apt-get install build-essential bison openssl \
libreadline6 libreadline6-dev curl git-core zlib1g \
zlib1g-dev libssl-dev libyaml-dev libsqlite3-0 \
libsqlite3-dev sqlite3 libxml2-dev libxslt-dev autoconf
```

When those libraries are finished installing, execute this command from your Terminal to install RVM:

```
$ bash < <(curl -s https://rvm.beginrescueend.com/install/rvm)
```

This fetches RVM and installs it to your home directory.

Next, run this command so that RVM and its files are available every time you start a new Terminal session:

```
$ echo '[[ -s "$HOME/.rvm/scripts/rvm" ]] && \
source "$HOME/.rvm/scripts/rvm"' >> ~/.bashrc
```

Finally, close and restart your Terminal session to ensure that RVM is now available.

Installing Ruby with RVM

With RVM installed, you can now install Ruby 1.9.2 with this command:

```
$ rvm install 1.9.2
```

Then, to use this version of Ruby, you type the following:

```
$ rvm use 1.9.2
```

For the purposes of this book, you may want to set this to the default version of Ruby:

```
$ rvm --default use 1.9.2
```

Now, test things by installing the Cucumber library that we use in Recipe 34, *Cucumber-Driven Selenium Testing*, on page 242. From the Terminal, type this command:

```
$ gem install cucumber
```

That's it! Ruby and its prerequisites are now installed, and you can now use tools like Cucumber, Sass, Guard, and Jekyll in your web development projects.

Bibliography

[Bur11]   Trevor Burnham. *CoffeeScript: Accelerated JavaScript Development*. The Pragmatic Bookshelf, Raleigh, NC and Dallas, TX, 2011.

[CADH09] David Chelimsky, Dave Astels, Zach Dennis, Aslak Hellesøy, Bryan Helmkamp, and Dan North. *The RSpec Book*. The Pragmatic Bookshelf, Raleigh, NC and Dallas, TX, 2009.

[CC11]   Hampton Catlin and Michael Lintorn Catlin. *Pragmatic Guide to Sass*. The Pragmatic Bookshelf, Raleigh, NC and Dallas, TX, 2011.

[Hog10]   Brian P. Hogan. *HTML5 and CSS3: Develop with Tomorrow's Standards Today*. The Pragmatic Bookshelf, Raleigh, NC and Dallas, TX, 2010.

[Swi08]   Travis Swicegood. *Pragmatic Version Control Using Git*. The Pragmatic Bookshelf, Raleigh, NC and Dallas, TX, 2008.

[WH11]   Matt Wynne and Aslak Hellesøy. *The Cucumber Book: Behaviour-Driven Development for Testers and Developers*. The Pragmatic Bookshelf, Raleigh, NC and Dallas, TX, 2011.

Index

Go Beyond with Rails and NoSQL

There's so much new to learn with Rails 3 and the latest crop of NoSQL databases. These titles will get you up to speed on the latest.

Thousands of developers have used the first edition of *Rails Recipes* to solve the hard problems. Now, five years later, it's time for the Rails 3.1 edition of this trusted collection of solutions, completely revised by Rails master Chad Fowler.

Chad Fowler
(350 pages) ISBN: 9781934356777. $35
http://pragprog.com/titles/rr2

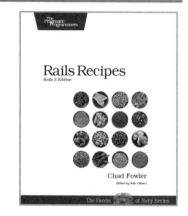

Data is getting bigger and more complex by the day, and so are your choices in handling it. From traditional RDBMS to newer NoSQL approaches, *Seven Databases in Seven Weeks* takes you on a tour of some of the hottest open source databases today. In the tradition of Bruce A. Tate's *Seven Languages in Seven Weeks*, this book goes beyond your basic tutorial to explore the essential concepts at the core of each technology.

Eric Redmond and Jim Wilson
(330 pages) ISBN: 9781934356920. $35
http://pragprog.com/titles/rwdata

Welcome to the New Web

You need a better JavaScript and more expressive CSS and HTML today. Start here.

CoffeeScript is JavaScript done right. It provides all of JavaScript's functionality wrapped in a cleaner, more succinct syntax. In the first book on this exciting new language, CoffeeScript guru Trevor Burnham shows you how to hold onto all the power and flexibility of JavaScript while writing clearer, cleaner, and safer code.

Trevor Burnham
(136 pages) ISBN: 9781934356784. $29
http://pragprog.com/titles/tbcoffee

CSS is fundamental to the web, but it's a basic language and lacks many features. Sass is just like CSS, but with a whole lot of extra power so you can get more done, more quickly. Build better web pages today with *Pragmatic Guide to Sass*. These concise, easy-to-digest tips and techniques are the shortcuts experienced CSS developers need to start developing in Sass today.

Hampton Catlin and Michael Lintorn Catlin
(100 pages) ISBN: 9781934356845. $25
http://pragprog.com/titles/pg_sass

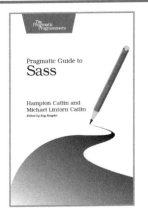

Pragmatic Guide Series

Get started quickly, with a minimum of fuss and hand-holding. The Pragmatic Guide Series features convenient, task-oriented two-page spreads. You'll find what you need fast, and get on with your work.

Need to learn how to wrap your head around Git, but don't need a lot of hand holding? Grab this book if you're new to Git, not to the world of programming. Git tasks displayed on two-page spreads provide all the context you need, without the extra fluff.

NEW: Part of the new *Pragmatic Guide* series

Travis Swicegood
(168 pages) ISBN: 9781934356722. $25
http://pragprog.com/titles/pg_git

JavaScript is everywhere. It's a key component of to-day's Web—a powerful, dynamic language with a rich ecosystem of professional-grade development tools, infrastructures, frameworks, and toolkits. This book will get you up to speed quickly and painlessly with the 35 key JavaScript tasks you need to know.

NEW: Part of the new *Pragmatic Guide* series

Christophe Porteneuve
(150 pages) ISBN: 9781934356678. $25
http://pragprog.com/titles/pg_js

Testing is only the beginning

Start with Test Driven Development, Domain Driven Design, and Acceptance Test Driven Planning in Ruby. Then add Shoulda, Cucumber, Factory Girl, and Rcov for the ultimate in Ruby and Rails development.

Behaviour-Driven Development (BDD) gives you the best of Test Driven Development, Domain Driven Design, and Acceptance Test Driven Planning techniques, so you can create better software with self-documenting, executable tests that bring users and developers together with a common language.

Get the most out of BDD in Ruby with *The RSpec Book*, written by the lead developer of RSpec, David Chelimsky.

David Chelimsky, Dave Astels, Zach Dennis, Aslak Hellesøy, Bryan Helmkamp, Dan North
(448 pages) ISBN: 9781934356371. $38.95
http://pragprog.com/titles/achbd

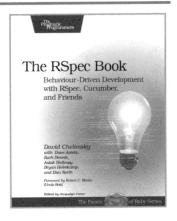

Rails Test Prescriptions is a comprehensive guide to testing Rails applications, covering Test-Driven Development from both a theoretical perspective (why to test) and from a practical perspective (how to test effectively). It covers the core Rails testing tools and procedures for Rails 2 and Rails 3, and introduces popular add-ons, including RSpec, Shoulda, Cucumber, Factory Girl, and Rcov.

Noel Rappin
(368 pages) ISBN: 9781934356647. $34.95
http://pragprog.com/titles/nrtest

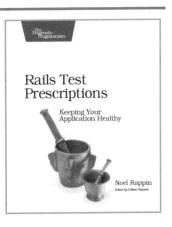

Advanced Ruby and Rails

What used to be the realm of experts is fast becoming the stuff of day-to-day development. Jump to the head of the class in Ruby and Rails.

Rails 3 is a huge step forward. You can now easily extend the framework, change its behavior, and replace whole components to bend it to your will, all without messy hacks. This pioneering book is the first resource that deep dives into the new Rails 3 APIs and shows you how to use them to write better web applications and make your day-to-day work with Rails more productive.

José Valim

(180 pages) ISBN: 9781934356739. $33

http://pragprog.com/titles/jvrails

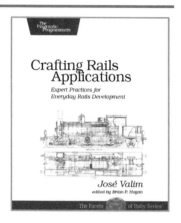

As a Ruby programmer, you already know how much fun it is. Now see how to unleash its power, digging under the surface and exploring the language's most advanced features: a collection of techniques and tricks known as *metaprogramming*. Once the domain of expert Rubyists, metaprogramming is now accessible to programmers of all levels—from beginner to expert. *Metaprogramming Ruby* explains metaprogramming concepts in a down-to-earth style and arms you with a practical toolbox that will help you write great Ruby code.

Paolo Perrotta

(240 pages) ISBN: 9781934356470. $32.95

http://pragprog.com/titles/ppmetr

Learn a New Language This Year

Want to be a better programmer? Each new programming language you learn teaches you something new about computing. Come see what you're missing.

You should learn a programming language every year, as recommended by *The Pragmatic Programmer*. But if one per year is good, how about *Seven Languages in Seven Weeks*? In this book you'll get a hands-on tour of Clojure, Haskell, Io, Prolog, Scala, Erlang, and Ruby. Whether or not your favorite language is on that list, you'll broaden your perspective of programming by examining these languages side-by-side. You'll learn something new from each, and best of all, you'll learn how to learn a language quickly.

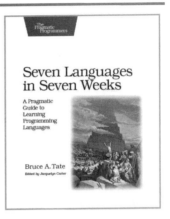

Bruce A. Tate
(300 pages) ISBN: 9781934356593. $34.95
http://pragprog.com/titles/btlang

Bill Karwin has helped thousands of people write better SQL and build stronger relational databases. Now he's sharing his collection of antipatterns—the most common errors he's identified out of those thousands of requests for help.

Most developers aren't SQL experts, and most of the SQL that gets used is inefficient, hard to maintain, and sometimes just plain wrong. This book shows you all the common mistakes, and then leads you through the best fixes. What's more, it shows you what's *behind* these fixes, so you'll learn a lot about relational databases along the way.

Bill Karwin
(352 pages) ISBN: 9781934356555. $34.95
http://pragprog.com/titles/bksqla

The Pragmatic Bookshelf

The Pragmatic Bookshelf features books written by developers for developers. The titles continue the well-known Pragmatic Programmer style and continue to garner awards and rave reviews. As development gets more and more difficult, the Pragmatic Programmers will be there with more titles and products to help you stay on top of your game.

Visit Us Online

This Book's Home Page
http://pragprog.com/titles/wbdev
Source code from this book, errata, and other resources. Come give us feedback, too!

Register for Updates
http://pragprog.com/updates
Be notified when updates and new books become available.

Join the Community
http://pragprog.com/community
Read our weblogs, join our online discussions, participate in our mailing list, interact with our wiki, and benefit from the experience of other Pragmatic Programmers.

New and Noteworthy
http://pragprog.com/news
Check out the latest pragmatic developments, new titles and other offerings.

Save on the eBook

Save on the eBook versions of this title. Owning the paper version of this book entitles you to purchase the electronic versions at a terrific discount.

PDFs are great for carrying around on your laptop—they are hyperlinked, have color, and are fully searchable. Most titles are also available for the iPhone and iPod touch, Amazon Kindle, and other popular e-book readers.

Buy now at *http://pragprog.com/coupon*

Contact Us

Online Orders:	*http://pragprog.com/catalog*
Customer Service:	*support@pragprog.com*
International Rights:	*translations@pragprog.com*
Academic Use:	*academic@pragprog.com*
Write for Us:	*http://pragprog.com/write-for-us*
Or Call:	+1 800-699-7764